An Introduction to Labor Arbitration

An Introduction to Labor Arbitration

CHARLES S. LaCUGNA

PRAEGER

New York
Westport, Connecticut
London

Library of Congress Cataloging-in-Publication Data

LaCugna, Charles S.
   An introduction to labor arbitration / Charles S. LaCugna.
      p.   cm.
      Bibliography: p.
      Includes index.
      ISBN 0–275–93047–5 (alk. paper)
      1. Arbitration, Industrial—United States.   I. Title.
   KF3424.L33   1988
   344.73′0189143—dc19
   [347.304189143]   88–5810

#17549683

Library of Congress Catalog Card Number: 88–5810

ISBN: 0–275–93047–5

First published in 1988

Praeger Publishers, One Madison Avenue, New York, NY   10010
A division of Greenwood Press, Inc.

Printed in the United States of America

The paper used in this book complies with the
Permanent Paper Standard issued by the National
Information Standards Organization (Z39.48–1984).

10 9 8 7 6 5 4 3 2 1

To Catherine

Contents

Preface

For many years the Federal Mediation and Conciliation Service (FMCS) and the American Arbitration Association (AAA) have sponsored annual labor arbitration conferences in Washington, Oregon, Idaho, Montana, and Alaska. As a frequent panelist and observer, I noted that labor-management practitioners frequently asked questions on the fundamental theory, practice, and procedure of labor arbitration. At one planning session for an FMCS conference, I suggested that FMCS schedule a panel, entitled *Fundamentals of Arbitration*, specifically designed for labor-management practitioners who had no experience or limited experience in arbitration. The panel on the fundamentals of arbitration became very popular and now is a fixture in many conferences in the Northwest. To prepare material for these conferences, I searched the literature for a useful, comprehensive, and basic book on labor arbitration. My search convinced me that inexperienced practitioners need a clear, simple, concise, elementary book, an introductory book that defines terms common in labor arbitration and explains the origin, legal context, theory, and practice of labor arbitration: Hence the title, *An Introduction to Labor Arbitration*. For further study, the reader can profitably consult the primary sources listed in the bibliography, and in particular, Robert Coulson, *Labor Arbitration—What You Need to Know*; Owen Fairweather, *Practice and Procedure in Labor Arbitration*, which discusses the legal relationship between court decisions and arbitral decisions; the annual *Proceedings* of the National Academy of Arbitrators (a storehouse of information and debates on current developments in arbitration practice); *The Future of Labor Arbitration in America*, seven papers of the Wingspread Conference sponsored by the AAA; *How Arbitration*

Works, by Frank and Edna Elkouri; Maurice Trotta, *Arbitration of Labor-Management Disputes*; Paul Prasow and Edward Peters, *Arbitration and Collective Bargaining*; Dennis Nolan, *Labor Arbitration Law and Practice*; Walter Baer, *The Labor Arbitration Guide*; Sam Kagel, *Anatomy of a Labor Arbitration*; and *Grievance Arbitration in the Private Sector*, a bibliography on labor arbitration compiled by the AAA.

In the spirit of arbitration practice, I purposely have omitted footnotes, legal citations, lengthy quotations, discussions of specialized or abstruse topics, foreign phrases, legal jargon, facts or figures, results of scientific surveys, and discussions of hypothetical or speculative questions. I have not used the cumbersome "he/she"; the pronoun "he" always refers to both male and female. Above all I have studiously avoided a common and fundamental error made by speakers and writers: to compare judicial theory and practice with the theory and practice of labor arbitration.

The plan of the book is simple. I define terms commonly used in labor arbitration; trace the origin of labor arbitration and the legislative and judicial decisions that shape labor arbitration and within which labor arbitration operates; analyze the grievance-arbitration clause; and state and illustrate from my own cases the principles that govern my practice before, during, and after a hearing. Finally, I set down my conclusions and reflections on labor arbitration.

Acknowledgments

I am grateful to the administration of Seattle University, in particular to David Pollick, Dean of the College of Arts and Sciences and Sr. Christopher Querin, S. P., Chairperson of the Political Science Department, for making typing help available to me; and to Bob Novak, librarian for inter-library loan service; to James L. Macpherson, former Regional Director of the Federal Mediation and Conciliation Service, to Norman Lee, present District Director of the Federal Mediation and Conciliation Service, and to Neal Blacker, Regional Director of the American Arbitration Association (AAA), for the many invitations to participate in conferences on labor arbitration; to Manhattan College, Fordham University, University of Notre Dame, and the University of Washington for my education; to all labor-management practitioners who have selected me to serve as grievance mediator, mediator, fact finder, and arbitrator; to all writers on arbitration, especially those members of the National Academy of Arbitrators who have contributed to the Academy Proceedings; to those persons who had the wisdom and foresight to develop labor arbitration; and to James L. Macpherson, Doug Hammond, Glenn Burgeson, Robert Sutermeister, Philip Kienast, Robert Burke, Lafayette Harter, Chuck Namit, and Jeffrey Thimsen for commenting on all or portions of the text. A special thanks to Earl R. Baderschneider of the AAA who made valuable suggestions and read the portion of the text that refers to the AAA, and to Walter Mercer, Regional Attorney for the National Labor Relations Board (NLRB), for reading the section on the National Labor Relations Board.

I also am grateful to the American Arbitration Association (AAA) for permission to quote from the *Voluntary Labor Arbitration Rules*, and again to the AAA, the Federal Mediation and Conciliation Service, and the National Academy of Arbitrators for permission to reprint and quote from the *Code of Professional Responsibility for Arbitrators of Labor Management Disputes* (1974).

An Introduction to Labor Arbitration

Definitions

In *United Steelworkers v. Warrior and Gulf Navigation* (1960), the Supreme Court defined the collective bargaining agreement as "a generalized code to govern a myriad of cases which the draftsmen cannot wholly anticipate." The collective bargaining agreement is "more than a contract," it covers the whole employment relationship and calls into being "a new common law, the common law of a particular industry or of a particular plant." The written agreement is not "the exclusive source of rights and duties; it includes also those practices and understandings which implement and furnish the context of the agreement". The written agreement governs an industrial community and establishes "a system of industrial self-government," ... "an agreed-upon rule of law" that regulates all aspects of a "complicated relationship," from the most crucial to the most minute over an extended period of time. The written document is "a compilation of diverse provisions" because parties must reach agreement on many matters: some provisions are automatically applicable, others require reason and judgment in their application, and still others are an expression of hope and good faith. Therefore, a collective bargaining agreement, whether long or short, embraces not only the customary "wages, hours, and conditions of employment"; in addition, "it almost always includes a grievance-arbitration clause because a written agreement, no matter how diligently drafted, cannot adequately reflect the many ambiguities, understandings, concessions, customs, and past practices that characterize a unique labor relationship."

The Court stated that the grievance procedure is "the very heart of the system of industrial self-government ... a vehicle by which meaning and content are given to the collective bargaining agreement ... a part of the continuous collective bargaining process" because the parties themselves seek to resolve a dispute over the interpretation and application of the agreement. The arbitration procedure is their own private judicial system, "a system of private law" to resolve those disputes that they cannot resolve in the grievance procedure.

THE DIFFERENCE BETWEEN GRIEVANCE ARBITRATION AND INTEREST ARBITRATION

Grievance or "rights" arbitration is arbitration of a dispute over the interpretation or the application of the terms of an existing agreement; "interest" arbitration is arbitration of a dispute over new contract terms. This book discusses only grievance arbitration.

COMPULSORY AND VOLUNTARY ARBITRATION

Arbitration, by definition, is voluntary because parties freely agree to arbitrate a labor dispute. The phrase "advisory arbitration" contains an inherent contradiction because an arbitrator neither dispenses advice nor makes recommendations; he renders a final and binding decision. However, compulsory arbitration does exist. Congress has ordered federal agencies and federal unions to arbitrate grievance and interests disputes, and most states and some cities have passed compulsory arbitration statutes for police officers, firefighters, and a few other categories of public employees.

ARBITRATION AND MEDIATION

Arbitration is fundamentally different from mediation. Although both a mediator and an arbitrator are third party neutrals, a mediator (sometimes called a conciliator) does not arbitrate; he does not adjudicate the merits of a labor dispute. The Federal Mediation and Conciliation Service describes a mediator as one who functions informally, and meets separately and jointly with the parties to help them find a mutually acceptable solution. A mediator gets stalled negotiations going again; he seeks to improve the bargaining atmosphere, encourages mutual discussion, explores alternative solutions, suggests specific contract clauses that have worked well elsewhere, and provides needed economic data and other information. In contrast, an arbitrator does not help the parties reach their own solution; he does not facilitate collective bargaining. An arbitrator adjudicates: he hears, receives, and evaluates evidence and argument; he then deliberates and issues a decision, called an award.

ARBITRATORS AND JUDGES

It is easy but incorrect to compare arbitrators to judges and to compare arbitral proceedings to court proceedings because both adjudicate and both processes are judicial processes. However, an arbitrator should not be called a judge or a "hybrid" or "quasi" judge because he is not an elected or appointed public official whose primary function is to interpret and apply public law. A person who serves as an arbitrator simply should be called "arbitrator" because he is a private adjudicator, a person selected and removable at will by the parties. An arbitrator's primary function is to interpret and apply the collective bargaining agreement, which is a private agreement, not public law.

There are marked and substantial differences between arbitral and court proceedings. Court proceedings are formal and complex, governed by public law. In contrast, arbitral proceedings, improperly called "trials" or "quasi" judicial proceedings, are flexible, informal, private, speedy, relatively inexpensive, and governed by a collective bargaining agreement. Advocates in court proceedings are attorneys, officers of the court; advocates in arbitration need not be attorneys, and lawyer advocates in arbitration do not use the technical language common to courts.

Parties prefer arbitration to court adjudication because labor arbitrators possess an expertise that the Supreme Court said is "foreign to the competence of courts, even the ablest judge." In the majority opinion in *Steelworkers v. Warrior and Gulf Navigation Co.*, Justice William O. Douglas said that parties submit a dispute to a labor arbitrator because they have "confidence in his knowledge of the common law of the shop," they trust "his personal judgment to bring to bear considerations which are not expressed in the contract as criteria for judgment," and they expect that his judgment of a particular grievance will "reflect not only what the contract says" but, insofar as the collective bargaining agreement permits, "such factors as the effect upon productivity of a particular result, its consequences to the morale of the shop," and "whether tensions will be heightened or diminished." The Court believed that "the ablest judge cannot be expected to bring the same expertise and competence to bear upon the determination of a grievance because he cannot be similarly informed."

1

Congress and Labor Arbitration

Labor arbitration, a unique U. S. contribution to the resolution of labor disputes, came into existence after Congress passed the National Labor Relations Act (NLRA) in 1935. Before the NLRA (commonly called the Wagner Act), all federal legislation—the Arbitration Act of 1888, the Erdman Act of 1898, the Clayton Anti-Trust Act of 1914, the Newlands Act of 1918, the Adamson Act of 1916, and the Railway Labor Act of 1926—sought to remedy some labor ill, but the legislation never granted employees the right to bargain collectively with employers. Although the Great Depression and the advent of the New Deal created a political climate favorable to organized labor, and although the Norris-LaGuardia Act of 1932 granted organized labor a shield against judicial interference in organized labor activity, unions did not enjoy the legal right to bargain wages, hours, and conditions of employment with employers until Congress passed the NLRA.

THE NATIONAL LABOR RELATIONS ACT OF 1935
(THE WAGNER ACT)

In 1933 Congress passed the National Industrial Recovery Act (NIRA) to promote economic recovery from the Great Depression, to quiet industrial unrest, and to prevent strikes. Section 7(a) of the NIRA granted employees the right to organize and to bargain collectively with employers but the Supreme Court declared the Act unconstitutional in *Schecter Poultry Corp. v. United States* (1935). The American Federation of Labor immediately mounted a vigorous campaign for legislation that would guarantee unions the legal right to bargain collectively with their employers. Two months after the Court declared the NIRA unconstitutional, Congress passed the Wagner Act whose immediate purpose was to diminish the causes of labor disputes that burdened or obstructed interstate and foreign commerce. The Wagner Act recognized that many employers had denied employees the right to organize and to bargain collectively, and that there was an inequality of bargaining strength between employer and employees that burdened interstate commerce.

Section 201 of the Act declared that:

It is hereby declared to be the policy of the United States to eliminate the causes of substantial obstruction to the free flow of commerce and to mitigate and eliminate those obstructions when they have occurred by encouraging the practice and procedure of collective bargaining and by protecting the exercise by workers of full freedom of association, self-organization and designation of representatives of their own choosing, for the purpose of negotiating the terms and conditions of their employment or other mutual aid or protection.

The Wagner Act (National Labor Relations Act of 1935), a legal milestone for organized labor, radically changed the relationship between employers and employees. Before the Wagner Act, the employer, legally and economically superior, could and did establish all conditions of employment. Even if an employer had entered into a collective bargaining agreement (usually a skeletal and generalized agreement, in effect only a memorandum of understanding), the enforcement of such an agreement depended entirely on the good will of the employer. The Wagner Act declared that employees not only had the right to form, join, or assist a labor organization, they also had the right to bargain collectively through representatives of their own choosing and to engage in concerted activities for the purpose of collective bargaining or other mutual aid or protection. Henceforth, an employer was legally bound to bargain collectively with a properly designated union on wage, hours, and working conditions. The Wagner Act made the resulting collective bargaining agreement a legally enforceable contract.

Organized labor, particularly the Congress of Industrial Organization (CIO), immediately began to exercise its right to enter into collective agreements with employers. Unions sought to bargain new and better wages, hours, and conditions of employment, and to retain those workplace practices favorable to labor. Employers sought to limit union incursions into previosuly unchallenged managerial prerogatives and to spell out, as unambiguously as possible, those rights that they had reluctantly agreed to share with a union. Collective bargaining had begun. Parties began to fashion detailed provisions on wages, hours, and working conditions. The language of these early-day agreements was necessarily loose and ambiguous because parties, novices in drafting language, wrote hastily or ineptly, and employers had neither the desire nor the experience to enter into collective bargaining agreements. To resolve these disputes, parties turned to arbitration and, in particular, to the American Arbitration Association (AAA), an organization established in 1926 to arbitrate disputes primarily over commercial contracts. In response to a growing demand for labor arbitration, the AAA established a Voluntary Industrial Tribunal, promulgated rules of procedure, fashioned model arbitration clauses for inclusion into collective bargaining agreements, and established a panel of labor arbitrators. Among the first to use the services of the AAA were the Actors' Equity Association, the Dramatists' Guild, the Authors' League, the Screen Actors' Guild, and the American Federation of Radio Artists.

After the Wagner Act, parties experimented and refined arbitration procedures, but it was only after the government established the National War Labor Board that arbitration became fixed in U. S. arbitration practice. The National War Labor Board of World War II not only greatly stimulated the use of arbitration, it also sharpened the distinction between grievance and interest arbitration. During World War II, management and labor acceded to President Roosevelt's request for a no-strike, no-lockout agreement. The tripartite War Labor Board, empowered to "finally determine" all labor disputes, became a "court of last resort": it either arbitrated a grievance or an interest dispute, or it ordered parties to submit their dispute to private arbitrators or to Board-appointed arbitrators. The Board also ordered management and labor to use their own grievance procedure, if they had one, or to include an arbitration clause in their agreements. The Board suggested that large employers employ a permanent arbitrator, usually called an umpire, to resolve disputes over the interpretation and application of an agreement. By the end of World War II, management and labor had accepted grievance arbitration as a method for settlement of disputes over contract terms.

After the war, a presidential Labor-Management Conference (1945) gave further impetus to grievance arbitration. A twelve-member labor and management committee unanimously endorsed arbitration of grievance disputes but rejected compulsory arbitration of interest disputes. The committee recommended that the grievance and arbitration procedure be simple and clear; be readily understood by all employees, union officials, and management representatives; be open to all grievances; provide a method of presentation—a method of appeal from one step to another; and be designed to facilitate the settlement of grievances as soon as possible after they arise. The committee also recommended that the grievance procedure provide adequate stated time for the presentation of grievances, the rendering of decisions, and the taking of appeals; that the grievance be reduced to writing after informal discussions; that both parties have an adequate opportunity to investigate grievances; and that they provide for priority handling of grievances on discharge, suspension, or other disciplinary action. In addition, the committee recommended that employers and unions inform and train their representatives in the proper functioning of the grievance procedure and their responsibilities under it. The committee emphasized that the objective of the grievance procedure was to achieve sound and fair settlement, not win cases; that foremen and supervisors should consider the filing of grievances an aid in discovering and removing causes of discontent; that routine support of earlier decisions by representatives when such decisions are wrong should be discouraged; that management and union officials should be willing to give adequate time and attention to the handling and disposition of grievances; and that management and union representatives should be thoroughly familiar with the entire collective bargaining agreement.

The committee recommended that parties adopt an arbitration clause to resolve unsettled grievances over the interpretation or application of the agreement but only after they had exhausted the grievance procedure. The decision of the arbitrator was to be final and binding and the arbitrator would only interpret and apply the existing provisions of the agreement. Both parties were to share the cost of arbitration equally.

THE LABOR MANAGEMENT RELATIONS ACT OF 1947 (LMRA)

To deal with the economic and political unrest after World War II and to meet the many and persistent criticisms, Congress amended the National Labor Relations Act in 1947. Commonly known as the Taft-Hartley Act, the amended National Labor Relations Act contained three provisions that had a profound and favorable impact on grievance arbitration.

First, Section 201 of the Act unequivocally favored and established a national policy of voluntary settlement for private disputes. The Act declared that:

(a) sound and stable industrial peace and the advancement of the general welfare, health, and safety of the Nation and the best interest of employers can most satisfactorily be secured by the settlement of issues between employers and employees through the processes of conference and collective bargaining between employers and the representatives of their employees;

(b) the settlement of issues between employers and employees through collective bargaining may be advanced by making available full and adequate government facilities for conciliation, mediation, and voluntary arbitration to aid and encourage employers and the representatives of their employees to reach and maintain agreements concerning rates of pay, hours, and working conditions, and to make all reasonable efforts to settle their differences by mutual agreement reached through conferences and collective bargaining or by such methods as may be provided for in applicable agreement for the settlement of disputes.

Second, Section 203 of the Taft-Hartley Act created the Federal Mediation and Conciliation Service (FMCS), successor to the U. S. Conciliation Service, as an independent federal agency whose primary function was to mediate labor disputes that interrupted the free flow of commerce. FMCS does not arbitrate, but it fosters arbitration. I discuss the FMCS procedure for nomination, retention, and selection of arbitrators elsewhere in the book.

Third, the Taft-Hartley Act allows unions to sue and be sued by employers in federal district court. Section 301(a) provides that:

Suits for violation of contracts between an employer and a labor organization representing employees in an industry affecting interstate commerce as defined in this Act, or between any such labor organizations, may be brought in any district court of the United States having jurisdiction of the parties, without respect to the amount in controversy or without regard to the citizenship of the parties.

Section 301(b) provides that:

Any labor organization which represents employees in an industry affecting commerce as defined in this Act and any employer whose activities affect commerce as defined in the Act shall be bound by the acts of its agents. Any such labor organization may sue or be sued as an entity and in behalf of the employees whom it represents in the courts of the United States.

Section 301, seemingly innocuous, has had far-reaching influence on labor arbitration because it reversed the common law doctrine that only individual work agreements were enforceable contracts and that unions could neither sue nor be sued because unions were incorporated associations. Significantly, Section 301 compelled the U. S. Supreme Court to define the nature and legal status of arbitration.

THE CIVIL SERVICE REFORM ACT OF 1978

The Executive Orders

In 1883 Congress passed the Civil Service Act, commonly known as the Pendleton Act, which provided that only Congress had the right to regulate wages, hours, and other conditions of employment for federal employees. In 1912 Congress passed the Lloyd-Lafollette Act which gave federal employees the right to lobby Congress and the right to join labor unions. However, the Wagner Act and the Taft-Hartley Act specifically forbade federal employees to strike because public sector employees were not yet organized politically into strong unions and Congress believed that the Civil Service System provided job security, pensions, and compensation superior in some respects to those enjoyed by employees in private industry. When private employees forged ahead of public sector employees in compensation and benefits, federal and other public sector employees, especially those in teaching and in the uniform services, began to organize into public unions. These public employees sought the right to bargain collectively with their employers and the concomitant right to grievance arbitration. Public sector employees lobbied state legislatures for the right to bargain collectively with public employers. As a result, some categories of public employees in some states have won a limited right to strike in addition to some combination of mediation and fact finding. Further, many states mandate the compulsory arbitration of interest disputes of certain categories of public employees.

However, Congress resisted efforts of federal unions to win collective bargaining rights. Congress feared that the joint determination of wages, hours, and conditions of employment would derogate from the sovereignty of the federal government and lead to increased taxes and to strikes against the government. Nonetheless, in 1962, President Kennedy promulgated Executive Order 10988, "Employee-Management Cooperation in the Federal Service." The Order reaffirmed the right of federal employees to join or not join unions, and granted federal unions the right to bargain collectively with federal agencies and the right to negotiate a grievance procedure. However, the Order allowed only "advisory" arbitration and specifically forbade arbitration of interest disputes.

To meet the complaints of both management and labor about Executive Order 10988, and, in particular, the criticisms of the dispute settlement machinery, President Nixon issued Executive Orders 11491 and 11616, which radically changed the grievance and interest arbitration provisions of Executive Order 10988.

Although Executive Order 11491 abolished "advisory" arbitration and authorized the use of binding arbitration, an agency could still object to an arbitrator's award by filing an "exception" with the newly created Labor Relations Council. If either management or labor filed an exception, the Council would issue a final and binding award. Executive Order 11491 also specified that the parties could not use the grievance procedure to resolve disputes for which statutory appeal procedures existed. Furthermore, the Order allowed an employee or group of employees to present and to adjust grievances without the intervention of the exclusive representative, but only if the exclusive representative had been given the opportunity to be present at the adjustment. Only an agency and an exclusive representative had the right to invoke arbitration and to file an exception to an arbitrator's award with the Labor Relations Council.

Executive Order 11491 created the Federal Service Impasses Panel, an agency of the Council, to consider and ultimately dispose of impasses over new terms of a collective bargaining agreement. At the request of either party, the Panel could, at its discretion and under its regulations, recommend third-party fact finding with recommendations or arbitration for the resolution of the impasse. If the panel authorized parties to proceed to arbitration, a dissatisfied party could appeal an arbitrator's award to the Federal Labor Relations Council.

Executive Order 11616 specified that a negotiated grievance procedure had to be the exclusive method to resolve contractual grievances, and only grievances over the interpretation or application of the agreement would be subject to the negotiated grievance procedure.

The Civil Service Reform Act of 1978 (CSRA)

Title VII of the Civil Service Reform Act, a historic milestone in federal civil service legislation, created a statutory labor-management system which superseded all executive orders. In 1977 a presidential task force reviewed the existing labor-management relations and identified a variety of problems. Structurally, CSRA abolished the Civil Service Commission and replaced it with two agencies, the Office of Personnel Management (OPM) and the Merit Systems Protection Board (MSPB). CSRA retained the Federal Service Impasses Panel, but it replaced the Federal Labor Relations Council with the Federal Labor Relations Authority (FLRA).

Title VII of CSRA, entitled "Federal Service Labor-Management Relations," prescribes the rights and obligations of the federal employees and establishes procedures designed to meet the special requirements and needs of the government. The Federal Labor Relations Authority (FLRA), an independent, neutral, full-time agency within the executive branch, establishes policies, determines appropriate units for labor organization representation, supervises or conducts elections to determine whether a labor organization is the exclusive representative, prescribes criteria, and resolves issues on national consultation rights, on the need for agency rules or regulations, and on the duty to bargain in good faith. FLRA resolves unfair labor practice complaints and exceptions to arbitrators' awards.

Resolution of Negotiation Impasses. The Federal Service Impasses Panel helps to resolve negotiation impasses between agencies and exclusive representatives. If mediation by the Federal Mediation and Conciliation

Service (FMCS) or another third party fails to resolve a negotiation impasse, either party may request the Federal Service Impasses Panel to consider the matter. The Panel, or its designee, may investigate the impasse and recommend fact finding. If parties cannot resolve the impasse, the Panel takes "whatever other action is necessary" that is "not inconsistent with other portions of the Statute" to resolve the impasse. Parties may proceed to binding arbitration but only if the Panel approves.

Grievance Arbitration. Under CSRA all collective bargaining agreements must contain a grievance and arbitration procedure. CSRA defines a grievance broadly: "any matter relating to employment . . . any claimed violation, misinterpretation, or misapplication of any law, rule, or regulation affecting conditions of employment." CSRA also defines management rights broadly: "nothing shall affect the authority of any management official of any agency . . . to determine the mission, budget, organization, number of employees, and internal security practices of the agency." In accordance with applicable laws the agency has the authority "to assign work, to make determination with respect to contracting out, and to determine the personnel by which agency operations shall be conducted." With respect to filling positions, the agency has the authority "to make selections for appointments from among properly ranked and certified candidates for promotion, or any other appropriate source" and "to take whatever action may be necessary to carry out the agency mission during emergencies." CSRA directs parties to devise a fair and simple grievance procedure, which is the exclusive remedy for grievances within its coverage, provides for expeditious disposal of grievances, assures the rights of an exclusive representative to present and process grievances either in its own behalf or on behalf of an employee in the unit represented by the exclusive representative, assures the right of an employee to present a grievance on his own behalf, assures the right of an exclusive representative to be present during the processing of a grievance, provides for binding arbitration, and resolves arbitrability questions. Only an exclusive representative or an agency can invoke arbitration.

Either party may file an "exception" to an arbitrator's award with the FLRA. If FLRA finds the award deficient because it is contrary to law, rule, or regulation, or deficient "on the grounds similar to those applied by federal courts in private sector labor-management relations," FLRA may take any action it considers necessary, consistent with applicable laws, rules, or regulations. If neither party files an exception to an award within 30 days, the award is final and binding. The "other grounds" on which the FLRA can modify or vacate an arbitrator's award are the same limited grounds courts have used. Specifically, FLRA can modify or vacate an award if the award is founded on a non-fact; the award does not "draw its essence" from the collective bargaining agreement; the arbitrator "exceeded his powers"; the award is incomplete, ambiguous, contradictory, or incapable of fulfillment; or the arbitrator failed to admit relevant and material evidence. Courts have no power to review an unappealed award or an award found deficient by the FLRA unless the dispute also involves an alleged unfair labor practice.

2
The Courts and Labor Arbitration

Section 301 of the Taft-Hartley Act has had far-reaching and favorable influence on labor arbitration: it made unions legal equals to employers. As legal equals, unions sued employers in federal court to enforce collective bargaining agreements. The suits compelled the Supreme Court to define the nature and the legal status of labor arbitration.

TEXTILE WORKERS' UNION V. LINCOLN MILLS

In *Textile Workers' Union v. Lincoln Mills*, 353 U. S. 448 (1957), the union sued the employer to compel arbitration under Section 301 of the Taft-Hartley Act. Two questions were before the court: first, should federal or state courts enforce collective bargaining agreements, and second, what were the applicable rules for the construction of a collective bargaining agreement? The Court held that Section 301 authorized federal courts to fashion a body of federal law for the enforcement of collective bargaining agreements. After a review of the legislative history, the Court said:

Plainly the agreement to arbitrate grievance disputes is the quid pro quo for an agreement not to strike. Viewed in this light, the legislation does more than confer jurisdiction in the federal courts over labor organization. It expresses a federal policy that federal courts should enforce these agreements on behalf of or against labor organizations and that industrial peace can be best obtained only in this way. The substantive law to apply in suits under Section 301 is federal law which the courts must fashion from the policy of our national labor laws. Federal interpretation of federal law will govern, not State law.... State law will be absorbed as federal law and will not be an independent source of rights.

In 1960 the Court answered other questions on the nature and legal status of arbitration in the celebrated *Steelworkers Trilogy*.

UNITED STEELWORKERS V. WARRIOR AND GULF NAVIGATION COMPANY

In *United Steelworkers v. Warrior and Gulf Navigation Company*, 363 U. S. 574 (1960), the union had sought to compel arbitration of a subcontracting dispute, but the employer refused to submit to arbitration. The employer argued that it had no obligation to proceed to arbitration because it had never agreed to arbitrate subcontracting issues.

The Court noted that the choice was between the adjudication of cases in courts with established procedures or the settlement of cases in the informal arbitration tribunal. The Court clearly favored arbitration of labor disputes as a substitute for industrial strife.

In the commercial case, arbitration is the substitute for litigation. Here arbitration is the substitute for industrial strife. Since arbitration of labor disputes has quite different functions from arbitration under an ordinary commercial agreement, the hostility evinced by the courts toward arbitration of commercial agreements has no place here. For arbitration of labor disputes under collective bargaining agreements is part of the collective bargaining process itself.

The Court agreed with the employer that arbitration was a matter of contract: a party could not be required to submit to arbitration any dispute which it had not agreed to submit to arbitration, yet, to be consistent with congressional policy in favor of settlement of disputes by the parties through the machinery of arbitration, the Court concluded that:

Judicial inquiry under 301 must be strictly confined to the question whether the reluctant party did agree to arbitrate the grievance or did agree to give the arbitrator power to make the award he made. An order to arbitrate the particular grievance should not be denied unless it may be said with positive assurance that the arbitration clause is not susceptible of an interpretation that covers the asserted dispute. Doubts should be resolved in favor of coverage.

Further, it concluded that:

In the absence of any express provisions excluding a particular grievance from arbitration, we think only the most forceful evidence of a purpose to exclude the claim from arbitration can prevail, particularly where, as here, the exclusion clause is vague and the arbitration clause quite broad. Since any attempt by a court to infer such a purpose necessarily comprehends the merits, the court should view with suspicion any attempt to persuade it to become entangled in the construction of the substantive provisions of a labor agreement, even through the back door of interpreting the arbitration clause, when the alternative is to utilize the services of an arbitrator.

The Court defined arbitration:

as the means of solving the unforeseeable by molding a system of private law for all the problems which will generally accord with the variant needs and desires of the parties. And, apart from matters that parties specifically exclude, all of the questions on which the parties disagree must therefore come within the scope of the grievance and arbitration provisions of the collective agreement. It, rather than a strike, is the terminal point of a disagreement.

The Court also defined the arbitrator's function and powers.

An arbitrator is not a public tribunal imposed upon the parties by superior authority which the parties are obliged to accept. He has no general charter to administer justice for a community which transcends the parties. He is rather part of a system of self-government created by and confined to the parties.... The labor arbitrator's source of law is not confined to the express provisions of the contract, as the industrial common law, the practices of the industry and the shop is equally a part of the collective bargaining agreement although not expressed in it.

The Court placed great confidence in arbitrators. The Court said that parties select an arbitrator because they have "confidence in his knowledge of the common law of the shop" and because they "trust his personal judgment to bring to bear considerations which are not expressed in the contract." They expect that his judgment of a particular grievance will reflect "not only what the contract says" but, insofar as the collective bargaining agreement permits,

such factors as the effect upon productivity of a particular result, its consequence to the morale of the shop, his judgment whether tensions will be heightened or diminished.... The ablest judge cannot be expected to bring the same experience and competence to bear upon the determination of a grievance because he cannot be similarly informed.

UNITED STEELWORKERS V. AMERICAN MANUFACTURING COMPANY

In the second *Trilogy* case, *United Steelworkers v. American Manufacturing Company*, 363 U. S. 564 (1960), the employer had refused to arbitrate a seniority grievance although the agreement contained an arbitration clause for the resolution of disputes over the interpretation and application of the agreement. The union sued in federal court to compel arbitration. The lower courts upheld the employer on the grounds that the grievance was frivolous and baseless. The Court reversed the lower courts and held that courts were to determine only the question of substantive arbitrability, not the merits of a grievance. The Court said:

The function of the court is very limited when the parties have agreed to submit all questions of contract interpretation to the arbitrator. It is then confined to ascertaining whether the party seeking arbitration is making a claim which, on its face, is governed by the contract. Whether the moving party is right or wrong is a question of contract interpretation for the arbitrator. In these circumstances, the moving party should not be deprived of the arbitrator's judgment when it was his judgment and all that it connotes that was bargained for.

The courts therefore have no business weighing the merits of the grievance considering whether there is equity in a particular claim or determining whether there is particular language in the written instrument which will support the claim. The agreement is to submit all grievances to arbitration, not merely those the court will deem meritorious.

UNITED STEELWORKERS V. ENTERPRISE WHEEL AND CAR CORPORATION

In the third *Trilogy* case, *United Steelworkers v. Enterprise Wheel and Car Corporation*, 363 U. S. 593 (1960), the employer refused to proceed to arbitration, the district court compelled arbitration, and an arbitrator issued a decision, but the circuit court refused to enforce an arbitrator's award. In *Enterprise Wheel*, the Court held that courts must refuse to review arbitral awards because court review would undermine the federal policy that favors arbitration of labor disputes. The Court said:

the question of interpretation of the collective bargaining agreement is a question for the arbitrator. It is the arbitrator's construction which was bargained for and so far as the arbitrator's decision concerns construction of the contract, the courts have no business overruling him because their interpretation of the contract is different from his.

The Court also said that courts could not review the arbitrator's judgment on the appropriate remedy. The Court reasoned that if a district or circuit court could review an arbitrator's judgment, the arbitrator's judgment would not be final and binding.

When an arbitrator is commissioned to interpret and apply the collective bargaining agreement, he is to bring his informed judgment to bear in order to reach a fair solution. This is especially true when it comes to formulating remedies. The draftsmen may have never thought of what specific remedy should be awarded to meet a particular contingency.

The Court opinion continued:

An arbitrator is confined to interpretation and application of the collective bargaining agreement; he does not sit to dispense his own brand of industrial justice. He may, of course, look for guidance from many sources, yet his award is legitimate only so long as it draws its essence from the collective bargaining agreement. When the arbitrator's words manifest an infidelity to its obligation, courts have no choice but to refuse enforcement of the award.

JOHN WILEY AND SONS INC. V. LIVINGSTON

In *John Wiley & Sons Inc. v. Livingston*, 848 S. Ct. 909 (1964), the employer argued that the union could not invoke arbitration because the union had not pursued the grievance in the first two steps of the grievance procedure in a timely manner. The employer argued that the question whether procedural requirements have been met must be decided by a court, not by an arbitrator. The Court disagreed. It held that because procedural issues, such as timeliness, are often intimately connected with the merits of the dispute and because court review of the alleged procedural defects would unreasonably delay resolution of a grievance, an arbitrator, not a court, should decide questions of procedural arbitrability.

Once it is determined that the parties are obligated to submit the subject matter of a dispute to arbitration, procedural questions which grow out of the dispute and bear on its disposition must be left to the arbitrator.

To summarize these landmark cases: courts are to decide questions of substantive arbitrability; arbitrators are to decide questions of procedural arbitrability. Today, the general practice is to submit the question of substantive arbitrability to an arbitrator.

3
Court Review of Arbitration Awards

Although the Supreme Court held that an arbitrator's award was "final and binding," that judicial inquiry should be "strictly confined" to the question of substantive arbitrability, that the function of the courts is "very limited" when the parties have agreed to arbitrate, and that the courts have "no business" weighing the merits of a grievance, courts have reviewed arbitration awards on a variety of grounds. Courts have either vacated or modified an award because they concluded that an award did not "draw its essence" from the collective bargaining agreement, or that the arbitrator "exceeded his jurisdiction," was "without authority to act," "altered, modified or added to" the collective bargaining agreement, or handed down his "own brand of industrial justice."

THE U. S. ARBITRATION ACT (1925)

Although Congress passed the U. S. Arbitration Act of 1925 to resolve maritime disputes, courts have used it to vacate or modify a labor award:

(a) Where the award was procured by corruption, fraud or undue means; (b) Where there was evident partiality or corruption in the arbitrators or either of them; (c) Where the arbitrators were guilty of misconduct in refusing to postpone the hearing upon sufficient cause shown, or in refusing to allow evidence pertinent and material to the controversy; or of any other misbehavior by which the rights of any party have been prejudiced; (d) Where the arbitrators exceeded their powers, or so imperfectly executed them that a mutual, final, and definite award upon the subject matter submitted was not made.

The Act also empowers a court to modify or correct an award:

(a) Where there was an evident material miscalculation of figures or an evident material mistake in the description of any person, thing, or property referred to in the award; (b) Where the arbitrators have awarded upon a matter not submitted to them unless it is a matter not affecting the merits of the decision upon the matter submitted; (c) Where the award is imperfect in matter of form not affecting the merits of the controversy. The order may modify and correct the award, so as to effect the intent thereof and promote justice between parties.

ALEXANDER V. GARDNER-DENVER CO.

Courts review an arbitrator's award if a grievant's right to non-discrimination in employment is at issue. Title VII of the Civil Rights Act of 1964 declares that it is an unlawful employment practice for an employer, employment agency, or labor organization "to discriminate against any individual because of race, color, religion, sex, or national origin." In 1970, the Court, in *Hutchins v. U. S. Industries, Inc.*, 428 F. (2) 303 (1970) ruled that although an aggrieved employee had proceeded to arbitration, a federal court, not an arbitrator, was the final arbiter in discrimination disputes under Title VII. In *Caldwell v. National Brewing Company*, 443 F. (2) 1044 (1971), the Court held that a grievant could go directly to a federal court to obtain Title VII rights; a grievant need not invoke or exhaust the arbitration procedure. In *Rios v. Reynolds Metals Company*, 467 F. (2) 54 (1972), the Court held that a federal court may defer to an arbitration award. In *Rios* the Court deferred to the arbitrator's ruling. The Court said:

It must be plain that the arbitrator's decision in no way violates the rights guaranteed by Title VII. In addition, before deferring, the District Court must be satisfied that (1) the factual issues before it are identical to those decided by the arbitrator; (2) the arbitrator has power under the collective agreement to decide the ultimate issue of discrimination; (3) the evidence presented at the arbitral hearing dealt adequately with all factual issues; (4) the arbitrator actually decided the factual issues presented to the Court; and (5) the arbitration proceedings were fair and regular and free of procedural infirmities. The burden of proof in establishing these conditions of limitation will be upon the respondents distinguished from the claimant.

In *Alexander v. Gardner-Denver Co.*, 405 U. S. 36 (1974), the Court resolved the inconsistencies in the lower court decisions and fixed the relationship between the federal courts and the grievance arbitration machinery in the resolution and enforcement of an employee's rights under Title VII.

A black grievant had argued before an arbitrator that his discharge violated the "just cause" provision of the collective bargaining agreement. He alleged that the employer had discriminated against him because of race but he did so only at the last step of the grievance procedure. The arbitrator sustained the discharge, but he did not consider the racial discrimination issue. Although the agreement provided that the arbitrator's decision was to be "final and binding" upon the employer, the union and the employee filed a complaint with the Equal Employment Opportunity Commission (EEOC). EEOC concluded that there was no reasonable cause to find that the employer had violated Title VII of the Civil Rights Act. The lower courts ruled that the grievant had waived his right to sue under Title VII because he had chosen to arbitrate the grievance under the non-discrimination clause of the collective bargaining agreement.

The Supreme Court rejected the lower court's reasoning that because the grievant had proceeded to arbitration he had lost his right to sue under Title VII. The Court held that a prior arbitral decision does not foreclose an individual's right to sue in a federal court because courts have plenary powers to enforce statutes. Congressional policy against discrimination is of the "highest priority," and no statute divests federal courts of jurisdiction. The submission of a claim in the arbitral forum does not preclude a later submission to a judicial forum. The legislative history of Title VII manifests a congressional intent to allow an individual to pursue statutory rights independently of arbitration. The Court said:

> The clear inference is that Title VII was designed to supplement, rather than supplant, existing laws and institutions relating to employment discrimination. In sum, Title VII's purpose and procedures strongly suggest that an individual does not forfeit his private cause of action if he first pursues his grievance to final arbitration under the non-discrimination clause of a collective bargaining agreement.
>
> In submitting his grievance to arbitration, an employee seeks to vindicate his contractual right under a collective bargaining agreement. By contrast, in filing a lawsuit under Title VII, an employee asserts independent statutory rights accorded by Congress. The distinctly separate nature of these contractual and statutory rights is not vitiated merely because both were violated as a result of the same factual occurrence. And certainly no inconsistency results from permitting both rights to be enforced in their respectively appropriate forums.

The grievant had not waived his cause of action under Title VII because "there can be no prospective waiver of an employee's rights under Title VII." A union may waive certain statutory rights related to collective activity but Title VII stands on plainly different grounds; its strictures are absolute and represent a congressional command that each employee be free from discriminatory practices. Therefore, a waiver of these rights would defeat the paramount congressional purpose behind Title VII. An employee's rights under Title VII are not susceptible to prospective waiver. Although presumably an employee may waive his cause of action under Title VII as part of voluntary settlement, "mere resort to the arbitral forum to enforce contractual rights constitutes no such waiver". Furthermore, an employee's contractual right to submit a claim to arbitration is not displaced simply because Congress also has provided a statutory right against discrimination. Both rights have legally independent origins and are equally available to the aggrieved employee. The arbitrator's task, as proctor of the bargain, is to effectuate the intent of the parties. His source of authority is the collective bargaining agreement, and he must interpret and apply that agreement in accordance with the "industrial common law of the shop." The arbitrator, however, has "no general authority to invoke public laws that conflict with the bargain between the parties." An arbitrator has authority to resolve only questions of contractual rights, and his authority remains regardless whether certain contractual rights are similar, or duplicative of the substantive of the substantive rights secured by Title VII.

The Court also rejected the argument that later recourse to the judicial forum would be unfair to an employer. To rebut the argument that dual forums would give an individual "two bites of the apple," the Court countered:

This argument mistakes the effect of Title VII. Under the *Steelworkers Trilogy*, an arbitral decision is final and binding on the employer and employee, and judicial review is limited as to both. But, in instituting an action under Title VII, the employee is not seeking review of the arbitrator's decision. Rather, he is asserting a statutory right independent of the arbitration process. An employer does not have "two strings to his bow" with respect to an arbitral decision for the simple reason that Title VII does not provide employers with a cause of action against employees. An employer cannot be the victim of discriminatory employment practices.

The Court also rejected the argument that later resort to the judicial forum would undermine an employer's incentive to arbitrate, that it would be the "death knell" for arbitration clauses because the arbitrator's decision would no longer be final and binding. The Court said that an employer still had an incentive to arbitrate because an employer enters into an arbitration agreement as a quid pro quo for a union's promise not to strike.

It is not unreasonable to assume that most employers will regard the benefits derived from a no-strike pledge as out-weighing whatever costs may result from according employees an arbitral remedy under Title VII. Indeed, the severe consequences of a strike may make an arbitration clause almost essential from both the employees' and the employers' perspective. Moreover, the grievance-arbitration machinery of the collective bargaining agreement remains a relatively inexpensive and expeditious means for resolving a wide range of disputes, including claims of discriminatory employment practices.

The Court rejected the deferral standard because deferral would deprive the grievant of his statutory right to attempt to establish his claim in federal court. Also, deferral to arbitral decisions would be inconsistent with the purpose and procedures of Title VII which clearly indicates that Congress intended that federal courts are to exercise final responsibility for enforcement of Title VII. The Court also rejected the assumption that arbitral processes are commensurate with judicial processes and that Congress implicitly intended federal courts to defer to arbitral decisions on Title VII issues. The Supreme Court distinguished arbitral proceedings from judicial proceedings.

Arbitral procedures, while well suited to the resolution of contractual disputes, make arbitration a comparatively inappropriate forum for the final resolution of rights created by Title VII. This conclusion rests first on the special role of the arbitrator, whose task is to effectuate the intent of the parties rather than the requirements of enacted legislation. Where the collective bargaining agreement conflicts with Title VII, the arbitrator must follow the agreement. To be sure, the tension between contractual and statutory objectives may be mitigated where a collective bargaining agreement contains provisions facially similar to those of Title VII. But other facts may still render arbitral processes comparatively inferior to judicial processes in the protection of Title VII rights. Among these is the fact that the specialized competence of arbitrators pertains primarily to the law of the shop, not the law of the land.(*United Steelworkers of America v. Warrior & Gulf Navigation Co.*). Parties usually choose an arbitrator because they trust his knowledge and judgment concerning the demands and norms of industrial relations. On the other hand the resolution of statutory or constitutional issues is a primary responsibility of the courts, and judicial construction has proven especially necessary with respect to Title VII, whose broad language frequently can be given meaning only by reference to public law concepts. Moreover, the factfinding process in arbitration usually is not equivalent to judicial factfinding. The record of the arbitration proceedings is not as complete; the usual rules of evidence do not apply; and the rights and procedures common to civil trials such as discovery, compulsory process, cross examination, and testimony under oath are often severely limited or unavailable. And, as this Court has recognized, "arbitrators have no obligation to the court to give their reasons for an award" (*United Steelworkers of America v. Enterprise Wheel & Car Corp.*). Indeed, it is the informality of arbitral procedure that enables it to function as an efficient, inexpensive, and expeditious means for dispute resolution. This same characteristic, however, makes arbitration a less appropriate forum for final resolution of Title VII issues than the federal courts.

The Court rejected the deferral standard in *Rios* because deferral would make arbitration a procedurally complex, expensive, and time-consuming process, and judicial enforcement of the standard would require courts to make another determination of an employee's claim. Deferral might also adversely affect arbitration and the enforcement scheme of Title VII because employees might bypass arbitration and institute a lawsuit; they might fear that the arbitral forum would not adequately protect their Title VII rights. Hence, voluntary compliance or settlement of Title VII claims might be reduced, and the result might be more litigation, not less. The Court concluded that the federal policy favoring arbitration of labor disputes and the federal policy against discriminatory employment practices can best be accommodated by permitting an employee to pursue fully both his remedy under the grievance-arbitration clause of a collective bargaining agreement and his cause of action under Title VII. The federal court should consider the employee's claim *de novo*. The arbitral decision may be admitted as evidence and accorded such weight as the court deems appropriate.

The Court directed lower courts to give an arbitrator's award some weight but courts were to be "ever mindful that Congress, in enacting Title VII, thought it necessary to provide a judicial forum for the ultimate resolution of discriminatory employment claims." Courts had the duty "to assure the full availability of this forum."

VACA V. SIPES

Courts also review an arbitrator's award when an employee alleges that his union violated its statutory duty to fairly represent him in arbitration. In *Steele v. Louisville and Nashville Rd.* 323 U. S. 192 (1944) the Supreme Court held that because the NLRA conferred on a union the exclusive right to represent employees, a union had the duty to represent all employees "without hostile discrimination, fairly, impartially, and in good faith." In *Conley v. Gibson,* 355 U. S. 41 (1957), the Supreme Court applied the principle to collective bargaining. In *Vaca v. Sipes,* 368 U. S. 171 (1967), the Court applied the principle to arbitration.

In *Vaca,* an aggrieved employee alleged in court that the union arbitrarily, capriciously, and in bad faith had failed to take his grievance to arbitration. The employer had refusesd to reinstate the aggrieved employee because the company doctor had concluded that the grievant's blood pressure was too high. The union told the grievant to "get better medical evidence" before it would proceed to arbitration. After an unfavorable report from a doctor selected by the employee, the union refused to proceed to arbitration. The question before the Supreme Court was: Does a union's duty of fair representation require a union to process all grievances to arbitration? The Court found that, in this instance, the union did not breach its duty of fair representation and concluded that an employee does not have an absolute right to proceed to arbitration. A union must have and does have discretion to decide whether or not it will process a grievance to arbitration, a discretion "subject only to the duty to refrain from patently wrongful conduct such as racial discrimination or personal hostility." The union must be allowed "a wide range of reasonableness" to serve its members, but when a union exercises its discretionary power it must do so with "complete good faith and honesty of purpose."

A union does not have to take every grievance to arbitration; it may settle or drop a grievance. The Court said:

> A breach of the statutory duty of fair representation occurs only when a union's conduct toward a member of the collective bargaining unit is arbitrary, discriminatory, or in bad faith. Though we accept the proposition that a union may not arbitrarily ignore a meritorious grievance or process it in perfunctory fashion, we do not agree that the individual employee has an absolute right to have his grievance taken to arbitration regardless of the provision of the applicable collective bargaining agreement. In providing for a grievance and arbitration procedure which gives the union discretion to supervise the grievance machinery and to invoke arbitration, the employer and the union contemplate that each will endeavor in good faith to settle grievances short of arbitration. Moreover, both sides are assured that similar complaints will be treated consistently, and major problem areas in the interpretation of the collective bargaining contract can be isolated and perhaps resolved. And finally, the settlement process furthers the interest of the union as statutory agent and as coauthor of the bargaining agreement in representing the employees in the enforcement of the agreement.
>
> If a union's decision that a particular grievance lacks sufficient merit to justify arbitration would constitute a breach of the duty of fair representation because a judge or jury later found the grievance meritorious, the union's incentive to settle such grievances short of arbitration would be seriously reduced. The dampening effect on the entire grievance procedure of this reduction of the union's freedom to settle claims in good faith would surely be substantial. Since the union's statutory duty of fair representation protects the individual employee from arbitrary abuses of the settlement device by providing him with recourse against both employer and union, this severe limitation on the power to settle grievances is neither necessary nor desirable.

Vaca permits an employee to sue not only the union for its failure to represent him adequately but also the employer for a breach of the agreement. *Vaca* makes the employer liable for damages and the union liable for the additional damages caused by its failure to fairly represent the employee. An employee may recover damages only if he can prove a double breach, that is, the union did not fairly represent him and the employer violated the agreement. As a consequence, the employer's liability is dependent upon the union's guilt or innocence; both find themselves allied against the employee. If the employee does prove a double breach, the employer is liable for any damage caused to the employee from the time of the employer's breach of labor contract up to the time at which the union breached its duty of fair representation. The union is liable for all damages that accrue after the breach of its duty to fairly represent.

The Court said:

> The damages sought by [the grievant] were primarily those suffered by [him] because of the employer's breach of contract. Assuming for the moment that [he] had been wrongfully discharged, [the employer's] only defense to a direct action would have been the union's failure to resort to arbitration . . . and if that failure was itself a violation of the union's statutory duty to the employee, there is no reason to exempt the employer from contractual damages which he would otherwise have had to pay.

> The governing principle, then, is to apportion liability between the employer and the union according to the damage caused by the fault of each. Thus, damages attributable solely to the employer's breach of contract should not be charged to the union, but increases, if any, of those damages caused by the union's refusal to process the grievance should not be charged to the employer. In this case, even if the union had breached its duty by refusing to process the grievance over the grievant's discharge, all or almost all of [the grievant's] damages would still be attributed to his allegedly wrongful discharge by the employer.

HINES V. ANCHOR MOTOR FREIGHT, INC.

In *Hines v. Anchor Motor Freight, Inc.* 424 U. S. 544 (1976), the employer discharged certain employees for turning in expense vouchers for motel rooms that, according to motel records, were higher than the amount the drivers actually paid for the rooms. The employees asked the union business agent to investigate because they believed the clerk had altered the motel's records. The business agent promised to check with the motel, but he never did. The union processed the driver's grievance to arbitration, the arbitration board upheld the discharge, and the employees sued the union for a breach of its duty to adequately investigate their grievance and the employer for a breach of the agreement. During the proceedings, the motel clerk admitted that he had stolen the money and that the drivers were innocent. In court, the employer argued that the arbitration board's decision was final, binding, and non-reviewable by a court. The Court admitted that an arbitrator's decision is final and binding but held that an arbitrator's decision is not final and binding if a union violates its duty of fair representation when it processed a grievance. The Court found that the union had violated its duty of fair representation because it had processed the grievance in a perfunctory manner. A union cannot simply go through the motions when it processes a grievance: a union's decision to proceed, drop, or settle a grievance must be based on the merits of the grievance and on the wisdom of proceeding to arbitration. As long as a union gives a grievance the consideration it deserves and does not deal arbitrarily, discriminatorily, or in bad faith with an employee, the union's decision does not violate its duty of fair representation. A union does not breach its duty of fair representation if it makes a mistake or exercises bad judgment: the grievance process cannot be expected to be error free. The burden of proof is on an employee to show that a union has processed the grievance perfunctorily.

BARRENTINE V. ARKANSAS-BEST FREIGHT SYSTEM

In *Barrentine v. Arkansas-Best Freight System*, 101 S. Ct. 1427 (1981), the Supreme Court ruled that an employee's statutory rights under the Fair Labor Standards Act are also independent of an arbitrator's award. Barrentine and several fellow truck drivers filed a grievance which claimed they were entitled to compensation for "pre-trip inspections" of their trucks within the meaning of the collective bargaining agreement. A joint labor-management grievance committee rejected the grievance without explanation. The drivers then filed an action in federal district court and claimed entitlement to compensation under the Fair Labor Standards Act. They alleged that the union had breached its duty of fair representation. Upon review, the Court restated the principle in *Gardner-Denver*: an employee's statutory right is non-waivable; statutory rights under the Fair Labor Standards Act are subject to court action and are independent of arbitration rulings.

4

NLRB and Arbitration

The NLRB and an arbitrator may have concurrent jurisdiction over a dispute because a single employer act may be both an unfair labor practice and a violation of a collective bargaining agreement. As a consequence, a union may lodge an unfair labor practice charge before the NLRB and file a demand for arbitration for an alleged offense. The existence of two forums raises questions of jurisdiction.

In *Smith v. Evening News Association*, 371 U. S. 195 (1962), the Court held that neither the NLRB nor an arbitrator had exclusive jurisdiction to decide disputes over the interpretation or the application of the collective bargaining agreement. Either the NLRB or an arbitrator could remedy a breach of the agreement.

In *Carey v. Westinghouse Electric Corporation*, 375 U. S. 261 (1964), the Court ordered arbitration because it believed that arbitration may have a "pervasive and curative effect"; that arbitration may "as a practical matter, end a controversy or put into movement forces that will resolve it"; that arbitration achieves the objective of the statute; that arbitration promotes industrial peace and stability; and that arbitration avoids fragmentation of a dispute. However, "should the Board disagree with the arbitrator, the Board's ruling would, of course, take precedence."

In *NLRB v. C & C Plywood Corp.*, 385 U. S. 421 (1967), the Court held that the Board could, even in the absence of a grievance-arbitration clause, construe a collective bargaining agreement to discharge its duty because the Board construed the labor agreement not to determine contractual rights, but to determine statutory rights. Even if, as in *NLRB v. Acme Industrial Co.*, 385 U. S. 432 (1967), the agreement contains a grievance-arbitration clause, the existence of an agreement does not affect the Board's power to adjudicate unfair labor practice charges. The Court reasoned that the Board does not make a binding construction of the labor contract or intrude upon the domain of the arbitrator; the Board merely assists in the arbitral process.

In *NLRB v. Strong Roofing and Insulating Co.*, 393 U. S. 357 (1969), the Court reasserted its view that the Board's authority to remedy unfair labor practices was not affected "by any other means of adjustment" and "the Board may proscribe conduct which is an unfair labor practice even though it is also a breach of contract remediable as such by arbitration and in the courts." Furthermore, "it may also, if it is necessary to adjudicate an unfair labor practice, interpret and give effect to the terms of a collective bargaining contract."

Since the Board has the "undoubted" power to construe a collective bargaining agreement and to review an arbitration award to discharge its public duty, what is the attitude of the Board toward arbitration? Will the Board exercise its power before arbitration takes place? Will the Board defer to an arbitrator's award?

POST-ARBITRATION DEFERRAL

In *Spielberg Mfg. Co.*, 112 N. L. R. B. 1080, 1082 (1955), the Board said it would defer to an arbitration award if the award effectively disposed of an unfair labor practice charge, if proceedings were fair and regular, if all parties had agreed to be bound by an arbitrator's award, and if an arbitration award was clearly not repugnant to the purposes and policies of the National Labor Relations Act (NLRA). In *International Harvester Co.* (1962), the Board affirmed its policy not to exercise its authority over an arbitral award if an arbitrator's award procured the fundamental aims of the Act. The Board said that it would give "hospitable acceptance" to the arbitral process because the final and binding arbitration of grievances is "part and parcel of the collective bargaining process" and "a substitute for industrial strife," and effectuates federal policy. The Board voluntarily would withhold its authority to adjudicate an unfair labor practice charge over the same subject matter "unless it clearly appears that arbitration proceedings were tainted by fraud, collusion, unfairness, or by serious procedural irregularities or that the award was clearly repugnant to the purposes and policies of the Act." However, in *Raytheon Co.*, 140 N. L. R. B. 883 (1963), the Board modified the policy: it would not defer to an arbitrator's award if an arbitrator did not consider the unfair labor practice charge.

In *Olin Corporation and Local 8–77 Oil, Chemical and Atomic Workers International Union, AFL-CIO* (1984), an arbitrator had sustained the discharge of the president of the union for threatening a sick-out, participating in a sick-out, and failing to prevent a sick-out. The Board said it would defer to arbitration if it found that an arbitrator had adequately considered the unfair labor practice but only if (1) the contractual issue was factually parallel to the unfair labor practice issue, and (2) the arbitrator was presented generally with the facts relevant to resolving the unfair labor practice. In this respect, differences, if any, between the contractual and statutory standards of review would be weighed by the Board as part of its determination under the *Spielberg* standards of:

whether an award is "clearly repugnant" to the Act. And, with regard to the inquiry into the "clearly repugnant" standard, we would not require an arbitrator's award to be totally consistent with Board precedent. Unless the award is "palpably wrong," i.e., unless the arbitrator's decision is not susceptible to an interpretation consistent with the Act, we will defer.

Finally, we would require that the party seeking to have the Board reject deferral and consider the merits of a given case show that the above standards for deferral have not been met. Thus, the party seeking to have the Board ignore the determination of an arbitrator has the burden of affirmatively demonstrating the defects in the arbitral process or award.

PRE-ARBITRATION DEFERRAL

In *Collyer Insulated Wire*, 192 N. L. R. B. No. 150 (1971), the Board majority deferred to arbitration before the parties had proceeded to arbitration because the employer had no animus against the employees' exercise of their protected rights, the arbitration clause was very broad, the employer was willing to proceed to arbitration, and the dispute was "well suited to arbitration." Further, the arbitrator's interpretation of the contract might resolve both the unfair labor practice issue and the contract interpretation issue in a manner compatible with the purposes of the Act. The Board was of the opinion that grievance disputes "can better be resolved by arbitrators with special skill and experience in deciding matters arising under established bargaining relationships than by the application by this Board of a particular provision of our statute." However, to protect the statutory rights of the charging party, the Board retained jurisdiction "solely" to entertain an appropriate and timely motion for further consideration. For the Board to consider the matter, the Board required that the charging party show either that the dispute was not timely resolved in the grievance procedure, not submitted promptly to arbitration, or that the grievance or arbitration procedures were not fair and regular, or reached a result repugnant to the Act.

The Board minority vigorously criticized the majority's pre-arbitral deferral policy. The minority believed that the Board had abdicated its statutory duty to adjudicate the unfair labor practice provisions of Taft-Hartley. The minority wrote:

Congress has said that arbitration and the voluntary settlement of disputes are the preferred method of dealing with certain kinds of industrial unrest. Congress had also said that the power of the Board to dispose of unfair labor practices is not to be affected by any other method of adjustment. Whatever else these two statements mean, they do not mean that this Board can abdicate its authority wholesale.

The majority is so anxious to accommodate arbitration that it forgets that the duty of this Board is to provide a forum for the adjudication of unfair labor practices. We have not been told that arbitration is the only method; it is one method.

The Board minority believed that the Board could not legally defer to arbitration because private arbitrators had not right to interpret and apply public law: that function belonged to the NLRB. The Board minority also thought that *Collyer* pre-arbitration deferral sacrifices a party's legal access to the NLRB: pre-arbitration defferal was tantamount to compulsory arbitration and a waiver of statutory rights.

In *United Technologies Corporation* (1984), the Board reaffirmed *Collyer*. The Board noted that arbitration had gained widespread acceptance, occupies "a respected and firmly established place" in federal labor policy, and has become entrenched in U. S. jurisprudence. The Supreme Court in *Lincoln Mills* and the *Trilogy* had sanctioned arbitration as a preferable instrument for preserving industrial peace; courts and administrative bodies supported and gave deference to the arbitral process; and the Board itself had fostered a climate in which arbitration could flourish. The Board observed:

Despite the universal judicial acceptance of the *Collyer* doctrine, however, the Board in *General American Transportation* abruptly changed course and adopted a different standard of arbitral deferral, one that we believe ignores the important policy considerations in favor of deferral.

The *General American Transportation* majority essentially emasculated the Board's deferral policy, a policy that had favorably withstood the tests of judicial scrutiny and of practical application. They did so for reasons that are largely insupportable. Simply stated: *Collyer* worked well because it was premised on sound legal and pragmatic considerations.

It is fundamental to the concept of collective bargaining that the parties to a collective bargaining agreement are bound by the terms of their contract. Where an employer and a union have voluntarily elected to create dispute resolution machinery culminating in final and binding arbitration, it is contrary to the basic principles of the Act for the Board to jump into the fray prior to an honest attempt by the parties to resolve their disputes through that machinery. For dispute resolution under the grievance-arbitration process is as much a part of collective bargaining as the act of negotiating the contract. In our view, the *statutory* purpose of encouraging the practice and procedure of collective bargaining is ill served by permitting the parties to ignore their agreement and to petition this Board in the first instance for remedial relief.

The Board said that its policy of deferral to arbitration was not an abdiction of its statutory power; it was the prudent exercise of restraint, a postponement of the process to give the parties' own dispute resolution machinery a chance to succeed. The Board could always invoke its power to review an arbitral result inconsistent with *Spielberg*. The Board also said that the burden of persuasion "rests with the General Counsel to demonstrate that there were deficiencies in the arbitral process which required the Board to ignore a determination of an arbitrator and subject the case to review." The Board strongly and unequivocally affirmed its policy of "full, consistent, and evenhanded deference to a significant process within our national labor policy" because *Collyer* favors the use of private, expeditious, inexpensive dispute resolution machinery negotiated by the parties.

5

The Influence of Private Organizations
on Labor Arbitration

Three private organizations, the American Arbitration Association, the National Academy of Arbitrators, and the Society of Professionals in Dispute Resolution, have had and continue to have great influence on labor arbitration.

THE AMERICAN ARBITRATION ASSOCIATION (AAA)

The American Arbitration Association has had an enormous and favorable influence on labor arbitration. It was the first private organization to establish panels of arbitrators and develop rules of procedure that today govern many proceedings. Significantly, the AAA unequivocally distinguished between mediation and arbitration. In pre–Wagner Act days, a neutral mediated and, if necessary, arbitrated. Practitioners and scholars differed over the nature of the arbitration process. Noble Braden, who is affiliated with AAA, asserted that arbitration is essentially a judicial process. When parties agree to submit contractual disputes to an arbitrator, they create a private judicial forum. The arbitrator's sole function is to adjudicate and to determine contractual rights and duties of the parties, not to help them find an acceptable solution, give unsolicited advice, or mediate or compromise the dispute. George Taylor was a well-known neutral in the early days of arbitration. He thought that the grievance arbitration process included both the "mediation process" and the "judicial process." Today, the view of the AAA prevails: arbitration is judicial, a process clearly separate and distinct from mediation.

THE NATIONAL ACADEMY OF ARBITRATORS (NAA)

The National Academy of Arbitrators (NAA), founded in 1947 by persons who served on or for the War Labor Board, exercises great influence on the theory and practice of labor arbitration. Today, the Academy holds annual conventions, publishes proceedings, and monitors arbitration developments. The Academy welcomes applicants of good moral character who have had substantial and current experience as impartial arbitrators of labor-management disputes or applicants who have had limited experience but are recognized "through scholarly publication or other activities" as impartial authorities on labor-management relations. NAA is not an agency for the selection or appointment of arbitrators.

Article II, Section 1, of the NAA Constitution sets forth the purposes of the Academy:

to establish and foster the high standards of integrity, competence, honor, and character among those engaged in the arbitration of industrial disputes on a professional basis;

to adopt and encourage the acceptance of or an adherence to canons of ethics to govern the conduct of arbitrators; to promote the study and understanding of the arbitration of industrial disputes;

to encourage friendly association among the members of the profession;

to cooperate with other organizations, institutions, and learned societies interested in industrial relations; and to do any and all things which shall be appropriate in the furtherance of these purposes.

The Academy views the work of labor arbitrators as a profession, and it strives to implement its objectives through papers and discussions at its annual meetings and through its various standing and special committees. The Bureau of National Affairs publishes the annual *Proceedings*, a valuable and extensive commentary on labor arbitration.

THE SOCIETY OF PROFESSIONALS IN DISPUTE RESOLUTION (SPIDR)

The increased use of arbitration and the prominent role of neutrals in dispute settlement prompted some members of the NAA in the early 1970s to organize the Society of Professionals in Dispute Resolution (SPIDR), whose main purpose is "to enhance professional skills of mediators, conciliators, factfinders, arbitrators, hearing officers, trial examiners and other neutrals in dispute resolution." SPIDR seeks to expand the role of neutrals in dispute resolution; advance the educational and professional interests of neutrals; recruit and train neutrals; develop innovative impasse resolution techniques; serve as a clearinghouse for information and research data; increase public understanding of negotiation, mediation, conciliation, factfinding, and arbitration; and represent the interests of professional neutrals.

SPIDR holds annual conferences and publishes the quarterly *SPIDR-NEWS*, its annual *PROCEEDINGS, OCCASIONAL PAPERS*, and SPIDR-PLACE, a nationwide listing of employment opportunities for neutrals.

In pre-Wagner days there were no professional part-time or full-time arbitrators. Parties usually selected a prominent person in the community—a judge, clergyman, or professor. Advocates before these non-professional arbitrators were non-professional practitioners—workers, business agents, foremen, or operating officials—concerned primarily with a "practical" solution to a dispute, not with a judgment on the merits of a contract dispute. An arbitrator, usually a friend of the parties, served as mediator, not as arbitrator.

Today, a growing number of labor relations professionals draft detailed collective bargaining agreements that contain elaborate grievance and arbitration clauses. Today, arbitrators are highly skilled professionals: professors, attorneys, judges, labor-management practitioners, and others who have extensive knowledge and experience in labor relations. Today, lawyers and labor relations practitioners specialize in labor arbitration and spend a large part of their time in preparation and presentation of arbitration cases. Reporting services print arbitral awards; practitioners routinely cite, criticize, and praise these decisions. Some colleges and universities offer courses in arbitration; and the AAA, the Industrial Relations Research Association (IRRA), FMCS, and Public Employment Commissions provide forums and practice sessions on arbitration. The arbitration of labor grievances has increased enormously since 1935 and has become a way of life in U. S. labor relations.

6
The Grievance Procedure: Prelude to Arbitration

THE PURPOSE OF THE GRIEVANCE PROCEDURE

The Supreme Court has called the grievance procedure "the very heart of the system of industrial self-government," a "vehicle by which meaning and content is given to the collective bargaining agreement." In the words of the Bureau of Labor Statistics, the grievance procedure provides "a means by which an employee, without jeopardizing his job can express a complaint about his work or working conditions and obtain a fair hearing." The language of collective bargaining agreements varies but the meaning is the same. Simply stated, the purpose of the grievance procedure is to resolve disputes fairly and expeditiously, "to create and maintain labor relation harmony" ... "to adjust all complaints, disputes, controversies or other terms of the agreement," or to dispose of grievances "amicably." In different language, the grievance procedure is the "means for the orderly and expeditious adjustment of grievances of individuals or groups of employees or the employer," or the "mutually acceptable method for prompt and equitable settlement of a grievance."

The value of the grievance procedure cannot be overestimated. It channels conflicts into a political-legal mechanism which makes it possible for parties to construe the written agreement according to changing circumstances. It can prevent minor misunderstandings and problems from becoming major problems, it can serve to locate sensitive problem areas, and it can encourage an employee to air his complaint without fear of retaliation and in the knowledge that his grievance will be considered fully.

THE SCOPE OF A GRIEVANCE PROCEDURE

An employee may feel aggrieved, or he may feel that he has been badly or unfairly treated or that the employer violated the agreement, but he is not a grievant unless the matter is grievable, that is, unless he is contractually entitled to process his grievance in the grievance procedure. The scope of the grievance procedure, broad or narrow, determines grievability.

Broad Provisions of Grievability

If the scope of a grievance procedure is broad, an aggrieved employee can process any and all grievances and complaints. Some managements favor a broad grievance procedure because they believe it fosters harmonious labor relations. The following is a sample of a broad provision: "Should any difference of opinion, controversy or dispute arise between the parties, such difference of opinion, controversy or dispute shall constitute a grievance." A provision is broad if the language refers to "any question or dispute"; "any provision of this agreement or memoranda, or supplemental agreements covering wages, hours, and other terms and conditions of employment"; "any controversy or dispute" to "a claim" by a teacher or group of teachers that the School District has violated, misinterpreted, or misapplied "any provision" of the agreement or to a claim that there has been "unfair, inequitable or unwise treatment of the grievant by the employer." The following provision from an agreement between a federal agency and a union is very broad.

A grievance means any complaint:

A. by an employee(s) concerning any matter relating to the employment of the employee; or

B. by the Union concerning any matter relating to the employment of any employee; or

C. by any employee(s), the Union or the Administration concerning: the effect or interpretation or claim of breach, of a collective bargaining agreement; or

D. any claimed violation, misinterpretation or misapplication of any law, rule or regulation affecting conditions of employment.

To make sure that all grievances are grievable, parties sometimes provide the following or similar language:

If either party considers a grievance non-grievable or non-arbitrable, the original grievance will be considered amended to include this issue. The parties agree to raise any questions of grievability or arbitrability of a grievance prior to the limit for the written answer in the final step of this procedure. All disputes of grievability and arbitrability shall be referred to as threshold issues in the related grievance, except where the parties agree to hear the threshold issue and merits of the grievance separately.

Restricted Provisions on Grievability

In contrast to the wide open definition of a grievance, an agreement may restrict the scope of grievable matter to "disputes arising under the agreement," or to disputes that arise "under the terms of the agreement and existing employer practices." An agreement may exclude specific subjects from the grievance procedure even if the subject matter is mentioned elsewhere in the agreement; for example: "Merit increases shall not be subject to the grievance procedure" or "Job classifications and the rates thereof will not be subject to the grievance procedure or arbitration." Parties specifically have excluded the following matter from the grievance procedure: the Retirement Income Program, the Health Insurance Agreement, the Supplemental Unemployment Benefit Plan, contracting out of work, "all matters for which law mandates another method of review," "any decision and substance of a performance evaluation," "any decision to grant or disallow a request for authorized leaves and absences," political activities, suspension or removal in the interest of national security, an examination, a certification, an appointment, and "classification of any position which does not result in the reduction in grade or pay of an employee."

The next provision reflects federal sector practice. "Grievances on the following matter are excluded from the scope of this procedure:

1. any claimed violation of 5 USC 73 relating to prohibited political activities;

2. retirement, life insurance or health insurance;

3. a suspension or removal under 5 USC 7532 relating to national security;

4. any examination, certification, or appointment; or

5. the classification of any position which does not result in the reduction in grade or pay of any employee."

THE STRUCTURE OF A GRIEVANCE PROCEDURE

A committee of the National Labor-Management Conference (1945) unanimously recommended that a grievance procedure provide adequate and stated time limits for the presentation of grievances, the rendering of decisions, and the taking of appeals; require parties to formulate the issues at the earliest possible moment; allow them the right to discuss the issue informally and later reduce it to writing, if necessary; encourage representatives to settle at the lower levels grievances which do not involve broad questions of policy or of contract interpretation; delegate sufficient authority to representatives to resolve grievances which do not involve broad questions of policy or of contract interpretation; delegate opportunity for both parties to investigate grievances; and provide for a priority system for discharge, suspension, or other disciplinary action.

THE PRESENTATION OF A GRIEVANCE

Informal Presentation of a Grievance

An agreement may encourage a grieving employee to present his grievance "through informal communication." Another may stipulate that "nothing in this article is intended to preclude or prohibit informal discussion of a potential grievance." Another agreement provided that a grievance may not be processed "until there is evidence that informal two-way communications have failed to resolve the issue." To permit and encourage informal presentation of a grievance, parties sometimes agree that "neither party will be represented by an attorney in any of the steps of the grievance procedure except by mutual agreement."

Formal Presentation of a Grievance

If parties are unable to resolve a dispute informally, who can formally present a grievance to the employer? The Wagner Act gave an individual employee or group of employees the right to present grievances to an employer and to adjust the grievances without the intervention of the bargaining representative, but Taft-Hartley added the qualifier "so long as the adjustment is not inconsistent with the terms of the collective bargaining agreement" and "so long as the bargaining representative had been given opportunity to be present at such adjustment."

Agreements vary. Some allow an employee to present his grievance; others allow or require the grievant to go with a union representative to present a grievance on his behalf. For example: "At least one Association representative shall be present at any grievance meetings, hearings, appeals." Another agreement reads: "A grievant may be represented at all stages of the grievance procedure by himself or, at his option, by an Association representative selected by the Association." Somewhat differently: if a union representative does not represent a grievant, "the union shall have the right to be present and to state its views at all stages of the grievance procedure." Similarly, "The grievance shall first be presented by the aggrieved employee in person, and if he so desires, in the presence of his steward or foreman. The steward shall be given an opportunity to be present at the adjustment of the grievance."

In some cases a union representative has the right "to originate the complaint, in writing, for an individual employee other than through an employee or shop steward and to seek adjustment with the company." A different agreement reads: "The Union shall not be required to press employee grievances if, in the union's opinion, such grievances lack merit." In stronger language, employees, whether union members or not, "shall have no independent unilateral privilege or right to invoke grievance procedures or to complain against the Union for failing or refusing to file a grievance unless the Union is guilty of arbitrary or unfair representation." In contrast, a teacher may present and adjust a grievance independently of the union "so long as the resulting adjustment does not conflict with the terms of this contractual agreement between the district and the association and is in accordance and subject to the conditions and limitations provided by law."

The following provision from the federal sector reflects the law.

Section 3—Exclusivity.

Grievances may be initiated by employee(s) covered by this agreement and/or their union representative or by the administration. Representation of bargaining unit employees shall be the sole and exclusive province of the union. This is the exclusive procedure available to bargaining unit employees, the Union or the Administration for the resolution of grievances.

Section 4—Representation

A. Bargaining unit employee(s), filing a grievance under this procedure, may represent themselves or be represented only by a designee of the Union.

B. Upon filing of a grievance, whether an employee is self-represented or represented by a designee of the Union, the Union has the right to be present during the grievance proceeding.

C. Where the grievant elects union representation, meetings and communications with regard to the grievance attempts at resolution shall be made through the designated union representative.

Employer Grievances

Although grievances are overwhelmingly employee or union grievances, an agreement may specifically state that the employer is contractually entitled to file a grievance. Thus, "The grievance procedure shall be available to the union and to the company as well as to the employee," or "The employer shall present claims or grievances in writing through its representative to the union."

TIME LIMITS FOR FILING A GRIEVANCE

Parties stipulate time limits for filing and processing grievances through the various steps of the grievance procedure to resolve them efficiently, expeditiously, and to prevent their festering or becoming stale. Parties recognize time limits as substantive obligations when they agree that time limits "shall be strictly observed" unless extended by written agreement of the parties; or they provide that if a grievant or a union fails to comply with time limits, "it shall be deemed as acceptable of the employer's disposition of the claim," "shall constitute a waiver of the grievance," or "shall not be considered at a later date."

Time limits must be specific. General and vague time provisions, as "at a reasonable time and place," "with reasonable promptness," or "from the time an employee had knowledge or should have had knowledge of its occurrence" lead to disputes on timeliness. To avoid disputes over timeliness, parties specify that the number of days within each step "shall be considered maximum"; that time limits are "exclusive of Saturdays, Sundays and the holidays"; that "days" shall mean "the contracted work days"; or that time provisions exclude "vacation, sick leave or leaves of absence" from time limit counting.

STEPS IN THE GRIEVANCE PROCEDURE

The number of steps in a grievance procedure varies with the size of the union and the employer. Most grievance procedures have three steps; a few have four, five, or six steps.

Step One

The purpose of the first step is to give the employer and the union an opportunity to find and exchange facts, define the issue, and locate the provision(s) alleged to be violated. The spirit of step one is to "settle grievances at the lowest possible level." To do so, parties agree to a full exchange of all available evidence and information, and "if new factual information or evidence comes to the knowledge of one party, notice of such information shall be served on the other party's representative, and a meeting held as soon as possible at a mutually agreeable time." To guarantee full exchange of information, to prevent distortion of a grievance, and to pinpoint the issue at step one, an agreement may require the grievant and the union to write the name(s), and position(s) of the employee who brings the grievance; a clear and concise statement of the grievance and all relevant facts; the employee's understanding of his contractual rights; the specific provision of the agreement allegedly violated by the employer; the remedy or relief sought by the employee; the signature of the aggrieved employee; and the name and position of the person other than the aggrieved employee who files the grievance. One agreement stipulated that "A grievance that does not conform with the written requirements may be rejected. Resubmission will be allowed, provided it is received by the appropriate official within seven (7) calendar days following rejection and provided it conforms with the requirements of this subsection."

The following form illustrates the practice.

GRIEVANCE REVIEW REQUEST

To: _____

   Name   Title

   Grievant's Name _____

   Position _____

   Address _____

   Dept. _____

1. Consistent with the procedure for adusting grievances, I have taken the following options: (Indicate specifically by name and title who has officially received the grievance to date)

   Level 1 _____   Conference Date _____

2. The nature of my grievance is:

3. The adjustment I am recommending is:

Signature _____   Date _____

Step Two

Step two allows higher officials in the organization to review the grievance. For example, "If the grievant is not satisfied with the disposition of the grievance at step one, or does not receive a decision within ten (10) working days, he may appeal the grievance in writing to the superintendent." At step two, a form may require a grievant to include "the responses of his supervisor," and "the grounds for considering the decision unsatisfactory" at step one, and the appeal "shall also state the names of all persons officially present at the prior hearing who shall receive a copy of the appeal." Similarly, if no satisfactory agreement is reached in step one, the matter shall, within five working days after it was first brought to the attention of the company, "be reduced to writing" and "be submitted to a higher official designated by the company."

Step Three or Higher Steps in a Grievance Procedure

Step three and higher steps allow an appeal to still higher officials, for example, to "the highest administrative officers of the union and the employer," to "the Board of Directors through the Superintendent or through the Chairman of the Board," to "the Commissioner or such supervisor of the Department or Agency," to "the Employee Relations

Manager of the Company in writing to be handled at a time mutually agreed to by the Plant Manager or his representatives and the Council representatives."

At the last step of the grievance procedure each party should have all the available facts, the other party's interpretation and application of the provisions alleged to be violated, and the remedy sought by the grieving party.

BYPASSING THE LOWER STEPS OF THE GRIEVANCE PROCEDURE

To expedite the resolution of certain kinds of grievances, an agreement may stipulate that "grievances on unjust or discriminatory dismissals or grievances concerning layoffs due to reduction in force shall be initiated in Step 3 of the grievance procedure," or grievances over actions taken by the Agency officials against field station employees "may be grieved directly to arbitration." If management initiates a grievance, it "shall be filed with the local union president, or designee, and shall constitute Step 3 of the negotiated grievance procedure."

SPECIAL PROVISIONS IN THE GRIEVANCE PROCEDURES

Experience and circumstances have prompted parties to write special provisions into their grievance procedure. For example: If an employee participates in grievance adjustment proceedings, whether as a grievant, a witness, or a representative of the union, he "shall not suffer any restraint, interference, discrimination, coercion, or reprisal on account of his participation in the grievance adjusting process." If a union processes a grievance during the regular workday, the employer shall provide "released time for all participants in the investigation and processing of grievances, including the grievant, Association representatives, and witnesses." If meetings extend beyond the regular working hours, "employees shall be paid at time and a half." Another agreement stipulated that "reasonable time during work hours will be allowed for employees and union representatives to discuss, prepare for, and present grievances, including attendance at meetings with management officials concerning the grievance." If a union requests permission to examine records, equipment, materials, and the workplace, "such examination will not be unnecessarily delayed or restricted by the Company." Furthermore, "all documents, communications, and records dealing with the processing of a grievance shall be filed separately from the personal files of the participant." If an employee is discharged or voluntarily terminates his employment, the union "may continue to process on behalf of the employee any grievance claim filed prior to his discharge or voluntary termination if such a claim would result in a monetary award under provision of this agreement." Similarly, if an employee dies, "the union may continue to process or initiate on behalf of his legal heirs" any grievance claim filed prior to or after the death, if such claim would result in a monetary award under provisions of this agreement.

MEDIATION OF GRIEVANCE DISPUTES-BEFORE ARBITRATION

Many stoutly proclaim the virtues of arbitration, but arbitration divides the parties because it creates winners and losers. Hence, some writers and practitioners suggest that parties should experiment with grievance mediation by inserting grievance mediation before arbitration because mediation is an extension of collective bargaining. It is also informal, promotes amicable relations, requires no record, saves time and arbitration costs, gives a grievant his day in court, prevents surprise awards, and allows parties to save face. Others point out that grievance mediation lengthens the process, adds cost, conditions parties to rely on the mediator, and does not and cannot resolve disputes over contractual rights.

Grievance mediation might improve the relationship, clarify the issue, and perhaps lead one party to recognize the weakness of its position. However, mediation cannot succeed unless the parties are willing to settle, unless they make the effort to do so, and unless they submit their whole relationship to grievance mediation.

DISTRESSED GRIEVANCES

A grievance procedure becomes "distressed" when parties overload the procedure by routinely filing non-meritorious grievances to harass the other party. To remedy a distressed procedure parties might change the procedure, trade off grievances, clarify the written language, hold expedited arbitrations, or submit the whole relationship to a review by a neutral party for recommendations.

WORDS TO GRIEVE BY

Grievances arise when parties use vague, ambiguous and general language, as in the following words identified by the AAA: ability, absolutely, adequate, almost, capacity, completely, day, equal, forthwith, frequent, fully, habitually, high degree, immediately, minimal, minimum, necessary, normal, periodic, possible, practical, properly, qualification, reasonable, regular, substantially equal, sufficient number, and with all dispatch.

7

The Arbitration Clause

If parties cannot resolve disputes in the grievance procedure, they proceed to arbitration in accordance with their arbitration clause. The arbitration clause controls and determines all procedural and substantive matters before, during, and after the arbitration. The procedural and substantive details of arbitration clauses may differ but the matters discussed below, found in many agreements, reflect the general practice.

HOW TO INITIATE ARBITRATION PROCEEDINGS

The grieving party may initiate arbitration by filing a *Demand for Arbitration* with the other party, or both parties may agree to a *Submission Agreement*. Thus, an arbitration clause may read: "Either party may within five calendar days . . . serve on the other party a written demand for arbitration." A *Demand for Arbitration* may require that the requesting party (usually the union) specify the name and address of the parties, the effective dates of the collective bargaining agreement, the text of the arbitration clause, a brief statement of the issue to be arbitrated, the relief sought, and the dated signature of the union or employer official authorized to demand arbitration. On the other hand, an arbitration clause may direct parties to attempt "join in a written submission," which "shall state the issue or issues and the specific clause or clauses of this agreement which the arbitrator is to interpret or apply." Somewhat differently: "Parties may independently file submission briefs to the arbitrator not less than fourteen (14) days prior to the hearing with a copy to the other party." One agreement directed each party to file "its version of the dispute" with the arbitrator who shall determine "the issues subject always to the scope of this agreement." If parties are unable to agree on a formulation of the question, an agreement may require parties to submit to arbitration "the dispute over the wording of the issue which is to be arbitrated"; may direct parties to file "a written statement," or "a separate submission"; or permit the arbitrator to "determine the issue or issues to be heard, provided that said issue or issues are arbitrable."

Under AAA rules, parties may initiate either a *Demand for Arbitration* or jointly execute a *Submission Agreement*. AAA Rule 7 specifies that either party may initiate arbitration "By giving written notice to the other party of intention to arbitrate (Demand), which notice shall contain a statement setting forth the nature of the dispute and the remedy sought." Under AAA rules the moving party must file with the Regional Office "three copies of said notice, together with a copy of the collective bargaining agreement, or such parts thereof as relate to the dispute, including the arbitration provisions." After an arbitrator is selected and appointed, a party cannot enter a new or different claim except with the consent of the arbitrator and all other parties. AAA Rule 8 obligates the party upon whom the *Demand for Arbitration* is made to file "an answering statement with the AAA within seven days after notice from the AAA," and the responding party "shall simultaneously send a copy of its answer to the other party." Failure to file an answer does not delay the arbitration. AAA Rule 9 allows parties to file jointly at any Regional Office of the AAA "two copies of a written agreement to arbitration (Submission), signed by the parties and setting forth the nature of the dispute and the remedy sought."

It is my practice to ask each party to file a separate or a joint pre-hearing statement (not a brief) on the facts that led to the dispute and a formulation of the question(s). If the parties agree on these two matters, the joint agreement becomes the *Submission Agreement*. If the parties cannot agree on the facts or the question(s), we discuss this matter at the hearing.

The *Submission Agreement* has great value: it specifies the arbitrator's jurisdiction, gives the parties another chance to resolve the grievance, saves hearing time, can replace the hearing, and alerts the arbitrator to the agreed upon facts and question(s) before him.

THE RIGHT TO INVOKE ARBITRATION

Who has the right to proceed to arbitration? An agreement may read that "only the union or management" may refer to arbitration any griev-ance that remains unresolved after the final steps, or "the grieving party" shall give notice in writing to the opposite party but must do so "within 30 calendar days after receipt of the written decision" in the final step of the grievance procedure. Another provision reads, "a grievant" may request his association in writing to submit his grievance to arbitration, but if the association determines that the grievance is over the interpretation, meaning, or application of any of the provisions of the agreement, "the association" shall give written notice to the superintendent "within fifteen (15) school days after receipt of the request from the aggrieved person," or, very directly, a grievance "only at the option of the association" may be submitted before an impartial arbitrator.

HEARINGS IN THE ABSENCE OF ONE PARTY

To hold a party to its obligation to arbitrate a grievance, an agreement may authorize an arbitrator to proceed to arbitration "after written notice" to a recalcitrant party and "to render his decision upon the evidence produced by the party appearing." AAA Rule 27 stipulates that "unless the law provides to the contrary, the arbitrator may proceed in the absence of the party who, after due notice, fails to be present or fails to obtain an adjournment."

EXCHANGE OF INFORMATION

To forestall "surprise" evidence and to ensure that parties have exchanged all information, parties provide that "neither party shall be permitted to assert in the arbitration proceeding any evidence which was not submitted to the other party before the completion of Step 3 proceedings." Similarly, "During arbitration, neither the employer nor the Union will be permitted to assert any grounds not previously disclosed to the other party at the last step of the grievance procedure."

THE SCOPE OF THE AGREEMENT

A grievance may be grievable but not arbitrable. The scope of the arbitration agreement may be very broad or very narrow. A broad provision may subject "all grievances whether or not founded in the agreement" or "any dispute or controversy arising during the life of this agreement" to arbitration. In even broader language, the arbitration machinery shall be applicable to "any and all disputes, complaints, controversies, claims, or grievances whatsoever."

Parties sometimes limit the scope of the arbitration to "a dispute, grievance, or difference involving a violation of this agreement," or to "any alleged violation of the terms or provisions of this agreement or difference of opinion as to its interpretation and/or application."

Parties may specifically and expressly exclude certain subject matter, even grievable matter, from arbitration. For example: "The arbitrator shall have no authority to consider matters relating to management prerogatives, or any other matter not specifically set forth in this agreement," or "job classification shall be subject to the first three steps of the grievance procedure but shall not be subject to step 4 or step 5 of the arbitration procedure." Similarly: "The base rate review may be made the subject of a grievance but such grievance will not be subject to arbitration," and, contrary to the general practice, "Nothing in these working conditions pertaining to discipline shall be the subject of arbitration between the parties." Further, "Grievances on consuming intoxicants in the plant, fighting in the plant, thievery, refusal to accept an assignment in an individual's classification and infractions of current attendance requirements shall not be arbitrable."

I have read agreements that exclude the following subjects from arbitration: health and safety, hours of work, distribution of overtime, premium-rate work, patents, layoff, recall transfer, promotion or demotion, training and retraining, wages, benefits, non-renewal of a teaching contract, and salary rates.

A VARIETY OF TIME LIMITS

To expedite proceedings, parties provide that failure to give timely notice "shall be deemed a settlement of the grievance on the basis of the previous step, and the grievance shall not be considered arbitrable," or they specify not only that a grievance must be brought to arbitration, "within but not later than 10 calendar days," but also that the arbitrator must issue his decision "within 15 days after the case is presented for arbitration." Furthermore, they specify that if an arbitrator fails to make a decision within the allotted time, either or both parties may request that "a new arbitrator be obtained." Parties may even agree to the opposite: "The failure of the arbitrator to render a decision within the aforesaid prescribed time shall not affect the validity of said award." Agreements usually permit parties to extend time limits "by mutual agreement" and allow a longer period "if the impartial person may not be able to comply with the time limit." However, "Either side can deny an arbitrator's request for a postponement beyond this 30-day period." Parties also specify that the arbitration must be held "at a mutually agreeable place and date on one of three dates submitted by the arbitrator," and that "any grievance submitted and determined in arbitration shall not be submitted again within 1 year from the date of its original submission." Parties sometimes allow "only ten (10) working days within which to submit post-hearing briefs" and post-hearing briefs shall be confined "to matters presented at the hearing," but "no briefs will be permitted except by mutual agreement of the parties." They also allow an arbitrator to extend the time for filing briefs "for good cause shown," but "in any case the arbitrator shall notify the other party, who shall also be entitled to the benefit of such additional time."

Under AAA rules, an arbitrator has 30 days after the hearing or the filing of briefs to issue his award. FMCS allows 60 days.

EVIDENCE AND WITNESSES

An agreement may provide that witnesses "shall be available as needed, but shall be restricted as to attendance to the time required for their testimony," and that they shall "testify under oath." An agreement may forbid an arbitrator "to interrogate witnesses at any time." Many agreements stipulate that "the arbitrator shall not follow the technical rules of evidence prevailing in a court of law or equity," but one agreement required the opposite: "Judicial rules of procedure shall be followed at hearings before the arbitrator." An agreement may empower an arbitrator to request, and the parties must produce, "such witnesses, records, and other documentary evidence he may require," and to "determine the relevancy of the evidence"; or it may direct an employer to make available to an arbitrator "the employer's pertinent books, vouchers, papers, and records." Furthermore, an arbitrator, at the request of either party or upon his own motion, may adjourn the hearing for a sufficient period "to enable either party to furnish additional evidence, oral or documentary, which, in the opinion of the arbitrator, is relevant to the issue or issues involved." In addition, an agreement may direct an arbitrator "to make his decision in the light of the whole record and ... decide the case upon the weight of all substantial evidence."

TRANSCRIPTS

Because transcripts delay proceedings and are expensive, parties sometimes specify that the cost of the transcript "shall be borne by the requesting party and such transcription shall be the exclusive property of the requesting party" or that they "shall share the cost and the right to the transcript" and that "both parties shall be entitled to obtain copies of the transcript." An agreement may authorize either an arbitrator or either party, "at his or their option," to employ the services of a stenographer or reporter at the hearings, and an agreement may unequivocally direct that "no official stenographic record of the arbitration shall be made."

PRIORITY IN SCHEDULING GRIEVANCES

To reduce costs, parties sometimes stipulate that grievances that entail a continuing liability "shall be given priority over all other grievances in the arbitration procedure," or that "first priority shall be given to discharge cases and second priority shall be given to cases involving continuing liability. Other cases shall be given priority according to the submittal date."

WITHDRAWAL OF A GRIEVANCE

An agreement may allow that a grievance "be withdrawn," or withdrawn "only by mutual consent," or withdrawn only "prior to the start of the hearing."

SEPARATE OR CONSOLIDATED GRIEVANCES

The following provisions illustrate the varying practice: "More than one grievance may be placed before a single board of arbitrators, if the parties so agree." I found its opposite: "If more than one issue or case is pending before the arbitration board, either party may demand that the issues be heard and adjudicated separately." One unusual clause stipulated that "there shall be no more than 10 cases, in total, submitted to arbitration in any calendar year during the life of this agreement." Similarly, "Neither the union nor the association may elect in excess of five cases for submission to arbitration in any calendar year."

THE ARBITRATOR

Nomenclature

Parties may call the person selected to serve as arbitrator an "impartial chairperson," "umpire", or simply, "arbitrator." An impartial chairperson is an arbitrator who serves as chairman of a tripartite board, a board composed of a neutral chairman, a representative of management, and a representative of labor. Writers and speakers incorrectly call partisan members of a tripartite board "arbitrators" or "partisan arbitrators." The correct name for panelists is "representatives in arbitration."

Impartial chairpersons of tripartite boards were common when "to arbitrate" meant either "to negotiate," "to mediate," or "to arbitrate." The National Labor Board used the tripartite format, a form familiar to parties, but parties now favor a single *ad hoc* arbitrator or a single permanent arbitrator. Knowledgeable and experienced employer-designated and union-designated members of a tripartite board provide pertinent and important information to the impartial chairperson. They make sure that he has a full and complete understanding of evidence and argument, especially in lengthy, complex, or technical disputes.

As chairperson of a tripartite board, I circulate a draft of my decision to the other board members and ask them to comment on the draft. If at all possible, we meet in executive session to discuss the factual accuracy of the text. After the executive session, I write the final opinion and award, which I send to advocates. A board member may write either a concurring or dissenting opinion or sign the opinion and award.

Some writers point out that a tripartite board gives parties "two bites of the apple," adds to the cost of proceedings, and delays the issuance of the award. Other writers say that tripartite boards provide an ideal forum to mediate the dispute. These writers raise an old and recurring question: should an arbitrator mediate? *The Code of Professional Responsibility for Arbitrators of Labor Management Disputes* allows an arbitrator to serve in a dual role as mediator and arbitrator, but it advises parties "to so advise the arbitrator prior to appointment." If an arbitrator accepts the dual appointment, he "must perform a mediation role consistent with the circumstances of the case." If the parties have requested arbitration and if one party requests mediation but the other party insists on its right to proceed to arbitration, an arbitrator must decline the request to mediate. The *Code* also says that an arbitrator may suggest that he mediate the dispute, but "to avoid the possibility of improper pressure, the arbitrator should not so suggest unless it can be discerned that both parties are likely to be receptive."

An arbitrator should not serve as mediator unless parties specifically ask him to do so in writing. An arbitrator's function is to arbitrate, to decide on the contractual merits of a contractual dispute, not to mediate, reconcile, or accommodate conflicting political or economic interests. My experience has been that representatives in arbitration do not change their views in executive session. Hence, the impartial chairperson is necessarily the sole arbitrator because his vote decides the issue.

An "umpire" is a full-time or part-time arbitrator who sits alone and serves for a specified period of time, usually for the duration of the agreement. A permanent umpire system in large industries, such as that between the United Auto Workers (UAW) and Chrysler, Ford, and General Motors, has many advantages: parties save time and money because the umpire becomes familiar with the industry and with the parties; he is always available; no time is lost in his selection; he can arbitrate many cases, and he can, especially in discharge and discipline cases, render consistent decisions. The permanent umpire system has two serious drawbacks: it may condition the parties to bypass the grievance procedure because parties can easily, though perhaps unwisely, submit frivolous and political disputes to the umpire, and, although parties can remove an umpire, it may be inconvenient or awkward. An *ad hoc* arbitrator is one who serves for a specific dispute. Today, the most common method of selection is *ad hoc* selection because parties can, by frequent or repeated selection, convert an *ad hoc* arbitrator into a permanent arbitrator.

AAA Rule 15 provides that if the arbitration agreement does not specify the number of arbitrators, "the dispute shall be heard and determined by one arbitrator, unless the parties otherwise agree."

Methods for the Selection of an Arbitrator

Parties must use the selection method provided for in the arbitration clause, but, if the agreed upon method fails or cannot be followed, or if the selected arbitrator fails to or is unable to act and a successor has not been duly appointed, parties may use the facilities of the American Arbitration Association, Federal Mediation and Conciliation Service, various state designating agencies, or another outside agency or person to select an arbitrator. The *Proposed Uniform Arbitration Act* would empower a court to appoint one or more arbitrators.

Mutual and Direct Selection of an Arbitrator. The best selection method is mutual selection, the selection of a person or persons "acceptable to both sides." For example, "[name] shall serve as a permanent arbitrator during the duration of this agreement, subject, however, to his removal by death, resignation, or his removal by either party," or "[Names of five individuals] are hereby appointed as a panel of arbitrators . . . who shall be chosen . . . as follows: Each party may strike two names from the panel and the remaining arbitrator shall serve in the case." Another option is for parties to agree upon a rotating list of three arbitrators listed in alphabetical order and the arbitrator at the top of the list "shall be scheduled to hear the grievance unless the employer and the union agree to select another arbitrator from the list."

Selection of an Arbitrator with the Assistance of a Neutral Agency. The AAA, FMCS, and State Employment Commissions provide a list of names from which parties can select an arbitrator. One agreement empowers a court, another a university president, and another a governor to appoint an arbitrator. The AAA, FMCS, and State Employment Commissions provide most of the lists.

The American Arbitration Association describes itself as a public service, not-for-profit private organization which offers dispute settlement services to business executives, individual employees, trade associations, unions, management, consumers, farmers, families, communities, and all levels of government. The AAA promotes arbitration, mediation, democratic elections, and other voluntary settlement procedures. Founded in 1926 in New York City, the AAA, with 31 regional offices in major cities through the United States, administers disputes in commercial construction, international trade, textile and apparel, automobile accident claims, insurance, labor-management relations, and interpersonal relations. In addition, the AAA serves as a national center for education, training, specialized publications, and research in alternative methods of dispute settlement.

The AAA offers its membership a variety of publications. The *Arbitration Journal* (quarterly) reviews court decisions, and publishes articles by scholars and practitioners in labor, commercial construction, accident claims, and international arbitration. The *Arbitration Times* (a quarterly newspaper), highlights current AAA activities and general dispute settlement news. It provides information about coming events sponsored by the AAA and contains news of other organizations involved in the dispute resolution process. The *Lawyers' Arbitration Letter* (quarterly) contains a comprehensive survey of a particular point of law in all areas of arbitration, foreign and domestic, at both the federal and state levels. The *Summary of Labor Arbitration Awards* (monthly) contains selected private sector arbitration awards in summary form. The *New York No-Fault Arbitration Reports* (monthly) contain selected summaries of awards from arbitrations conducted by the AAA under the New York State No-Fault Law. *Arbitration in the Schools* (monthly) summarizes arbitration awards of professional and non-professional employees of public and private educational institutions. *Labor Arbitration in Government* (monthly), a companion reporting service to *Arbitration in the Schools*, summarizes selected arbitration awards that involve city, county, state, and federal employees. *Punch List* is a periodic newsletter that highlights current uses and trends in arbitration and mediation for those in the construction industry. *Arbitration and the Law* (annual) is a comprehensive summary of the most significant developments in arbitration and law during the year, and, *Study Time* (quarterly) is a newsletter of comment and opinion on substantive and procedural matters for labor arbitrators who are contributing members of the AAA. The staff of the Lucius R. Eastman Arbitration Library of the AAA publishes a selected *Bibliography on Labor Arbitration*, a valuable compilation of arbitration literature. The AAA offers its members substantial discounts on AAA books and films, reduced rates for registration at AAA eduational conferences and training seminars, access to services and facilities of the Eastman Arbitration Library, and consultation services on problems or assistance in designing specialized arbitration systems.

AAA provides administrative services for a hearing. If it does not administer the hearing, AAA notifies an arbitrator that "under the agreement that we have with the parties, the services of the American Arbitration Association terminate upon your appointment," and that "all future communications will take place directly between you and the parties. Their names and addresses are shown below." AAA directs the arbitrator to forward a copy of the *Notice of Appointment* and the award when it has been rendered. AAA also encloses a case reporting form to be filled out and returned when the case is closed.

AAA maintains and constantly reviews and updates its National Panel of Arbitrators. Before the AAA lists a person on its National Panel, it scrutinizes professional qualifications, experience, competence, and impartiality of applicants to determine their acceptability to both labor and management.

Under the AAA *Voluntary Rules of Labor Arbitration*, parties may select an arbitrator in three ways: appointment from a panel, direct appointment, and appointment by advocates.

AAA Rule 12, *Appointment from Panel*, stipulates that if parties have not appointed an arbitrator and have not provided any other method of appointment, an arbitrator shall be appointed in the following manner:

Immediately after the filing of the Demand for Submission, the AAA shall submit simultaneously to each party an identical list of names of persons chosen from the Labor Panel. Each party shall have seven days from the mailing date in which to cross off any names objected to, number the remaining names indicating the order of preference, and return the list to the AAA. If a party does not return the list within the time specified, all persons named therein shall be deemed acceptable. From among the persons who have been approved on both lists, and in accordance with the designated order of mutual preference, the AAA shall invite the acceptance of an Arbitrator to serve. If the parties fail to agree upon any of the persons named, or if those named decline or are unable to act, or if for any other reason the appointment cannot be made from the submitted lists, the Administrator shall have the power to make the appointment from other members of the Panel without the submission of any additional lists.

AAA Rule 13, *Direct Appointment by Parties*, provides that if an agreement names an arbitrator or specifies a method of appointing an arbitrator, "that designation or method shall be followed. The notice of appointment, with the name and address of such Arbitrator, shall be filed with the AAA by the appointing party." If an agreement does not specify a period of time, "the AAA shall notify the parties to make the appointment and if within seven days thereafter such Arbitrator has not been appointed, the AAA shall make the appointment."

AAA Rule 14, *Appointment of Neutral Arbitrator by Party Appointed Arbitrators*, provides that if parties have appointed arbitrators and have authorized them to appoint a neutral arbitrator within a specified time, "the AAA may appoint a neutral arbitrator, who shall act as Chairman." If an agreement does not specify a period of time for appointment of a neutral arbitrator and parties do not make an appointment within seven days from the date of the appointment of the last party-appointed arbitrator, "the AAA shall appoint such neutral Arbitrator, who shall act as Chairperson." If parties have agreed that arbitrators appoint a neutral arbitrator from its Panel, "the AAA shall furnish to the party-appointed Arbitrators, in the manner prescribed in Section 12, a list selected from the Panel, and the appointment of the neutral Arbitrator shall be made as prescribed in such Section." The AAA notifies the arbitrator of his selection, and sends him an acceptance form which must be filed with the AAA prior to the opening of the first hearing (AAA Rule 16).

The following, a common and typical provision, authorizes AAA to supply an arbitration panel: "If the union and company representative do not agree on an arbitrator, he shall be chosen from a list of nine arbitrators proposed by the American Arbitration Association." The union and company are "to alternately strike one name from the list until only one name remains. The right to strike the first name shall be determined by lot." Similarly: "A request for a list of arbitrators may be made to the AAA by either party. The parties shall be bound by the rules and procedures of the AAA," or "The arbitrator shall be selected by the AAA in accord with its rules shall likewise govern the arbitration proceeding."

Congress established the Federal Mediation and Conciliation Service (FMCS) in 1947 as an independent agency. Although mediation is the most visible and primary function of the Service, the Service encourages arbitration through its Office of Arbitration Services (OAS). FMCS does not compel parties to agree on a particular arbitrator; influence, alter or set aside decisions of arbitrators; or compel, deny or modify payment of compensation to an arbitrator. FMCS publishes rules in a pamphlet, *Policies, Functions and Procedures*; maintains a roster of arbitrators; administers the procedures for arbitration services; assists, promotes, and cooperates in the establishment of programs for the training of new arbitrators; and collects information and statistics on arbitration. The Arbitration Review Board scrutinizes the qualifications of applicants for listing on its Roster and the qualifications of all persons already on its Roster. The Review Board makes recommendations to the Director of the Service for acceptance, rejection, or whether or not a person should be listed. Persons on the Roster are expected to conform to the ethical standards and procedures set forth in the *Code of Professional Responsibility for Arbitrators of Labor Management Disputes*, as approved by the Joint Steering Committee of the National Academy of Arbitrators, the AAA, and the FMCS.

To be listed on the Roster, an applicant must complete and submit an application form obtainable from the Office of Arbitration Services. Further, an applicant must be experienced and competent in labor relations; acceptable to labor and management; and able to conduct an orderly hearing, analyze testimony and exhibits, and prepare a clear, concise, and decisive award within specified time limits. OAS prefers applicants who have had previous arbitration experience, but it considers equivalent experience acquired in training, internship, or development programs. OAS does not list any person who serves as an advocate for either labor or management. The initial listing for three years is renewable every two years. The Service cancels a listed name if that person no longer meets the criteria for admission, if he is repeatedly and flagrantly delinquent in submitting awards on time, if he refuses to make reasonable and periodic reports to FMCS, if he is the subject of complaints by parties who use FMCS facilities, or if the record shows that OAS has often proposed his name but parties never or very seldom selected him. OAS gives a listed person the reason and at least 60 days notice before it cancels his name. It also gives the listed person an opportunity to respond before a hearing officer on the proposed cancellation.

The Service requires arbitrators to fill out and to return all documents, forms, and reports required by the Service and to inform OAS of changes in address, telephone number, or availability, and of any business or other connection with parties that might create or give the appearance of advocacy. The OAS requires arbitrators to prepare and periodically revise biographical information on the appropriate form but arbitrators may change fees, address, experience, or other relevant data.

OAS follows a very specific procedure when parties request a panel of arbitrators. The Service prefers a joint request, but it submits a panel if the requet is made by only one party. The Service encourages parties to use the *Request for Arbitration Panel*, form R–43, available at all FMCS offices. The *Request* asks parties to specify the issue, and to enclose a copy of the arbitration clause and a copy of the stipulation to arbitrate. If parties do not use form R–43, the letter of request must include the names, addresses, and phone numbers of the parties, the location of the hearing, the issue(s) in dispute, and the number of names desired on the panel. OAS submits the names of seven arbitrators unless the applicable collective bargaining agreement provides for a different number or unless parties themselves request a different number. OAS provides biographical data on an arbitrator's qualifications, experience, and fees. OAS assigns a control number to each case for identification. OAS considers the wishes of the parties, general acceptability, geographical location, general experience, availability, size of fee, and the need to expose new arbitrators to the selection process. OAS accedes to a joint request to include or exclude persons from a panel, but if only one party makes a request it will not be honored. OAS complies with requests for an additional panel if the request is permissible under the agreement or if the other party agrees. Parties are to notify the OAS after they select an arbitrator; in turn, OAS formally appoints him.

Parties select from FMCS panels in two ways. They may alternately strike a name from the panel until only one name remains, or they may rank each nominee by numerical preference. If one name remains, OAS appoints him as arbitrator. If parties rank persons on the panel, OAS appoints the person who has the lowest accumulated numerical number. OAS makes direct appointment of an arbitrator but only on a joint request.

The following and similar provisions of a collective bargaining agreement authorized FMCS to furnish panels: "The Director of the Federal Mediation and Conciliation Service shall be called upon to provide a panel of seven experienced arbitrators"; and "each party shall alternately strike a name from the panel until one remains. The person whose name remains shall serve as the arbitrator." Similarly, "The parties shall request that a list of Arbitrators be submitted by the Federal Mediation and Conciliation Service." "The parties shall ask for a list of seven (7) names," and "within five (5) days from receipt of the list each side shall alternately strike names until one name remains." If the remaining name is unacceptable to either or both parties, they may ask for a second list of seven (7) names but they must "within five (5) days of receipt of this second list . . . alternately strike names until one remains and the remaining name shall be the Arbitrator. The parties shall jointly notify the Federal Mediation and Conciliation Service of the name of the arbitrator selected." The following is a slightly different version. "The selection of an arbitrator shall be made from a panel or panels, not exceeding three, submitted by the Federal Mediation and Conciliation Service. . . . If the company and the union fail to agree on an arbitrator, the selection shall be made by the Federal Mediation and Conciliation Service."

Whom do parties select to serve as arbitrator? An arbitrator's acceptability, appointment, and reappointment depend on his performance, his conduct at the hearing, his relations with the parties, and in particular, the quality of his awards. Partiality and poorly reasoned or poorly written decisions make an arbitrator expendable. An arbitrator becomes expendable if he curries favor, philosophizes, engages in abstruse legal discussions, and writes unnecessarily long and unclear opinions. An arbitrator becomes expendable if he prolongs hearings unnecessarily, demands pre-hearing or post-hearing briefs against the wishes of the parties, cites learned tomes, neglects substantial evidence, reverses prior arbitration awards without substantial reason or explanation, writes decisions without substantial reason or explanation, suggests that parties write clear provisions, mistakes critical facts, and fails to appreciate the real issue. An arbitrator becomes increasingly acceptable if his conduct and awards manifest impartiality, integrity, independence, and courage to decide directly and forthrightly. An arbitrator is acceptable if parties conclude that he is not susceptible to pressure, blandishment, or threat of non-reappointment, if he comprehends and accurately restates the parties' contentions, if he understands the significance of the issues, if he is not easily hoodwinked by bluff or histrionics, if he makes an earnest and evident effort to inform himself fully, and if his final judgment is the product of deliberation and reason against the standards entrusted to him.

Unions, employers, law firms, and personnel directors rightfully pay close and considerable attention to an arbitrator's experience, education, temperament, fair-mindedness, insight, intelligence, and especially to his past decisions, because selection is central to winning. They keep a biographical sketch of acceptable arbitrators, they accumulate and evaluate hearsay and direct observations about his performance, and they collect and research his opinions in the various reporting services. Parties select an arbitrator who manifests an understanding of the human conflicts embedded in labor arbitration, a person familiar with personnel policies and industrial discipline, and a person who will write a clear, concise, reasoned, decisive, and a "best and honest" opinion. Experienced practitioners do not select an arbitrator who praises the losing party with language but rules against it. Parties do not select an arbitrator who "splits the difference." They know when they have a "loser." Experienced practitioners do not judge an arbitrator's competence solely by his published awards; they do not keep a "box score" because they know that an arbitrator's competency, independence, and impartiality are unrelated to the number of his published awards. An arbitrator's reputation precedes him; he cannot blame others if he is not selected. He alone is responsible for his decisions. Expendability is an occupational hazard.

Ethical Standards and Qualifications of Arbitrators

Arbitrators on FMCS or AAA panels must conform to the ethical standards and procedures set forth in the *Code of Professional Reponsibility of Arbitrators of Labor Management Disputes*, as approved by the National Academy of Arbitrators, AAA, and FMCS. In *Study Time* (July 1985), the AAA reaffirmed its policy of strict neutrality in listing and appointing arbitrators. AAA reminded arbitrators that Section 3, "Responsibilities to Administrative Agencies," of the *Code of Professional Responsibility for Arbitrators of Labor-Management Disputes* requires arbitrators "not seek to influence an administrative agency by any improper means, including gifts or other inducements to agency personnel." The AAA has unequivocally stated: "IT IS AAA POLICY FOR ITS EMPLOYEES NOT TO ACCEPT GIFTS" because acceptance of a gift might be or appear to be construed as an expectation of preferential treatment. The AAA enforces its policy strictly and requests arbitrators to observe the *Code* and assist AAA personnel in doing the same.

The *Code*, a privately developed set of standards of professional behavior, lists the essential personal qualifications of an arbitrator: honesty,
integrity, impartiality, and general competence in labor relations. The
Code directs arbitrators to exercise good judgment, to be fair, not to
hestitate to rule decisively for one party, not to compromise or split
awards, and to decline appointment, withdraw, or request technical assistance if a particular case is beyond his competence. The *Code* leaves
it to each arbitrator to determine whether he includes "Labor Arbitrator"
or similar notation on letterhead, cards, or announcements, but the *Code*
says that it is inappropriate for an arbitrator to list memberships or offices
held in professional societies.

The *Code* obligates an arbitrator to disclose directly or through the
administrative agency any current or past connections or advocacy status
with an employer or union, and to disclose "any close personal relationship or other circumstance" which might reasonably raise a question as
to his impartiality before he serves as arbitrator. If an arbitrator did not
know these circumstances before he accepts an appointment, he must
disclose this information when it becomes known to him. The burden
of disclosure rests on the arbitrator.

AAA unequivocally requires disclosure. AAA Rule 11 says that:

> No person shall serve as a neutral Arbitrator in any arbitration in which that
> person has any financial or personal interest in the result of the arbitration,
> unless the parties, in writing, waive such disqualification.

AAA Rule 17 requires that before a prospective neutral arbitrator
accepts appointment he "shall disclose any circumstances likely to create
a presumption of bias" which the arbitrator believes might disqualify
him as an impartial arbitrator. The AAA immediately discloses this information to the parties. If either party declines to waive the presumptive
disqualification, the vacancy will be filled in accordance with the applicable provisions of the AAA Rules.

The AAA *Acceptance Appointment Form* reminds an arbitrator that the
Code requires disclosure and directs the arbitrator to disclose any current
or past relationship with the employer or labor organization, or any close
personal relationship or other circumstances "which might reasonably
raise a question as to your impartiality." If the arbitrator is or has served
as an advocate, AAA reminds him to disclose "any pertinent pecuniary
interest" before he accepts appointment.

Sometimes an agreement may impose the same obligation to disclose
"any circumstances likely to create a presumption of bias" which might
disqualify him as an impartial arbitrator, or "cause either party to object
to him acting as arbitrator."

Prudence and common sense dictate that an arbitrator disqualify himself if he has any financial interest in the company, if he has represented either party in the recent past, if he has or has had social or athletic contact with a grievant, or if he is a grievant's neighbor or church associate. Prudence also dictates that an arbitrator not accept rides to and from the hearing room without mutual consent of the parties, not have lunch or dinner with either party, not accept phone calls from a grievant, and not accept gifts or loans from advocates. Courts have said that an arbitrator should not only be neutral, he must also appear to be neutral. All doubts should be resolved against accepting an appointment.

The *Code* says that an arbitrator need not tell the parties that he has lectured and participated in AAA and FMCS conferences. Nonetheless, a professor-arbitrator should disclose that he has directed an advocate's graduate thesis or has had a close work relationship with the advocate.

The *Code* directs arbitrators to keep proceedings confidential unless the requirement is waived by both parties. He should discuss proceedings only with persons who have "a direct interest" in the proceedings, not invite persons to the hearing without prior consent, and not press parties for consent to publish an opinion. The *Code* captures the spirit and tone of the relationship that should exist between the arbitrator and the parties: an arbitrator should handle all matters "in a manner that fosters complete impartiality." AAA Rule 45 explicitly requires that "there shall be no communication between parties and a neutral Arbitrator other than at oral hearings." Any other oral or written communications from the parties to the arbitrator "shall be directed to the AAA for transmittal to the Arbitrator."

The *Code* directs arbitrators to accept the parties' decision to settle an issue(s) at any stage of the proceedings, to maintain adequate records to support charges for fees and expenses, to charge only the amount actually incurred, and to give a detailed accounting to the parties or to the administrative agency on request.

In *Study Time* (No. 2, 1987), the American Arbitration Association reported that the Special Committee on Professionalism of the National Academy of Arbitrators looked at what is considered a "declining level of respect" for the observance of its ethical *Code*. The committee deplored "the open solicitation of work, long delays in issuing awards, and suspect billing practices—all demonstrating a growing insensitivity to *Code* requirements." The committee recommended that the Academy devote at least one session each year at its annual meeting and its annual education conference to a study of the *Code* provisions. The committee also felt that it was necessary to publicize more effectively the *Code* and Academy complaint procedure and that innovations in Academy and appointing-agency procedures be undertaken.

Tenure of Arbitrators

All arbitrators, even "permanent" umpires, have no tenure because they serve at the will of the parties. A "permanent" umpire can be dismissed but only in accordance with the collective bargaining agreement. The following clause allows parties to dismiss an umpire at will: "If either party desires to remove the umpire, that party shall notify the other party and the arbitrator in writing of its decision and such notification shall constitute removal."

Limits to an Arbitrator's Power

An arbitrator has jurisdiction only over that portion of the agreement that parties specifically and expressly delegate to him. The following provision expresses this postulate of arbitration:

The arbitrator, who shall function in a judicial and not a legislative capacity, shall have only such jurisdiction and authority as is specifically granted to him by this Agreement. The arbitrator shall be limited to determining whether or not the Company (Union) has violated or failed to apply the specific provision or provisions of the Agreement as initially presented in the grievance. The arbitrator shall have no power to destroy, change, add to, or delete from any of the specific terms of this Agreement. The arbitrator shall be required to provide his decision in accordance with the express language of the Agreement.

Parties commonly use the following boilerplate language to express the same idea. Thus: "The arbitrator shall have no power to alter, add to, or in any way amend the provisions of this agreement." Similarly, parties often limit an arbitrator's inquiry and decision "to the specific area of the Agreement as cited in the grievance form." They even prohibit him from substituting his knowledge "for the express provisions of the contract" or they caution him not "to make any decision which requires the commission of an act prohibited by law or which is violative of the terms of this Agreement."

One agreement empowers the arbitrator "to determine the applicability of a previous award and opinion to a pending issue if a party claims that a previous award is final and binding on a pending dispute," but, somewhat differently, "No arbitration decision shall be used as a precedent for any subsequent case." Similarly, an arbitration award "shall not, on renewal of this agreement or negotiation of a new agreement, constitute a binding agreement." Another agreement permits an arbitrator to interpret the award "so far as necessary to clarify the same, but without changing the substance thereof, and such interpretation or construction shall be binding upon all parties." One agreement allows the arbitrator to "reverse, modify, or affirm his original decision if the parties point to an error in fact or an ambiguity in the relief granted within 6 workdays after receipt of the award."

CSRA breaks new ground. It grants an arbitrator "full authority to award appropriate remedies including reasonable legal fees, pursuant to the provisions of Section 702 of the Civil Service Reform Act, in any case where he deems it be warranted."

COST OF ARBITRATION

Agreements commonly stipulate that "the fees and expenses of an arbitrator shall be borne equally by the parties to this agreement," each party shall be responsible for the costs and expenses of its appointed member" and "they shall share equally in the expenses and fees of the Chairperson of the Board of Arbitration."

An agreement may provide that "the loser shall pay the fees of the impartial chairperson and the costs of preparing the transcript." Similarly, "The arbitrator, in making the award, shall stipulate which party is the loser," and the expenses of the American Arbitration Association, including the compensation to the chairperson of the arbitration board, "shall be paid by the party losing the case." However, if neither party wins a clear decision, "the Chairman of the Arbitration Board shall decide which party shall be assessed the cost" or "as, in the arbitrator's judgment, is equitable." To deter a union and an employer from referring trivial complaints to arbitration, a joint conference committee or an arbitration board "may assess the cost of any case against the party presenting such trivial or undeserved case or cases to trial, otherwise the cost shall be divided equally between the two parties."

AAA Rule 44 provides that the expenses of the arbitration (other than the costs of the stenographic record), including required traveling, other expenses of the arbitrator and of AAA representatives, and the expense of any witness, or the costs of any proofs produced at the direct request of the arbitrator, "shall be borne equally by the parties unless they agree otherwise, or unless the arbitrator in the award assesses such expense or any part thereof against any specified party or parties." Section 10 of the *Proposed Uniform Arbitration Act* provides that "unless otherwise provided in the agreement to arbitrate, an arbitrator's expense and fees, together with other expenses, not including counsel fees, incurred in the conduct of the arbitration "shall be paid as provided in the award."

Arbitrator's Fees and Expenses

An arbitrator may charge a daily rate or an hourly fee and bill parties for incurred expenses. An arbitrator may specify the number of hours that constitute a hearing day, for example, a six, seven, or eight hour day, and an arbitrator may adjust his charge for a hearing held during the evening, or on Saturday or Sunday. An arbitrator also charges either an hourly rate or daily rate for study and writing time, and for travel time, cancellations, and postponements.

FMCS permits each of its nominees or appointees to charge per diem fee and other predetermined fees. FMCS specifies the arbitrator's maximum per diem fee and the existence of other predetermined fees, if any, in the biographical sketch that FMCS sends the parties when they request a panel. The stated fees control any dispute over fees. To change his fee and charges an arbitrator must give FMCS at least 30 days advance notice.

Payment for a Transcript of the Hearing

Because a transcript is expensive, parties may agree that "neither party shall be required to pay any part of the cost of a stenographic record without its consent," or that "the cost of such transcript shall be borne equally by the parties." If only one party desires a transcript, "the other party shall not receive a copy thereof" or, if one party refuses to agree to share the cost of a stenographic record, "its refusal is not a waiver of its right of access to the record." Somewhat differently: If a party wants an official stenographic record of the testimony, that party "shall so advise the other party and shall arrange for the taking of such stenographic record," or "the requesting party shall pay the cost of such record ...and shall furnish the original transcript to the arbitrator.

Payment for Advocates and Witnesses

An agreement may provide that the Chairman of the shop committee and the president, or duly designated representative of the union, shall be paid for the time spent in arbitration "if it occurs during their regular working hours." Similarly, the employer "shall pay for time lost from regular working hours if one additional employee is required as a witness in arbitration." However, in disciplinary grievances, "two employees may be paid for time lost from regular working hours if required as witness," but "in no case shall the number of employees paid by the company exceed four." Alternatively, "Each party shall pay one-half of the aggrieved employee's time lost from work for appearance at the arbitration proceedings," and, differently, "No employee shall be paid for time lost, while acting as a represenative of the brotherhood during arbitration proceedings."

Administrative Fees

AAA charges an administrative or filing fee; FMCS does not. FMCS allows an arbitrator to charge an administrative fee if an arbitrator spends time and expense on pre-hearing matters. FMCS requires that an arbitrator make known to the parties all other fees and charges not specified in the biographical sketch which FMCS sends to the parties immediately after his appointment. Although FMCS does not attempt to resolve fee disputes, it requests parties to notify it if an arbitrator deviates from its policies. FMCS encourages parties to settle disputes but it allows an arbitrator to charge a cancellation fee after parties have selected him and notified him and agreed to a date. FMCS allows its arbitrators to charge a cancellation fee "whenever he receives insufficient notice of settlement to enable him to rearrange his schedule of arbitration hearings or working hours" and for the time he spends arranging or rearranging dates. FMCS has noted that because its service is free, it is not uncommon for parties to notify the arbitrator that they have resolved the dispute just prior to a scheduled hearing.

The *Code* requires an arbitrator to notify parties not only of his fees and expenses but also of his charges for hearing time, his per diem hearing fee, and his fee for hearing days of varying lengths. The *Code* allows an arbitrator to charge for study time, necessary travel time if this time is not included in charges for hearing time, postponement fee, cancellation fee, and office expenses.

My hearing day is a seven hour day; my fee schedule for cancellations and postponements is as follows:

If the parties cancel or postpone the arbitration more than 48 hours prior to the scheduled hearing date, the parties will be charged a half day's fee to be borne equally by both parties. If they cancel or postpone the arbitration within 48 hours of the scheduled hearing date, the parties will be charged one day's fee to be borne equally by both parties. If one party changes the scheduled hearing date, at any time, that party will be charged the total day's fee.

8
Preparation for the Arbitration Hearing

To present his side of the grievance effectively to the arbitrator at the hearing, an advocate must prepare himself thoroughly.

DESIGNATION OF THE ADVOCATE

Parties may select any person to represent them. In the past, a business agent or a personnel director represented parties. Today, law firms that specialize in labor arbitration represent parties in arbitration. Knowledgeable advocates expedite and regularize the process because they know how to formulate a submission agreement, how to present evidence and examine witnesses, and how to write an incisive brief. They do not harass or intimidate witnesses, engage in emotional arguments, use the trite "immaterial, incompetent, and irrelevant" phrase, or use "technical" or obscure language.

INVESTIGATION OF A GRIEVANCE

To present the facts accurately and well, an advocate must investigate a grievance thoroughly and objectively. The following suggestions might help an advocate ascertain the specific answers to the questions who, what, when, where and why. Set down all the facts in chronological order; tape-record not only the facts but also the opinions and feelings of all witnesses immediately after the incident because recollections are then fresh and relevant exhibits readily available. It is difficult to get an accurate account of events after several months because memory dims, and witnesses confuse events or allow prejudices or personal motives to color their view of events. Record in detail the observations of witnesses, ask witnesses to sign a transcription of their statements, and then date the record. Anticipate the other party's version of the facts; get sworn affidavits from persons who may be unable or unwilling to attend the hearing. Study the grievant's personnel record thoroughly. Study the grievance record from the original filing to the demand for arbitration.

An advocate diligently gets answers to the following questions: What is the grievance? Did the parties comply with all the steps of the grievance procedure? Is the grievance grievable? Is the grievance arbitrable? What provision(s) has been allegedly violated? Examine the language of the agreement, review the history of the clause, study the grievance committee records, and determine if past practice has given a different meaning to the language. What article(s) of the collective bargaining agreement is relevant to the dispute? Does one section relate to another section? Does one section modify or qualify another section? Is one section inconsistent with another? Did any party disclose the intent of the clause when they proposed the language? Was the controverted section amended? Why, and who suggested the amendment? Are there applicable federal laws, rules, and regulations?

GATHERING RELEVANT EXHIBITS

What documents, papers, exhibits, or other evidence will you need to present? Get all the available, relevant, tangible evidence: the minutes of the parties' prior meetings, the current agreement, prior agreements, personnel records, disciplinary documents, the employer's work rules, posted notices, memoranda of understanding, plans or photographs of the work area, charts, maps, medical and police records, copies of prescriptions, telephone bills, copies of by-laws, municipal ordinances, statues, and court decisions. Get affidavits and depositions. Make three readable packets of all written evidence: one for the other party, one for the arbitrator, and one for the witness as he testifies.

Does the other party have any document(s) you need? Ask for a copy before the hearing. If the other party refuses, ask the arbitrator to sign an easily available standard subpoena form. Be ready to show an arbitrator why you need the subpoena(s). Many states and the federal government have arbitration statutes that authorize court enforcement of arbitration subpoenas. Some federal courts hold that arbitrators have no subpoena power under the U. S. Arbitration Act. CSRA confers subpoena authority on agencies but excludes arbitrators from that list. Section 7 of the *Proposed Uniform Code* would grant the subpoena power to an arbitrator to compel the attendance of witnesses and the prodution of books, records, documents, and other evidence.

PREPARATION OF WITNESSES

Prepare and review questions you will ask your witnesses and anticipate those of the opposing advocate. Direct witnesses to stay calm, to tell the truth, to testify in their own words and from their own knowledge, and to answer only the questions asked. A witness who volunteers information may prompt the advocate to explore new areas on cross-examination. Warn them not to argue with the opposing advocate. Select persons who have expertise or direct knowledge and those persons whose demeanor is the most direct and forthright. Avoid a shy or hesitant witness, if possible. Coordinate the testimony of all witnesses at a meeting to eliminate gaps, conflicts, and redundancies in the testimony. Show all witnesses how their testimony fits into the total presentation of the case. At the initial interview with witnesses write out the questions, tape the answers, and review the questions and answers. In the follow-up interview, add or eliminate questions. Summarize the substance of the testimony of each witness and instruct each witness not to testify on any other matter. Assume the role of an advocate for the other party and ask your witnesses questions an opposing advocate might ask. Explain the hearing procedure and the role each witness plays in the procedure. Show witnesses relevant documents: it helps a witness recall and reconstruct events. Instruct your witnesses to dress as they usually dress, to listen to the questions carefully, not to anticipate questions or to answer before they know the question. Instruct your witnesses to ask the questioner to repeat the question if they do not understand the question, and not to lose their tempers. Tell your witnesses not to offer cute answers, to admit when they do not know the answer, not to volunteer information, not to anwer "yes" or "no" unless that is the correct answer, not to answer compound questions, and not to talk to the other side about their testimony. Instruct your side not to make any vocal or facial demonstrations.

PREPARATION OF AN OPENING STATEMENT

An *Opening Statement* contains a brief summary of salient facts, pinpoints the issue, sets forth what a party expects to prove, and asks for a remedy. Its chief purpose is to alert an arbitrator to the issues in disputes. I have written two opening statements as guides to help parties prepare one.

For the Union:

Mr. Arbitrator, the Union will show that the Employer violated Article X, Section 2 of the collective bargaining agreement, entitled *Seniority* because (a) the language must be given its ordinary not a technical meaning; (b) past practice supports the Union's interpretation and appliation of the agreement; (c) industry practice also supports this interpretation and application of the Agreement; and (d) other reasons support the Union's contention that the employer violated the collective bargaining agreement.

The union will call on (a) Mr. A. who will testify to . . . ; (b) on Mr. B. who will testify that . . . ; the Union will introduce Exhibit No. 1 which will show that . . . ; Exhibit No. 2 will show that. . . . If the arbitrator considers the union's evidence and arguments, he must conclude that the employer violated the collective bargaining agreement. The union asks the arbitrator to order the employer to promote the grievant to the journeyman machinist job.

For the Employer:

Mr. Arbitrator, the employer will show that the grievant was discharged for just cause.

The arbitrator must agree with the employer if he considers (a) the grievant's work record which will be introduced as Exhibit 1; (b) Exhibit 2 will show his many violations of work rules; (c) management and other employees will testify about his poor attitude and his indifference to his work; and (d) Exhibits 3, 4, 5, and 6 record his absences and tardies. The employer asks the arbitrator to dismiss the grievance. No remedy is appropriate.

PRE-HEARING CONFERENCES

Parties have a right to a pre-hearing conference, but in most cases it is unnecessary because parties can determine procedural questions (the proper subject matter for a pre-hearing conference), by mail or phone, or in a *Submission Agreement.* To forestall a pre-hearing conference, I direct each party, two weeks before the hearing, "to file and exchange no later than (date) a statement of the facts that led to the dispute, and a formulation of the question(s)." Pre-hearing statements or facts stipulations are invaluable: they compel the parties to reduce the facts and the question(s) to writing and they familiarize the arbitrator with the facts and issues before the hearing. If the parties submit contradictory facts or if they formulate the question(s) differently, an arbitrator knows what to look for at the hearing. A *Submission Agreement* eliminates the need for a pre-hearing conference or pre-hearing statements.

THE DATE, TIME, AND PLACE OF THE HEARING

It might be difficult to agree upon the date and place of the hearing because parties have to dovetail the schedules of an arbitrator, the advocates, and the witnesses. AAA Rule 10 states that if the collective bargaining agreement or the *Submission Agreement* does not specify the locale, or if there is a dispute over the locale, "the AAA shall have the power to determine the locale." AAA mails notices of the time and place of the hearing to all parties at least five days prior to the hearing.

It is my practice, immediately after I am notified of my appointment, to offer the parties, in writing, my earliest and most convenient available date. Each party then accepts or rejects the date until we agree on one. If we cannot coordinate dates readily, I ask the parties to submit three dates acceptable to them. I then select one of these dates. I confirm all arrangements in writing. Before the hearing, I also advise the parties that if they cancel or postpone the scheduled hearing date, they automatically incur an administrative/docket fee according to the following time schedule.

If the parties cancel or postpone the arbitration 48 hours prior to the scheduled hearing date, the parties will be charged an administrative/docket fee equal to one-half the per diem fee to be borne equally by both parties. If the parties cancel or postpone the arbitration within 48 hours of the schedule hearing date, they will be charged a full day's fee to be borne equally by both parties. If one party cancels or postpones the scheduled hearing date, the moving party will be charged the total day's fee. My per diem fee is ($ amount) for a seven (7) hour hearing day; study and writing time at ($ amount) per hour. Expenses as incurred. I will send you a detailed accounting of my fees and expenses.

PHYSICAL ARRANGEMENTS FOR A HEARING ROOM

Parties should appoint some person to arrange for a table, chairs, coffee, and tea. Almost any seating arrangement for a conference in a well lighted and comfortable room will do.

THE USE OF TRANSCRIPTS

Transcripts, although useful, are expensive; they also delay the award. Transcripts might be necessary, and perhaps indispensable, when parties disagree over critical facts, when the question of the credibility of a witness is at issue, when technical or complex issues are being disputed, or when one party foresees the possibility of court or FLRA review.

AAA Rule 21 allows a party to request a stenographic record. If parties agree to a transcript, the transcript becomes the official record of the proceeding and must be available to the arbitrator and to the other party for inspection at a time and place determined by the arbitrator.

According to the *Code* the transcript becomes the official record of a hearing "only when both parties agree to a transcript or an applicable law or regulation so provides." The *Code* allows an arbitrator to seek to persuade the parties not to use a transcript, or to use a transcript only "if the nature of the case appears to require one." If an arbitrator requires parties to provide a transcript, he must make this requirement known to both parties prior to his appointment. If the parties do not agree to have a transcript, an arbitrator may permit one party to take a transcript at its own cost. An arbitrator may also make arrangements to give the other party access to a copy, if a copy is provided to the arbitrator.

The *Code* allows an arbitrator to tape a hearing as a supplement to note taking without prior approval of the parties, but an arbitrator should not insist on a tape recording if either or both parties object. It is my practice to inform the parties that "the hearing will not be transcribed unless one or both parties provides for a court reporter." I tape the hearing to relieve myself of tedious note taking and to review the testimony. After I issue an award, I erase and reuse the tapes. In one case, a union taped the hearing and sent me the tapes and the transcription of the tapes. I sent the package back unopened because one party's tape and its transcription are not the official record. One writer thought that neither notes nor tapes provided an adequate basis on which to base a decision. A fair hearing requires a transcript: there are no "minor" disputes and there is no "bargain basement" arbitration.

9

At the Arbitration Hearing

The U. S. Arbitration Act sets forth the fundamental principle that governs the arbitration hearing, namely, "The arbitration shall be conducted in accordance with rules and procedures agreed upon by the parties, or in the absence of such agreement, by rules and procedures determined by the arbitrator." The practice varies. Parties sometimes determine the rules of procedure for the arbitration hearing either in their arbitration clause or in a *Submission Agreement,* or they leave the determination of the rules to the arbitrator. If parties designate the AAA as the administrative agency in the collective bargaining agreement, the rules of the AAA (the *Voluntary Labor Arbitration Rules* quoted throughout the text), govern the arbitration. These time-tested and very specific rules guarantee due process which the *Code* defines as "a fair, adequate hearing which assures that both parties have sufficient opportunity to presesnt their respective evidence and argument." AAA Rule 33 stipulates that if a party knowingly proceeds to arbitration, that party waives its right to object to AAA rules if the other party did not comply with all the requirements of the rules. AAA Rule 46 empowers the arbitrator to interpret and apply the rules "insofar as they relate to his powers and duties." If there is more than one arbitrator and if a difference arises among them on the meaning or application of the rules, "the matter shall be decided by majority vote." If a majority is unobtainable, either the arbitrator or a party may refer the question to the AAA for final decision, and "all other Rules shall be interpreted and applied by the AAA."

ROLE OF THE ARBITRATOR

The *Code* directs arbitrators to grant an advocate full freedom to present his case in his own way. Although an arbitrator should not interfere in any way, he may question a witness when "necessary and advisable." One writer approved "reasonable intervention" on the part of the arbitrator and suggested that an arbitrator intervene if he concludes that an advocate is "inexperienced" or is "purposely doing an inadequate job" because the arbitrator has a professional obligation to render a fair decision based on a complete exploration of the facts.

An activist role is alien to arbitration: an arbitrator should listen and seldom ask questions. No matter how objective or well meaning an arbitrator's questions may be, experience and court cases show that one party can easily interpret an arbitrator's question(s) as "making the case" for the other party. Parties, for a variety of reasons, might want to withhold evidence or refuse to call witnesses. Each party must prepare and present its case; the arbitrator must rule on the record before him even if the record is inadequate and even if advocates "did not do a good job" or were inexperienced.

PHYSICAL ARRANGEMENTS

The employer sits on one side of a rectangular table, the union sits on the other side facing the employer, and the arbitrator sits at the end of the table. Advocates take a seat nearest to the arbitrator; the witness chair is to the right of the arbitrator, and the court reporter (if there is one) to the left of the arbitrator or in another convenient place.

ATTENDANCE

The hearing is private, and open, as AAA Rule 22 says, only to those persons who have "a direct interest" in the arbitration. The *Code* directs arbitrators to admit only "persons involved directly" unless the parties agree or applicable law requires or permits it. An agreement may specifically restrict the persons who can be present at the hearing. For example, "Only the following persons may attend arbitrations: the first step supervisor, four additional company representatives, the grievant, four local union representatives and witnesses and counsel for both sides." If a party refuses to appear at the hearing, the arbitrator must decide whether he will hold a hearing in the absence of a party or postpone a hearing. AAA Rule 27 says that "unless the law provides to the contrary, the arbitrator may proceed in the absence of any party, who, after due notice, fails to be present or fails to obtain an adjournment." The *Code* directs arbitrators to consider all circumstances and to make sure that a recalcitrant party has been given adequate notice of the time, place, and purpose of the hearing. The arbitrator has the obligation to hold a hearing even in the absence of a party because an unwilling party must be held to its bargain to arbitrate a grievance, but before he does so, he should try to induce the unwilling party to appear. An arbitrator must require the attending party to present its cases; he cannot make an award solely on the non-appearance of the other party.

VISITS TO THE WORK SITE

AAA Rule 30 permits an arbitrator to visit the work site, if necessary, but only "after written notice to the parties" who may be present at such inspection. The *Code* allows an arbitrator to initiate a request to visit the work site and requires that the arbitrator comply with the request of any party to visit a work area.

PRESENCE OF THE GRIEVANT

A grievant has a right to be present at the hearing. If he is not present, an arbitrator must ascertain whether the grievant knew that an arbitration was being held on his behalf and whether he had received adequate notice of time and place of the hearing. An arbitrator should get this information into the record.

THIRD PARTY PARTICIPATION

An arbitrator should allow private counsel to represent a grievant but only if the union does not object. A grievant has no independent right to process a grievance; the union owns, protects, and applies the agreement. If the union represents the grievant, an arbitrator should grant a grievant's request to have a private attorney attend but not participate at the hearing.

SWEARING AN ARBITRATOR AND WITNESSES

Under AAA Rule 24, an arbitrator "may take an Oath of Office; and if required by law, shall do so." AAA requires an arbitrator to sign the AAA appointment form, which reads:

The undersigned, being duly sworn and being aware of the requirements for impartiality, hereby accepts this appointment and will faithfully and fairly hear and examine the matters in controversy between the above named Parties, in accordance with the Arbitration Agreement.

An arbitrator or any duly qualified person must swear witnesses if required by law or requested by either party. I always ask a witness to stand, raise his right hand, and answer the following question, "Do you swear to tell the truth and nothing but the truth, so help you God?" If a court reporter is present, the court reporter asks the question. Even if an oath or affirmation is not required by an agreement or by statute, a witness should always be sworn. Oaths dignify proceedings and remind a witness that he is expected to testify truthfully.

SUBMISSION OF JOINT EXHIBITS

Parties can expedite a hearing by submission of joint exhibits. I always ask advocates if they want to submit joint or separate exhibits. If parties agree on joint exhibits, I mark the applicable collective bargaining agreement Joint Exhibit No. 1; the complete written record of the grievance from the filing of the original grievance to the demand for arbitration Joint Exhibit No. 2; and subsequent joint exhibits as Joint 3, 4, and 5. If the parties do not submit joint exhibits, they mark each of their exhibits in numerical order as they present their case. Thus, an employer introduces its first exhibit as Employer Exhibit No. 1, and a union introduces its first exhibit as Union Exhibit No. 1.

The procedure to offer a document and to get it into the record is simple. The advocate hands the document to the arbitrator, who marks it for identification, for example, as Joint Exhibit #1 or Union Exhibit #1. The advocate asks for the admission of documents into the record. The arbitrator asks the opposing advocate if he has any objections to its admission. If there is no objection, the arbitrator accepts the document. If the opposing advocate objects to the admission of the document, the arbitrator hears argument on the objection from both sides. The arbitrator either sustains or overrules the objection. If the objection is overruled, the document is admitted; if the arbitrator sustains the objection, the document is not part of the record. Proceedings can be expedited if advocates have two copies of readable, well marked, and easily available exhibits in a packet, one for the other party and one for the arbitrator.

PRESENTATION OF THE CASE

Formulation of the Question

A clear, precise, and agreed upon formulation of the question is critical because it determines and limits an arbitrator's jurisdiction. Therefore, neither party can change the formulation without the consent of the other party. Ideally, parties should agree on the question(s) answerable by a "yes" or "no" before the hearing, but if they cannot agree on a wording of the question(s) before the hearing, each party should come to the hearing prepared with a version of the question(s). At the hearing, parties can then discuss and amend the other's draft formulation until parties agree on a particular formulation.

I press parties to agree on some wording of the question(s). In one case it took three hours; the temptation to shift the burden of the formulation of the question is great. An arbitrator should hesitate to formulate the question(s) for three reasons. First, parties cannot be relieved of their obligation to locate the cause of the dispute. Second, the arbitrator does not have the parties' intimate knowledge of the emotional, political, or legal context from which the dispute arose. Third, the arbitrator might not address himself to the real issue because he does not know what it is.

An arbitrator should formulate the question(s) if the agreement requires that "If the parties fail to agree on a joint submission of the issue for arbitration, each shall submit a separate submission and the arbitrator shall determine the issue or issues to be heard." If the parties, after extensive discussion, are either unwilling or unable to agree upon a formulation of the question(s), I ask each party to submit its formulation and to allow me to decide which formulation is the proper formulation in my opinion and award. Hence, the first question in my opinion becomes: What is the proper formulation of the question? Is the proper question the question as formulated by the union, or is the proper question the questioon as formulated by the employer? Another way to resolve an impasse over the formulation of the question is to incorporate the grievance into the question, thus: What shall be the disposition of the grievance filed on _____ by _____ ?

Here is an example of a clearly formulated question on a dispute over the interpretation or the application of contract language.

Did the Employer violate Article II, Section 3 of the collective bargaining agreement when the Employer denied overtime payment to the grievant?

The following is a common formulation for the discharge and discipline disputes.

(1) Did the Employer discharge (or discipline) the grievant for just cause?

(2) If not, what is the proper remedy?

The Opening Statement

Either party may start first but the customary practice is for the moving party to start first. The union starts first if the dispute is over the interpretation or application of the agreement; the employer starts first in disputes over discipline and discharge.

Sequestration of Witnesses

Witnesses are sequested to assure that one witness does not hear and later repeat what another witness has said. AAA Rule 22 empowers an arbitrator "to require the retirement of any witnesses during the testimony of the other witnesses." I always allow the grievant and his counterpart, usually the first line supervisor, to be presesnt for the entire hearing. Witnesses can be heard out of turn for good and sufficient cause.

Examination of Witnesses

Advocates examine witnesses to elicit the facts. Any procedure that affords a "full and equal opportunity to all parties for relevant proofs" will do (AAA Rule 26). Parties often use the simple and time-tested system of direct examination, cross-examination, redirect examination and recross-examination because it regularizes proceedings. Much or all examination and cross-examination of witnesses can be eliminated by stipulation of facts in a submission agreement.

Direct examination is the questioning of a party's own witness(es). In direct examination, a witness gives his name, position or title, and length of employment, and he testifies on what he said, did, or heard. The best questions are simple, direct questions that require a yes or no answer and questions that anticipate what the other party will ask. If an advocate introduces exhibits during the direct examination, the witness may attest to the authenticity of the exhibit.

On cross-examination, an advocate seeks to elicit, clarify, correct, and put into perspective those facts which a hostile witness might have colored, exaggerated, or omitted. In cross-examination an advocate seeks to reconcile or point to contradictory testimony and to test the memory, candor, reliability, or credibility of a hostile witness. To discredit a witness' credibility, an advocate simply points to contradictions or inconsistencies in testimony by other witnesses. Cross-examination should be short and focus only on clearly relevant, controverted, and important facts. Do not cross-examine a witness unless cross-examination is necessary to correct the factual record. You can always reserve the right to cross-examine the witness later in the hearing, if necessary.

After cross-examination, an advocate may question his witness on redirect examination, and the other advocate also may ask the witness more questions on recross-examination. The questioning continues until a witness has nothing further to add and until the advocates have no further questions. When the roster of witnesses for one side is exhausted, the opposing advocate presents witnesses in the same way until all witnesses are heard.

I agree with the recommendation of the Chicago Tripartite Committee that, except for unusual cases, an employer should not be allowed to call a grievant as the first witness in a discharge or discipline dispute. The committee would allow one exception: when the grievant might be the only person who knows what occurred and the circumstances surrounding the grievance. The committee said that "no other limitations should be placed by the arbitrator on the parties calling witnesses from the other side."

In arbitration each witness tells his version of the facts in his own way and without interruption. When you examine a witness, ask simple, clear, concise, and objective questions. Do not interrupt the other advocate; you have the right to cross-examine a witness. When cross-examining a hostile witness, do not use a sneering tone or snide remarks. Do not badger or intimidate a hostile witness. Avoid histrionics; do not interject arguments or evaluate facts. Avoid personal attacks, emotional outbursts, surliness, shouting, lectures, caustic remarks, declamations, and provocative language. These actions do not impress an experienced arbitrator.

Have your witnesses well prepared and readily available. Prove your case by your own evidence and witnesses. Do not assume that you can prevail by impeaching hostile witnesses. Be very careful when you cross-examine; the witness is a hostile witness. Do not ask leading questions on disputed matters. Do not ask a witness to interpret or apply the agreement. That is the arbitrator's task.

EVIDENCE IN ARBITRATION

Definition of Evidence

Evidence is the means an advocate uses to prove or disprove an alleged fact. Evidence that establishes a cause and effect relationship between the evidence and an alleged fact has probative value: it tends to prove. If the evidence is sufficient to convince the arbitrator, the evidence results in some degree of acceptable proof.

Presentation of Evidence

Who must present the evidence? The party that has the evidence must produce it and make it available to the other side, preferably before the hearing. An advocate has the right to object to improper evidence to alert the arbitrator to the possibility that evidence might be irrelevant or insignificant, but it is foreign to arbitration to interrupt and object constantly to evidence as "immaterial, incompetent and irrelevant." If a party makes an objection to the introduction of certain evidence, I ask the objecting party to state the reason(s) for the objection. Then, I invite the other party to rebut the reason(s) for the objection. After argument, I either grant, deny, or reserve judgement on the objection.

Admissibility of Evidence

In arbitration the question for the arbitrator is not "Is the evidence admissible?" but "How valuable is the evidence?" Labor arbitrators, unlike lay juries, need not be protected against spurious or doubtful evidence because they are professionals who know and value the common sense and wisdom embodied in court-tested rules of evidence. The spirit of arbitration is to admit all evidence, even hearsay, and immaterial and irrelevant evidence, "for what it is worth." Arbitration favors the liberal admission of evidence because, as some writers say, it might have a "therapeutic value": it can give an aggrieved employee an opportunity "to get something off his chest," to tell the boss his side of the story, or to vent his feelings, even if that "something" has no probative value or is contractually irrelevant. AAA Rule 28 allows parties to offer and produce "whatever evidence they desire," and "conformity to legal rules of evidence shall not be necessary." Parties must present evidence "in the presence of all the arbitrators and all the parties except where any one of the parties is absent, in default, or has waived its right to be present."

Relevance and Weight of Evidence

The arbitrator determines the relevance and materiality of all evidence, and he can give an affidavit "only such weight as seems proper" after he considers any objections made against it (AAA Rule 29). The *Code* directs arbitrators to allow parties "full opportunity to offer all evidence and to give affidavits "such weight as the circumstances warrant," and to afford the other party "an opportunity to cross-examine the persons making the affidavits or to take their depositions or otherwise interrogate them."

To admit evidence means only that an arbitrator will consider it; it does not mean that he will give it any weight. An arbitrator prudently admits all evidence for two reasons. First, he knows little or nothing about the dispute; he cannot know if the evidence is relevant or irrelevant. Second, his award will not be overturned if he accepts this evidence but it might be overturned if he refuses to hear relevant evidence. Irrelevant or useless evidence can always be discarded. Labor arbitration favors the liberal admission of evidence and full, immediate exchange of all available evidence regardless of possession. If a party offers "surprise" evidence, the arbitrator must give the other party full opportunity to examine and rebut the evidence.

I accept all evidence "for what it's worth." When a school district sought to exclude certain evidence, I wrote:

> The District's narrow view on the admissibility of evidence ignores the uniqueness of arbitration proceedings. In marked contrast to the strict rules of evidence required in court proceedings, the arbitration forum liberally allows evidence, all sorts of evidence, even parol and hearsay evidence. Parties select the arbitration process to avoid the formal, technical, strict procedures because they have confidence in the experience and competence of their arbitrator to discern the probative value of the offered evidence. Arbitration relies on more rather than fewer facts: arbitration ensures that each party gets a full hearing even if, technically, all facts are not relevant. Arbitration awards can be vacated on the ground that "We didn't get a chance to present our whole case," but never on the ground that "We were allowed to say just what we thought." In addition, one of the rules of the American Arbitration Association which governs this dispute stipulates that "conformity to legal rules shall not be necessary." Further, were the arbitrator to rule against the admissibility of this evidence, and the injured party could not air his alleged pain, suffering, or injustices, he would not get his "day in court." For all these reasons, I must, and do admit all the evidence submitted by the Association in its pre-hearing Brief and at the hearing.

Rules of Evidence

Three committees of the National Academy of Arbitrators considered the question: Are court "rules of evidence," essentially exclusionary rules, applicable to arbitration? The New York committee thought that the court rules of evidence were inapplicable to arbitration but recommended that the Academy develop rules on the admissibility of evidence; the Pittsburgh committee recommended that the Academy retain only the "common sense" of court rules; the Chicago committee concluded that it would be both unsound and unwise to attempt to prescribe a fixed set of procedural rules comparable to judicially adopted rules of procedure. Court rules of evidence are foreign to arbitration. Arbitral and judicial proceedings, only facially similar, cannot and should not be compared because the two processes are distinctly and uniquely different.

The Value of Evidence

The value of evidence varies. The best evidence is written, real, tangible evidence because it is objective evidence that proves a fact without inference or deduction. The best evidence can be found in personnel and payroll records, production records, charts, maps, machinery, official time records, blueprints, tools, overtime records, correspondence, minutes of bargaining sessions, photographs, tapes, models of trucks, medical records, and official public documents. Original records are better than copies. Copies of written records are acceptable so long as there is no question of authenticity. A visit to the work site can be tangible and valuable evidence. Circumstantial evidence (a number of facts taken together or a web of circumstances), is evidence that reasonably points by inductive logic to a particular conclusion. Circumstantial evidence is real but indirect evidence and may be valuable evidence if corroborated by objective evidence. If not corroborated by objective evidence, circumstantial evidence is suspect because a false conclusion might be drawn from circumstantial evidence.

Oral testimony is valuable evidence if the witness testifies on what he saw, did, or heard. However, a witness may fail to tell the truth. To impeach a witness, an advocate adduces contrary testimony; points to internal inconsistencies in the testimony; or shows that the witness was biased, hostile, under the influence of drugs, or had lied previously. For example, an employee might assert before an unemployment commission that he is unable to work, and he might assert before an arbitrator that he is able to work.

If witnesses contradict each other, whom is an arbitrator to believe? Writers suggest that an arbitrator notice how a witness testifies. Was he elusive? Was he alert, quick, and intelligent, or slow and dull? Is he a truthful person? Has he a bias or interest in the outcome? Does his testimony form a consistent whole? Did the testimony "ring true"? In paraphrased language, the California *Code* suggests that a judge and a jury observe the demeanor of a witness while testifying and the manner in which he testifies; the character of his testimony; the extent of his capacity to perceive, to recollect, or to communicate any matter about which he testifies; the extent of his opportunity to perceive any matter about which he testifies; his character for honesty or veracity, or their opposites; the existence or nonexistence of a bias, interest, or other motive; a statement previously made by him that is consistent with his statement at the hearing; a statement made by him that is inconsistent with any part of his testimony at the hearing; the existence or nonexistence of any fact testified to by him, his attitude toward the action in which he testifies or toward the giving of the testimony; and his admission of untruthfulness.

I concur with the West Coast Area Tripartite Committee that there is no reliable and foolproof way to determine whether a witness is telling a lie or the truth. Credibility findings are only probability findings because a witness' testimony is often incomplete, vague, or inexact. A witness might not consciously lie, but his emotions may distort his perceptions, and his interests or self-image might misinterpret or recast events. Further, time dims the memory and view of events.

In the following case, whom was I to believe, the grievant or the undercover agent? Who was more likely to tell the truth? Who had the most to lose or gain from the testimony? An undercover agent and two other persons were on their way back from a fishing trip. They stopped at the grievant's residence to make a "back-up buy" of marijuana. When the grievant was asked if they could purchase marijuana, the grievant said that he could get the undercover agent a quarter pound of marijuana if the undercover agent would wait. The grievant left, came back, and delivered the marijuana to the undercover agent. The undercover agent paid the grievant for the quarter pound of marijuana. When the grievant offered to sell cannabinol to the undercover agent, the undercover agent said he was out of money. The grievant assured the undercover agent that his credit was good and said that he could give him the money at work. At the hearing, the undercover agent testified that he gave money to the grievant on company property for the cannabinol purchased the previous day. He also testified that, on the day of the sale, he simulated smoking a marijuana cigarette with the grievant. In sum, the undercover agent's testimony was that a sale of drugs took place on company property and that the grievant had possession of and smoked marijuana on company property. The grievant admitted that he sold illegal drugs to the undercover agent, but he twice flatly denied that he accepted any money for illegal drugs from the undercover agent on company property. The crux of the issue was the conflict in the testimony between the company's primary witness, the undercover agent, and the grievant's testimony. I wrote:

The undercover agent is far more credible than the Grievant. His testimony was consistent and professional; his demeanor confident, poised, and forthright. The undercover agent had worked for numerous counties, for twenty (20) police departments, had studied drug control at a University, had never used drugs himself, voluntarily took and successfully passed a polygraph test, had worked on over 500 cases, and was an experienced simulator.... The undercover agent had no reason to single out or harass the Grievant.

The Grievant was not a credible witness. He had a powerful and personal interest to deny that he ever sold or was in possession of illegal drugs on Company property. His two explanations were vague and his denials too pat. He lacked the spontaneity and freedom of spirit that accompanies true statements.

I concluded that the grievant probably sold or would sell drugs on company property. I wrote:

Although the affidavit in court proceedings is not determinative of this issue, the affidavit does supply external evidence that the Grievant trafficked in drugs outside of plant property. It is more than likely that, if the Grievant trafficked in drugs outside of plant property, he would not hesitate to continue to buy and sell on Company property because it was a common knowledge among employees that the Grievant was "the one to see" if anyone wanted drugs.

In another case, a dispute over a ten-day disciplinary suspension, I had to determine whether the grievant, an oil company employee on the picket line, or a former truck driver for another company was the credible witness. The truck driver testified that the grievant had slashed a truck tire with a screw driver; the grievant denied it. I believed the truck driver because he had nothing to gain or to lose by his testimony. He gave clear and specific testimony; he testified confidently, forthrightly, and uninhibitedly, but the grievant's testimony was unconvincing and unsatisfactory. He testified that he had brought the screw driver to fix a friend's chain saw, and that he merely rubbed the screw driver on the tire, and that an "inexplicable impulse caused him to do it."

Hearsay testimony, what a witness heard another say rather than what was said to him, is secondhand, doubtful, and unreliable evidence. Hearsay evidence is weak evidence because there is no opportunity to cross-examine the person who made the original statement and because a witness who offers hearsay evidence may be motivated by self-interest, malice, or spite. Furthermore, he might not repeat the information accurately. Hearsay evidence may be of value if it corroborates direct evidence.

An affidavit, a form of hearsay, is a sworn written statement by one who is unable to be present to testify. An affidavit has very limited value because an opposing advocate cannot cross-examine an absent person. A deposition is a written statement taken in the presence of advocates who have the opportunity to cross-examine the person who testifies. Depositions have value because they are subject to cross-examination.

Parol evidence is evidence that a party offers to assert that the written agreement is not the final or complete agreement between the parties. Parol evidence is of no value if an arbitrator finds the language of the agreement clear and unambiguous. Written evidence, for example, collateral agreements, minutes of negotiations, the history of a clause, may be valuable evidence if the contract language is ambiguous or if an agreement is silent on the disputed subject matter.

The "evidence" gathered from a polygraph is doubtful and scientifically unreliable evidence. Some believe that telling a lie causes psychological conflict. This, in turn, causes physiological changes in blood pressure, pulse rate, respiration rate, and muscular movements, which are measurable by the polygraph machine. There is no conclusive scientific proof that the machine can measure the quality of a statement, its truth or falsity. Further, the operation of the machine and an interpretation of the answers depends on the skill of the operator; there is no way to cross-examine the machine, and the machine itself may not be free from error.

Expert opinion and testimony is valuable because opinions and conclusions of a locksmith, engineer, doctor, scientist, and others can help an arbitrator draw correct inferences. The qualifications of an expert are open to challenge, and his opinion and testimony are open to cross-examination.

Compromise offers have no value because they are not evidence but rather political decisions made to resolve the dispute.

Sufficiency of Evidence

Some writers say that the moving party has a "burden of proof" and the burden at some point shifts from one party to the other party. This language and notion, taken from the law practice, is foreign to arbitration. An advocate's task is to "convince the arbitrator." A union advocate must convince an arbitrator that the employer did violate the agreement, an employer advocate must convince the arbitrator that it had just cause to discharge or discipline an employee.

How much evidence is needed? Writers also say that for certain offenses, like discharge, an advocate must offer the strictest proof, "proof beyond a reasonable doubt," which means "fully satisfied, entirely convinced, satisfied to moral certainty." For other offenses, an advocate must offer a "fair preponderance of the evidence," or "evidence sufficient to create in the minds of the triers of fact the conviction that the party upon whom is the burden has established its case." For other offenses, an advocate must offer "clear and convincing evidence" or "proof beyond a reasonable or well-founded doubt." I find the three standards taken from law practice vague, confusing, and irrelevant. I agree with the conclusion of the West Coast Tripartite Committee that these legal concepts are inappropriate to arbitration. The task of the moving party is to adduce sufficient evidence to convince the arbitrator.

RECESSES AND ADJOURNMENTS

AAA Rule 23 permits an arbitrator to grant a recess "for good cause shown" upon the request of a party or upon his own initiative: to stretch, to go to lunch, or to discuss the grievance. An arbitrator may adjourn the hearing to the following day or to another day, but if he adjourns the hearing indefinitely, he must give parties official written notice, either immediately or at a future date, of the time and place of the next hearing.

CLOSING STATEMENT OR POST-HEARING BRIEFS

AAA Rule 31 requires an arbitrator to ask parties if they have any further proofs to offer or witnesses to be heard before he invites an advocate to make a *Closing Statement*. After the closing statement, the arbitrator or the AAA tribunal clerk declares the hearing closed. The time limit within which an arbitrator must make an award begins immediately after the close of the hearing or after parties file briefs.

An advocate may make a closing statement or file a brief. A closing statement saves time and money, but to be effective, an advocate must be able to summarize facts clearly and argue cogently, convincingly, logically, and forcibly for his conclusion. An oral summation at the end of the hearing is not an adequate substitute for a brief: parties will not have sufficient time to organize facts and arguments, and an arbitrator may be too tired to understand and appreciate all the facts.

Before I formally close the hearing, I ask parties: "Have the parties received a full, fair, and impartial hearing?" After an affirmative answer, I ask the parties if they want me to send the opinion and award to another party, because sometimes advocates and principals work in different cities. Lastly, we agree on a time schedule for an exchange of briefs, if any, and the issuance of the opinion and award.

POST-HEARING BRIEFS

The *Code* permits an arbitrator to suggest to the parties that they are free to file or not file post-hearing briefs. I know that writing a brief is hard work, but a clear, concise, and well written brief ultimately decides the issue. An ideal brief sets forth the specific facts of the dispute in chronological order unless the parties have stipulated the facts in the *Submission Agreement*; it restates the question(s) agreed to in the *Submission Agreement* or at the hearing. A party cannot change the wording of a question because the arbitrator has authority only over the question as agreed to by the parties. An ideal brief sets forth the applicable principle of contract interpretation; makes a statement on who must convince the arbitrator; and argues forcibly.

To argue forcibly in a contract interpretation dispute, argue deductively, that is, proceed from the general principle of contract construction (the theory of the case) and apply the principle to the dispute. To be convincing in a discipline and discharge dispute, argue inductively, that is, gather a set of particulars that point to your conclusion; avoid analogical arguments and quotations from other arbitrators because analogical argument is the weakest form of argument: it assumes a nonexistent identity of facts, issues, and contract. Another arbitrator's award might be useful and instructive if it enunciates a valid principle or argues logically and coherently. Quotations from arbitral "authorities" carry little, if any, weight, because one "eminent" authority can be juxtaposed against another "eminent" authority, and there are no precedents in arbitration. However, arbitration awards, especially in discharge and discipline cases, might have some value because they show how arbitrators have wrestled with and applied the notion of fairness, justice, and equity to other circumstances.

In addition, a good brief impeaches testimony by citing contrary testimony, points clearly to the reasons why and how the arbitrator should rule, and specifies a clear and practical remedy that the arbitrator should award.

Poorly written briefs do not persuade. They do not serve the interest of the client. I have found the following books helpful: William Zinsser, *On Writing Well*; H. W. Fowler, *A Dictonary of Modern English Usage*; Roger Fowler, *Essays on Style and Language*; William Strunk and E. B. White, *Elements of Style*; and Sheridan Baker, *The Practical Stylist*. I have taken the following suggestions from these books. Use strong verbs in the active voice; write directly, affirmatively, and unequivocally; use the negative form only to contrast or juxtapose ideas; simplify sentences and eliminate most adjectives and adverbs after the first draft; write with nouns and verbs; replace phrases with a single word, preferably with a noun or a verb; limit sentences to 20 words or less; make sure that each sentence contains a subject, verb, and object, usually in that order; omit sentences with more than one subordinate clause; go from the known to the unknown; start every new paragraph with a new idea and a transitional sentence; write in the same person and verb tense; and avoid pretentions, imprecise, stilted, fashionable, or trendy language, such as viable, input, or orient. Use simple language, like "the union asserts" or "the employer concludes"; do not use nouns or adjectives as verbs, for example, optimize, prioritize, impact, interface, maximize, finalize, or target; use the precise word, for example, criterion is singular, criteria is plural; avoid redundancies; it is still a good rule not to split an infinitive; put the brief away for a day, and reread it for unity, coherence, emphasis, punctuation, readability, and direction. The time-honored adage says it concisely: "Rewriting is good writing."

10

After the Hearing

REOPENING OF THE HEARING

AAA Rule 22 permits an arbitrator to reopen the hearing on his own motion or on the motion of either party "for good cause shown, at any time before the award is made." An arbitrator must give one party an opportunity to agree to or to object to the other party's request to reopen a hearing, but he cannot reopen the hearing after he has issued a decision because then he will have lost authority over the matter. Furthermore, he cannot reopen the hearing if reopening prevents him from making a timely award, "unless both parties agree upon the extension of such time limit." If an agreement does not fix a time limit, an arbitrator may reopen a hearing, and he "shall have 30 days from the closing of the reopened hearings within which to make an award."

THE FORM OF AN OPINION AND AWARD

The *Opinion and Award,* sometimes called the decision or the award, is an arbitrator's oral or written decision on the question(s) before him. Although the Supreme Court said that an arbitrator need not give reasons for an award or write an opinion (Steelworkers v. Enterprise Wheel & Car Corp.), arbitrators commonly write opinions that are sometimes published by the reporting services. An arbitrator may issue an opinion in any form, oral or written, long or short, unless the collective bargaining agreement or the parties specify the form of the opinion. For example, the arbitrator "shall render his award in writing within fourteen (14) calendar days after submission", or he shall render his award "in writing together with his written findings and conclusions." Similarly, he shall render "a written decision which shall include the award and an opinion stating the specific provision(s) of the agreement relied on, the issue(s), reasoning, and facts upon which the decision is based." Alternatively, the Board's decision "shall contain a full statement of the grounds upon which the issue or issues have been decided," or he shall send "identical copies to both parties." Likewise, an arbitrator can issue an oral award "only when mutually agreed upon by both parties."

AAA Rule 38 requires that an award shall be "in writing" and signed "either by the neutral arbitrator or by a concurring majority if there be more than one arbitrator." Parties must advise AAA if they do not require the arbitrator to write an opinion. The *Code* also requires that the award "shall be in writing and signed by the arbitrators joining in the award."

An arbitrator issues a "bench" decision when he hands down his decision immediately after the hearing. The *Code* directs an arbitrator to render a bench decision if he accepted appointment on condition that he would issue one; if not, he should use his discretion. If only one party requests a bench decision and the other party objects, the arbitrator should not render a bench decision except under the most unusal circumstances.

It is unwise for parties to ask for an oral or even a brief-written bench decision, and it is doubly unwise for the arbitrator to grant one. The reason is simple: even an experienced arbitrator can be led astray by first impressions and articulate advocates. It is difficult, if not impossible, to absorb all the facts and arguments of a dispute in one sitting. An arbitrator needs time to deliberate and evaluate facts and arguments because there are very few, if any, "simple" cases; every dispute contains some contractual or political interest. Further, a losing party may easily, and perhaps rightly, equate an oral or a written bench decision with hasty judgment.

THE CONSENT AWARD

Parties ask an arbitrator for an "agreed" or consent award when they ask him to convert their settlement of a dispute into his award. AAA Rule 39 permits an arbitrator to "set forth the terms" of the agreed settlement in an award; the *Code* says that it is consistent with an arbitrator's professional responsibility to adopt a consent award but only if he believes that the award is "proper, fair, sound, and lawful." The *Code* cautions an arbitrator to be certain that he understands the suggested settlement adequately before he consents to the award, and if an arbitrator concludes that the parties did not disclose pertinent facts or circumstances, he "may request additional specific information and may question witnesses at a hearing."

INTERIM AWARDS

I think it wise for an arbitrator to issue an interim award whenever he must fashion a remedy. It is preferable for the parties to devise their own remedy within stated time limits because they must live with each other. However, prudence dictates that the arbitrator always should retain jurisdiction over the remedy just in case the parties cannot agree on a remedy.

TIME LIMITS ON FILING AN AWARD

An arbitrator must comply with all contractual time requirements. For example: The arbitrator must issue his award within "30 days after the date that the parties transmit their final statements and proofs." AAA Rule 37 requires an arbitrator to render his award "promptly" and "unless otherwise agreed upon by the parties, or specified by law, not later than 30 days from the date of closing the hearings." The FMCS requires an arbitrator to render an award "not later than 60 days from the date of the closing of the record as determined by the arbitrator, unless otherwise agreed upon by the parties or specified by law." The FMCS points out that an arbitrator's failure to render timely awards reflects on his performance and "may lead to his removal from the FMCS roster." FMCS directs parties to inform OAS whenever a decision is unduly delayed, and to notify OAS if and when the arbitrator cannot schedule a hearing and determine issues promptly. The *Proposed Uniform Code* would require an arbitrator to render his decision "within the time fixed therefore by the agreement or, if not so fixed, within such time as the court orders an application of a party." The *Code* states that a party waives its rights to object to a late award if it did not notify the arbitrator of its objection prior to the delivery of the award.

Parties usually grant an arbitrator's request to waive either contractual or administratively imposed time limits for illness or some other good reason.

DELIVERY OF AN AWARD

AAA Rule 40 says that the award is legally delivered when the AAA places an award or a true copy in the mail addressed to a party at its last know address or to its attorney, or delivers it by personal service, or files an award in the manner prescribed by law. FMCS no longer requires an arbitrator to file a copy of the award with OAS. The *Code* directs arbitrators to deliver a copy of the award to each party "personally or by registered mail, or as provided in the agreement."

CLARIFICATION OF AN AWARD

The *Code* directs arbitrators not to clarify or interpret an award or make comments on an award "except at the request of both parties, and unless the agreement provides therefore." The *Proposed Uniform Arbitration Act* would allow an arbitrator to modify or correct an award on the application of a single party or on submission by a court, if there was "an evident miscalculation of figures or an evident mistake in the description of any person, thing, or property referred to in the award," or if the award is "imperfect in a manner or form, not affecting the merits of controversy." To "clarify" an award can easily lead an unsuspecting arbitrator to say something that will only cause difficulties.

THE EFFECT OF AN ARBITRATOR'S AWARD

Agreements commonly specify that "the decision of the arbitrator shall be final and binding upon all parties to the dispute," and "enforceable against any of the parties to this agreement in a court of competent jurisdiction." One agreement makes the award "enforceable under the Arbitration Law of the State of New York." Another provides for enforcement thus: "Neither party shall institute any proceedings in a court of law or equity other than to enforce the decision and award of the arbitrator." One agreement allows a party to challenge a decision of an arbitrator "in a court of competent jurisdiction should either party fail to implement the decision," but if the initiating party does not prevail in the litigation, "such party shall bear the full costs of such action, including but not limited to the adverse party's court costs, legal fees and other related expenses incurred as a result of defending such action." In the federal sector, the following provision, or one similar to it, is common: "The arbitrator's decision shall be final and binding" but "either party may file an exception to the arbitrator's award in accordance with applicable law, rules, and regulations." Another agreement provides that if a party claims that an arbitrator's award is invalid under the laws of the State of California, "that party shall serve written notice to the other party within 10 days after receipt of the written award" and "shall proceed promptly with proceedings" seeking to modify or set aside the award. If parties agree that notice was not given, "such failure shall constitute a waiver of any legal objections to the award." Another agreement allows review of an arbitral or tripartite board decision by the international board of arbitration "in cases of alleged evasion, collusion, fraud, or bad faith."

ENFORCEMENT OF AN AWARD

If a party applies to a court to enforce an award, the AAA will furnish to that party "upon written request and at its expense, certified facsimiles of any papers in the AAA's possession that may be required in judicial proceedings" (Rules 41, 42).

PUBLICATION OF AN AWARD

An arbitrator cannot make an award public "unless this requirement is waived by both parties or disclosure is required or permitted by law," but an arbitrator may ask parties for their consent to publish an award either at the hearing or when he issues the award. The *Code* directs arbitrators to ask the following question in writing: "Do you consent to the submission of the award in this matter for publication?" If parties consent and later want to revoke their consent, they must notify the arbitrator "within 30 days after the date of the award"; failure to notify implies consent to publish.

The various reporting services cannot publish an arbitral opinion and award without the consent of the parties. If parties consent to the publication of an award, a reporting service might summarize an award, publish the whole text, or refuse to publish it. The AAA does not publish private sector awards without the consent of both parties because the AAA believes that the award is the property of the parties. AAA publishes public sector awards without the consent of either party because it believes these awards are public property, but AAA publishes only those awards that it considers instructive for persons other than the parties. The AAA publishes awards in its *Summary of Labor Arbitration Awards in the Private Sector, Labor Arbitration in Government,* and *Labor Arbitration in Schools.* AAA seeks to present the frequent issues, for example, absenteeism; tries to present a mixture of issues; and considers the geographical location of the decision and the decisions of new arbitrators. AAA does not publish sarcastic, pedantic, or poorly written awards.

Prentice-Hall publishes only a summary of private sector awards in its *Industrial Relations Guide* and selects those awards that it considers of current and timely interest and those awards that discuss management rights and an arbitrator's authority. The Bureau of National Affairs (BNA) publishes awards that it considers significant, logical and objective in *Labor Arbitration Reports.* BNA does not publish awards that hinge on the credibility of the witnesses or awards that have unique factual situations.

Published awards represent the accumulated experience and wisdom of arbitrators, a "sense of the most," and a guide to what might be reasonable and just, especially on remedies in discipline and discharge disputes. No prior award is a "leading case" or "landmark decision"; no previous award sets a precedent for other parties, or even for the same parties. A prior award between the same employer and the same union on a identical issue might, but does not necessarily, settle the issue because a sitting arbitrator must exercise independent and impartial judgment on the issue(s) before him.

ON THE WRITING OF AN AWARD

The Supreme Court noted that an arbitrator's decision must contain an "operative command," and the *Code* directs arbitrators to write a "definite, certain, and concise" award that meets the significant issues, is forthright, and avoids gratuitous advice or discourse not essential to the disposition of the issues. The *Code* allows an arbitrator to use an assistant for research, clerical duties, and for a preliminary draft of an opinion and award, but an arbitrator cannot allow another person to decide the issue without consent of the parties.

It is inappropriate for an arbitrator to allow another person to draft an opinion because the tone, style, and coloration of a drafter's language inevitably intrudes into and subtly becomes the arbitrator's language. Parties rightly expect an arbitrator to do the arduous work of drafting, editing, and re-editing the opinion. In September 1987 the Federal Mediation and Conciliation Service sent to all arbitrators, at the suggestion of the National Academy of Arbitrators, the Advisory Opinion of its Committee on Professional Responsibility and Grievances on the ethics of an arbitrator's conduct. The Committee interpreted and applied its *Code* to fifteen various circumstances. Opinion 12 states the same view:

If the style of the ultimate opinion is not that of the arbitrator, however, discerning parties may harbor doubts as to the extent of the assistant's participation in the decision-making process. Such doubts, even if unfounded, could be harmful to the arbitrator and to the process itself.

After the hearing, I ask the parties if they want a full opinion and award, a summary opinion and award, or an award only. When I write a full opinion and award, I set forth a chronological statement of facts from the filing and processing of the grievance to the demand for arbitration. A chronological statement of facts is important because it shows parties that I understood the context of the dispute and that I based my decision on the facts. Next, I restate the question(s) before me, reproduce the pertinent provision(s) in the agreement alleged to have been violated, discuss preliminary matters, state and explain how and why I ruled on motions, restate the position and the arguments of the parties, point to the principle(s) of interpretation or the reasoning I used to reach the decision, make a statement on the insufficiency of the losing party's argument(s), restate the question(s) before me, answer each question, and issue a specific and practical remedy.

A summary opinion and award omits facts and arguments; it sets forth only the decision and the main reason(s) for the decision. My summary opinions usually run one or two pages. A summary opinion and award saves time and money.

The award-only option contains only the decision but no reason(s) for the decision. Parties seldom avail themselves of the award-only option; a few ask for a summary opinion, but most ask for a full opinion.

Some expedited arbitration systems direct the arbitrator to write only the decision but no opinion. A decision without an opinion saves time and money, but it might cause a problem in federal sector arbitration because a reviewing federal judge or the NLRB would be deprived of the arbitrator's reasoning.

The written opinion is the touchstone of arbitral success or failure because the written opinion measures an arbitrator's competence, intelligence, and impartiality. To draft, redraft, excise, prune, and write strong, clear, and factually accurate opinions is not very glamorous. I stare at a blank page; I make false starts; I discard one draft, then many drafts. To reach a decision, I go over all the facts thoroughly and ask myself: what issue divides the parties? How does each party argue? How cogent is each argument? Who has the better argument or evidence? How persuasive is the evidence? If I conclude that one party prevails, what evidence substantiates my conclusion? Is there sufficient evidence to link the arguments and evidence with the conclusion? If parties cite prior awards, I scrutinize the principle in the award; I do not go to the library to research how other arbitrators have ruled. If a party cites one of my prior awards, I first determine if the award is applicable; if it is, I then determine whether the dispute before me is distinguishable from or applicable to the previous dispute. I must find sufficient, satisfactory, and cogent arguments to support my written conclusion. Doubt and confusion dissipate the more I think about the matter. After I arrive at a conclusion, I do not agonize over it: I argue forcefully for it. If I cannot convince myself about a particular conclusion, I reread the record and try to convince myself about the opposite conclusion.

Though arduous, to write a precise, clear, and well reasoned opinion is ultimately a rewarding and satisfying task. I write and rewrite until I am satisfied with the whole opinion. I try to show the losing party that I had no choice but to rule as I did. I write only on those matters relevant to the decision. I do not tell the parties how or why I struggled with a particular conclusion; I simply state: "The grievance is denied" or "The grievance is sustained." I write primarily for the grievant and supervisors in understandable, straightforward standard college English. I do not write for courts, NLRB, or reporting services, but I do seek to write a publishable opinion. I know that the less I say, the better the opinion. I know, and advocates readily admit, that they first skip the text of the opinion and go immediately to the award because winning is better than losing. Then advocates do read the opinion, with pleasure if they win, and very carefully and critically if they lose. Arbitration lore has it that experienced practitioners read the opinion, first to see where they went wrong, then to see where the arbitrator went wrong.

In *Study Time* (No. 2, 1987), the American Arbitration Association reported that the Special Committee on Professionalism of the National Academy of Arbitrators rendered its opinion of the "current level of quality" of arbitration awards. As quoted in *Study Time*, the Committee concluded:

> Opinions are often much too long and poorly written. Arbitrators too often base their rulings on principles taken, not from the parties' agreements, problems or needs, but from some treatise on arbitration or from published awards dealing with other parties, other agreements, and other problems. Theoretical principles are too often imposed on the parties, without regard to considerations of practicability or justice. Collective bargaining realities become obscured and play an insufficient role in the reasoning process. Self-restraint is often ignored and awards attempt to decide far more than need be decided.

The committee attributed the decline in the quality of awards to four causes: the enormous growth in arbitration, the frequent use of arbitration, the fact that many new persons with little or no background in collective bargaining or contract administration have become arbitrators, and the fact that an even larger number of arbitrators are dependent on cases for a livelihood. To upgrade the quality of arbitrator's work the committee rejected the notion that arbitrators be certified or licensed. The Committee suggested that Academy members participate in training programs for new arbitrators, and that before any person be placed on a panel he should undergo either an internship with an established arbitrator or a supervised apprenticeship program.

11

Principles of Contract Interpretation and Application

Participants at arbitration conferences and seminars frequently ask how arbitrators interpret and apply the language of an agreement. Contractual language may be clear, ambiguous, or silent on the disputed subject matter.

CLEAR CONTRACT LANGUAGE

Language may appear "clear" to one party but not to the other party, and even if parties agree that the language is "clear," they may disagree on its application. Controverted language becomes authoritatively clear when an arbitrator concludes and declares that the language has, and can have, only one meaning. If an arbitrator so finds and so declares, that meaning prevails. Hence, recourse to other principles of contract construction are unnecessary.

In one dispute an employer argued, and I found, that the language of the agreement was clear. Therefore, I had to reject the principles of contract interpretation that the union used to construe the language. I wrote:

The Company's main, cogent, and decisive argument that the clear and unambiguous contract language unequivocally retains to the Company the right to assign bargaining work is legally sufficient and superior to all Union arguments. Arguments from parol evidence, from putative intent, from past practice, and from burdensome performance, cannot have, and do not have any legal force because these canons of contract interpretation are inherently inferior to the clear contract language.

In a dispute over the meaning of the word "duration," I wrote:

The word is neither ambiguous nor vague; it is not open to interpretation and can have only one meaning. The simplest, true, and most direct meaning is: the new contract "becomes operative" on September 1. On September 1, the contract vested rights, imposed obligations, prescribed duties, and established a *modus vivendi et operandi*. The District's argument would render the September 1 date superfluous, without content, and without meaning, a conclusion at variance with the well established principle that every word, phrase, clause, and sentence must be given its full force and effect. The only possible conclusion is that the effective date must be September 1, particularly since it is the only date that appears in the legal instrument.

AMBIGUOUS LANGUAGE

Contract language is ambiguous when it is susceptible to various interpretations or applications. To resolve disputes over ambiguous contract language, an arbitrator may use a variety of well-known and long established principles of contract construction.

Past Practice

An arbitrator can use past practice as a useful guide to determine the meaning to be attached to ambiguous and general language.

Definition of Past Practice. A contractually binding past practice emerges when the claiming party can show by hard and sufficient evidence that the parties, by their actions, have implicitly consented to and fixed a certain mode of action over an extended period. The asserting party must show that the parties' continual, frequent, and uninterrupted action tacitly created a pattern of work habits that gave practical meaning to an ambiguous contract provision. The claiming party must show that both parties concurred in, and continued the practice over a long period of time, that they applied the practice uniformly and consistently, and that neither party protested or objected to the practice. In short, the claiming party must show that a past practice became the customary way to do things: a tacit agreement, an acceptable and reasonable interpretation of a vague provision, "the way to do things."

Example No. 1. An employer argued that past practice and the language of the agreement entitled an employee to take leave only with the written consent of the employer. The employer pointed to the clear language, which said that an employee "*may* be granted a leave of absence," with "the consent of the union and employer." The clear language left no room for doubt, speculation, or interpretation; an employee must have the employer's consent to take leave; if the employer did not consent to the request, an employee is not entitled to leave. Past practice was irrelevant in determining the rights of the parties because the language was plain, simple, complete, and unambiguous; the arbitrator had no choice but to interpret and apply the language literally; no interpretation was needed because the language spoke for itself.

Example No. 2. The union argued that past practice can, and in this case did, alter the meaning of the language. I wrote:

To prevail, the Union must show that the past practice has developed a uniform, constant, uninterrupted and uncontested pattern of action which has created a definite, certain and unequivocal *modus vivendi et operandi* which has modified the literal contractual language. The reasons for this strict requirement are simple: the Union has the burden of proof; past practice is not legally equal to contract language; clear contract language is always superior to past practice, no matter how well established; past practice is open to debate; clear language is not.

Example No. 3. In another case the union argued that a past practice had developed because the language has remained the same over 30 years, the company routinely granted leaves with or without reasons, no leave was ever denied until October 1976, and even in October 1976 the company ultimately granted the request. Nonetheless, the facts did not show that the parties had reached an unequivocal, definite, and mutual understanding that varied with the contractual language. I wrote:

Not only has a past practice not emerged, but the uncontroverted testimony by a Company official and a Union official was that the parties had reached a mutual and common understanding not contrary to, but in harmony with the literal meaning of the language.

Example No. 4. In another case the union failed to adduce sufficient evidence to show that past practice had nullified the express language of the agreement. I wrote:

It is true that past practice can have a force and vitality that could modify or even render obsolete express language. But, for past practice to be determinative and conclusive, the asserting party must show that the alleged past practice has existed for a long time, has become imbedded as general and customary usage, has created an uncontested *modus vivendi*, and has developed observable prescriptive rights. The Union failed to advance hard and conclusive evidence of a uniform, consistent, and uninterrupted past practice. In fact, the Union relied on the mixed and inconclusive evidence. The overwhelming evidence at the hearing, detailed in the Company's *Brief*, is that dispatchers worked a combination of shifts in rotation without the seniority rule.

Example No. 5. In another dispute, past practice filled a gap in a collective bargaining agreement. Employees had enjoyed a Christmas party on Christmas Eve for 30 years. The newly appointed manager sought to abolish the practice. The contract provided that:

Local rules and regulations covering working condition of labor of employees, which have been established by custom or local agreement and were in effect January 1, shall not be changed during the life of this agreement without mutual consent. Such future changes in local rules and regulations shall be reduced to writing.

The employer argued that the "binding quality of a past practice is due not to the fact that it is a past practice but rather to the agreement on which it is based." I wrote:

While this is generally true, in the specific case before me there is substantial evidence that both the Company and the Union had, at least tacitly, agreed to a half-day holiday on Christmas Eve. The Union had always assumed this understanding because the Company had always paid employees a full day's pay even if the employees did not attend the party and went home. Company supervisors even attended and contributed to these parties. Even if the Company had not intended, say in 1930, to grant a half-day holiday, the continual exercise of this right, uninterrupted by the Company, created prescriptive rights, i.e., legal rights which accrue with the passage of time.

Example No. 6. In this dispute, mutual consent abolished a past practice. An employer not only intended to, but actually did eliminate the past practice of "grandfathering." During mediation, the association had attempted but failed to place the phrase "fifth year certificate" on the salary schedule. The association's chief negotiator testified that the district and association had tentatively agreed to a salary schedule on February 3, which contained the phrase "45 credits after B.A. or 5th year." However, under cross-examination, the chief negotiator admitted that the phrase "or fifth year" was not initialed or signed, as is customary negotiation practice. Further, the mediator never informed the district that the association proposed to add the phrase "or fifth year." Still further, the complete tentative agreement which became the final agreement, contained no reference to the fifth year or standard certificate in the salary schedules.

I wrote:

Although the facts above are sufficient to show that the past practice was eliminated, the most decisive fact is the Association's signature on a Collective Bargaining Agreement which contained a clear, specific, and unambiguous listing of the requirements for advancement on the salary schedule without any reference to a "fifth year" or to certification. The simplest and most elementary postulate of contractual construction is applicable: clear language is always superior and preferable to all other criteria of textual construction. When the language is clear, no extrinsic aids are necessary; hence, past practice, which has cogency and vitality only if the language is vague, loses its force. It is impossible to conceive that the knowledgeable signatories were not keenly aware of the modifications in the salary schedule headings wrought by the 1977–1979 Collective Bargaining Agreement Schedule Headings of the 1974–1975, 1975–1976, and 1976–1977 contracts.

Example No. 7. In this dispute, a fixed, continuous past practice destroyed the force of clear language. Both the collective bargaining agreement and the employer's policy letters explicitly made theft of government property a dischargeable offense, and the grievant, a shop steward, was aware of the collective bargaining agreement and policy letters. The union argued that undercharging fellow employees for meals had become a past practice and could not be considered theft of government property.

For several years, food service contract employees, under a variety of management companies, had either received their meals free, or had paid less than the stated price at the dining halls where they worked. A previous Project Manager had directed cashiers to charge fellow employees only for a portion of the food purchased. Employees knew and participated in the practice, both as purchasers and as cashiers, the various managements had never promulgated a rule to contravene the practice until the new management terminated the grievant.

I concluded that past practice had destroyed the clear intent of the contract language. I wrote:

> It is a primary, sacrosanct, and well established principle of contract law that clear contract language is superior to past practice. But, a well established past practice can, and here did nullify the legal force of a clear rule. The parties, by their daily, continuous, uninterrupted actions had caused the rule to fall into desuetude. The past practice, not the clear rule, had concretely fixed the relations between the parties; it had given their relationship context, life, and vitality, and it had created and fixed a *modus vivendi et operandi,* an agreed upon, though tacit, method on how things were to be done. The past practice, known by all, applied uniformly and consistently by all, and uncontested by the employer, had created a prescriptive right, the right to food at less than the stated cost. Employees are legally entitled to the use and usufruct of this right.

> I found it hard to believe that the Project Manager, clearly an energetic and vigilant sort, was unaware of the practice. Even so, he should have been aware of the practice because it is his obligation to know what cashiers are doing. He should have known about the practice because his supervisors, who knew about and participated in the practice, should have told him about the practice.

Common Dictionary Usage

The general, ordinary, common usage and dictionary meaning of the language prevail over any other interpretation of disputed language unless the text clearly and unmistakably calls for a technical or other meaning. I used this principle in the two following cases.

Example No. 1. An employer had prevailed in negotiations: it successfully substituted the word "shall" in two paragraphs for the word "may." I had no choice but to give the word "shall" its imperative meaning because "shall" denotes a duty, an obligation; and to give the word "may" its permissive meaning because "may" denotes freedom to act or not act.

Example No. 2. A union had cited *Webster's New Collegiate Dictionary* and concluded that the expressions "shall be determined" and "acted upon" created an ambiguity which gave both the employer and a Review Committee final authority over leaves. I wrote that the word "determine" means to decide, to resolve, to end; and that the word "act" means to perform a special function, that is, to act as mediator or, to make a chair. I concluded that the union's interpretation of the language was faulty because the union had selected from the dictionary only words in the intransitive mood. I interpreted the phrase "the recommendation shall be acted upon by the District Board" to mean that the Board had the final authority upon a recommendation of the Review Committee to grant or deny leaves.

Technical Language

Words commonly used in industrial and labor relations are to be given that meaning which obtains in the industrial practice or in labor relations dictionaries.

Example No. 1. I applied this principle in a dispute over the meaning of the expression "Working with the tools." I wrote:

The plain and unambiguous contractual language derives its substantive meaning from the practice long found in the baking industry. The Union President, and the only witness on this point, testified that "working with tools" means the repair of broken down equipment and the maintenance of electrical, mechanical, hydraulic, and other kinds of machinery. It also included some supervisory functions, e.g., scheduling, paper work, ordering parts and preparing the budget. His testimony is the most authoritative: for many years he had negotiated industry-wide and multi-employer contracts, had policed these contracts, and in a real sense, "lived" with the contract.

Example No. 2. In the following dispute, parties disputed the meaning of the word "certification." The employer had argued that the word "certification" is ambiguous: "Certification" can mean either the signature date or the date when the Labor Board certified the local as the bargaining unit. Since the language is ambiguous, the arbitrator must resolve the dispute against the party who drafted it, the union. I wrote:

This argument incorrectly assumes that the word "certification" is ambiguous. As the Union pointed out, in the parlance, context, and general usage of labor relations, the word "certification" has a unique, special, fixed, and specific meaning, i.e., official recognition by the appropriate recognizing body that a labor organization is the exclusive bargaining agent for a unit of employees.

Even though the language is not "certification by the National Labor Relations Board," this technical meaning is the only meaning that can be read into the word "certification." The Union correctly noted and applied the firmly established and well-known postulate of contract construction: ordinary words must not be construed in their technical sense. The Employer's argument that the determination of legal right "should not turn upon technicalities of language used" would contravene this fundamental law of contracts. Parties used technical language purposely: to pinpoint and to focus upon special and specific objects, to reduce ambiguity, and to avoid disputes. If the arbitrator did not give the word "certification" its technical meaning, he would destroy its denoted meaning, rob it of its strength and vitality, and negate its intent: all results at variance with law of contracts.

The Context of the Language

Language must be construed in its entirety. Each word, phrase, clause, and sentence must be given that meaning which harmonizes with the rest of the text. No word will be considered superfluous. I used this principle in a dispute over the interpretation and application of an emergency leave clause. I wrote:

It is a well-known, long established, and commonly accepted principle of language construction that the meaning of controverted portions of a Collective Bargaining Agreement can be ascertained by an examination of its textual companions (*noscitur a sociis*). Here, Article III, entitled *LEAVES*, specifies the various kinds of leaves, viz., (a) *Sick Leaves,* (b) *Family Illness Leaves,* (c) *Emergency Leaves,* (d) *Bereavement Leaves*—all the way through (k) *Other Leaves.* Each leave has an operative paragraph, i.e., the paragraph specifies the conditions for the enjoyment of the named leave. To enjoy *Sick Leave,* an employee must be sick; to enjoy *Family Illness Leave,* there must be an illness in the family. Hence, a logical, reasonable, and harmonious reading of the whole text would be that to enjoy *Emergency Leave,* there must be an emergency.

History of the Intent of Parties in Negotiations

The history of negotiations, proposals for new language, rejected proposals, and the modification of prior language might point to the intent of ambiguous language. This principle helped me resolve a dispute over the meaning of personal leaves. I wrote:

The history of the 1976–77 negotiations, which led to the new and now disputed Section 12(c), also supports the District's contention that the *Emergency*

Leave clause of the new Collective Bargaining Agreement does not contain the *Personal Leave Clause.* In the 1976–77 Agreement, the *Personal Leave Section* 11(f) was an independent section in no way related to *Emergency Leave.* But the exercise of personal leave posed problems for the District: teachers could be, and were absent before and after long weekends; classes could not be easily or readily covered; theoretically, a large number of teachers could be absent on the same day. To solve this problem, the District proposed to eliminate the *Personal Leave* clause (11f). To meet the Association's resistance, the District offered to increase sick leave from ten days per year to twelve days per year in exchange for the personal leave clause. To assure the Association that personal emergencies would qualify under the new language, the District agreed to incorporate the words "for personal reasons" into the old *Emergency Leave* clause (11c). In exchange, the Association agreed to the inclusion of the phrase: "The intent of the above leave is to make it possible for employees to be absent for the stated reasons and not for personal pleasure or profit."

I concluded that the history of negotiations supported the district's conclusion that the parties had traded off "one day of personal leave for two days of sick leave, with personal emergencies qualifying for emergency leave."

Principles from the Law of Contracts

The following principles from contract law may help an arbitrator interpret ambiguous language. Enumerated, they are: (1). If parties enumerate or list items, an arbitrator may conclude that the enumeration, that is, the inclusion of some categories, means the exclusion of other categories; (2). If an agreement has a general and a specific provision on a particular subject, the specific contract language prevails over general language; (3). Subsequently adopted language prevails over past language; (4). A right, once acquired, is never ceded or forfeited without clear and unequivocal language that disestablishes the right; (5). Ambiguous language should be construed against the drafter because the drafter could have made the language clear (I have doubts about this principle because both parties agree to the ambiguous language, usually to avoid further argument. The non-drafting party can be held responsible for the language because it could have written or amended the ambiguous language); and, (6). Considerations of equity (I am suspicious of the equity considerations because the notion of equity is entirely subjective, and inevitably colored with interest).

The reader might consider the following question. If parties ask the arbitrator only to interpret and apply contract language, should an arbitrator adjudicate equity questions? Specifically, as in one case before me, the parties asked me to answer the question: "What is the Grievant's seniority date?" They did not ask me whether the grievant had unfairly lost his seniority rights. Did I have jurisdiction over the equities inherent in the dispute? The facts are simply stated: the grievant, a highly esteemed and very competent longtime bakery salesman, was hospitalized with Guillain-Barre syndrome, an illness that paralyzed and disabled him. During the grievant's illness and disability, the company and the union negotiated a new collective bargaining agreement that amended the seniority provision. The amendment erased the grievant's 24 years of accrued seniority.

I wrote:

Though not insensitive or unsympathetic to the Grievant's equity argument, I cannot consider it; if I did, I would exceed the scope of the submission, and I would furnish grounds for a vacation of the Award ... my jurisdiction extends solely over the interpretation and application of the written contract language, i.e. the contractual status of the Grievant's seniority rights. Further, equity inheres in the clear, explicit, and objective contract language because it embodies the parties' agreed upon notion of justice. And, the contract language, the only guide for the arbitrator, supersedes and is inherently superior to the Grievant's or the arbitrator's subjectively colored notion of justice.

The federal court vacated the award because I did not rule on the equity question. If I had ruled on the equity question might not the employer persuasively have argued that I had exceeded my jurisdiction?

ABSENCE OF CONTRACTUAL LANGUAGE

When an agreement is silent on a subject, management and labor rely on different principles to interpret and apply an agreement.

Management's View

Management advances the "residual rights" theory that asserts that because the agreement is silent on a particular subject, management has retained all rights over that subject. Management argues that the employer has retained not only its previously held right but also the discretionary power over the subject matter: an arbitrator has no jurisdiction over it; the matter is substantively inarbitrable. As a corollary, management also argues that the union has only those rights specifically mentioned and ceded to it in the express language of the agreement because the written agreement is the complete and only agreement between the parties. The union has no other rights.

To forestall any union claim over matters not mentioned in an agreement, management seeks to include a "zipper" clause into a collective bargaining agreement. A zipper clause seeks to limit a union's right to the expressed provisions of an agreement. It seeks to exclude all past practices and implied obligations, and to make the written agreement the complete, final, and only agreement between the parties. The following are examples of zipper clauses.

It is understood and agreed that with the exception of the expressed provisions of the collective bargaining agreement, the employer retains all rights and responsibilities that have been granted or imposed on it by law, rules, and regulations of federal, state, county, and all other regulatory agencies.

Another example: One zipper clause forbade an arbitrator to construe the agreement in a way that infringes or impairs "any of the normal management rights which are not inconsistent with the provisions of the Agreement." Another zipper clause specified that the enumeration of rights "shall not be deemed to exclude other rights not herein enumerated but shall be deemed representative and characteristic." Another clause sought to retain to a city government the "traditional rights to manage and direct the affairs of the city in all its various aspects and to manage and direct its employees." A company sought to retain all of its "customary, historical, and usual rights, powers, functions, and authorities."

The Union's View

A union argues that the written agreement is not and cannot be the exclusive source of its rights because a written agreement, an ever changing, living, and necessarily imperfect and inadequate document, never truly expresses the total, continuing, almost permanent labor relationship. A collective bargaining agreement incorporates past practices, past understandings, and the working environment. All are implied though unstated contractual obligations. A union also asserts that management has no reserved or residual rights; it has discretionary power only over the subject matter specifically mentioned to be under its exclusive control. Hence, disputes over a subject not mentioned in the agreement are grievable and arbitrable. The Supreme Court echoed this view in *United Steelworkers of American v. Warrior & Gulf Navigation Co.* when it declared that the past practices of the industry and the shop are "equally a part of the collective bargaining agreement although not expressed in it."

To preserve past practices and to forestall a "residual rights" interpretation of an agreement, a union seeks to include a "Past Practice" or a "Maintenance of Standards" clause into an agreement. For example: "All practices and conditions not specified in this contract shall remain the same for the duration of the contract." Similarly, "The Agreement shall not be interpreted and/or applied to eliminate or reduce prevailing practices in effect prior to the effective date of this agreement," and "Any rights and protection previously enjoyed by employees will continue in effect." Again, "Local working conditions now in effect shall remain in effect unless they are in conflict with the rights of employees under this Agreement or are changed by mutual agreement."

12
Arbitrability

The arbitrability issue, a question over the interpretation and application of an agreement, arises when a party, usually the employer, asserts that the dispute is substantively or procedurally inarbitrable, that is, the arbitrator has no jurisdiction over the dispute. A dispute is substantively inarbitrable if the employer can show that it never agreed to arbitrate the disputed subject matter. A dispute is procedurally inarbitrable if the employer can show that the union failed to abide by all or some provisions of the grievance procedure.

SUBSTANTIVE ARBITRABILITY

Who determines whether or not a dispute is substantively or procedurally inarbitrable? In *United Steelworkers v. Warrior and Gulf Navigation Co.*, the union sought to compel arbitration of a subcontracting dispute. The employer refused to go to arbitration because it believed that it had never agreed to arbitrate disputes over subcontracting. The Supreme Court reiterated the fundamental postulate of arbitration: a party cannot be required to arbitrate any dispute unless it has agreed to do so. In *Warrior and Gulf* the Court held that courts were to decide this question and directed them to compel arbitration "unless it may be said with positive assurance" that the parties excluded the matter from arbitration. "Doubts should be resolved in favor of coverage," and "Only the most forceful evidence of a purpose to exclude" removes the claim from arbitration. A court should view "with suspicion" any attempt to persuade it to become entangled in the construction of substantive provisions of a labor agreement by the "back door" of interpreting the arbitration clauses.

In *United Steelworkers v. American Manufacturing Company,* the Court reiterated its holding in *Warrior and Gulf.* It said that courts have no business weighing the merits of the grievance; courts were not to consider whether an agreement supports a claim. Parties have agreed to submit all grievances to arbitration, not merely those the court deems meritorious. The Court said:

> The function of the court is very limited when the parties have agreed to submit all questions of contract interpretation to the arbitrator. It is then confined to ascertaining whether the party seeking arbitration is making a claim which on its face is governed by the contract. Whether the moving party is right or wrong is a question of contract interpretation for the arbitrator. In these circumstances, the moving party should not be deprived of the arbitrator's judgment when it was his judgment and all that it connotes that was bargained for.

The National Academy of Arbitrators has proposed a Federal Labor Arbitration Act that would empower arbitrators to determine disputes over substantive arbitrability unless an agreement expressly provided to the contrary. The Academy's proposal reflects its conviction that because the parties have agreed to submit their disputes to arbitration, an arbitrator should also resolve the dispute over substantive arbitrability.

PROCEDURAL ARBITRABILITY

In *John Wiley and Sons v. Livingston,* the Supreme Court said that "procedural questions which grow out of the dispute and bear on its final disposition should be left to the arbitrator."

The spirit of arbitration on substantive and procedural arbitrability questions is summed up in the words of one agreement: "Neither party to this agreement shall refuse to proceed to arbitration upon the grounds that the matter in question is not arbitrable." To resolve substantive arbitrability disputes, parties simply empower an arbitrator to resolve them. Thus: "If the grievance is over the interpretation or the application of the agreement, such controversy shall be decided by the arbitrator." Similarly, "If there is a dispute as to whether or not a grievance is arbitrable, it shall be submitted to the arbitrator for determination." If so, he shall "first rule whether or not the subject is arbitrable" and "then he shall rule on the grievance." One agreement provided that "one arbitrator will determine the question of procedural arbitrability and another arbitrator will determine the merits of the dispute."

Timeliness

Employers often assert that a grievance is procedurally inarbitrable because the union or the grievant did not file on time or because there is no valid excuse for the non-observance of contractual time limits, or because the grievant did not file when he was "aware or should have been aware" that he might have a grievance. Parties recognize that filing on time is a substantive obligation. They agreed that "the time limits provided shall be strictly observed unless extended by written agreement of the parties."

The following cases show how and why I ruled on arbitrability disputes.

Example No. 1. A district argued that because a *Request Form* was not in the collective bargaining agreement, I had no jurisdiction over the dispute. There could be no grievance over a non-existing provision. Further, the agreement defined a grievance as "an alleged misinterpretation of or violation of terms and/or provision of this Agreement." If I assumed jurisdiction, I would add to the contract, a course denied me because the agreement said that "the arbitrator shall be without power or authority to add to, subtract from, or alter any of the terms of the Agreement." The association argued that any document, procedure, practice, or policy (here the *Request Form*), that is allegedly in opposition to or contrary to the agreement is arbitrable. I concluded that the grievance was arbitrable. I wrote:

It is true that the *Request Form,* the administrative mechanism to process travel reimbursement claims, does not appear in the Collective Bargaining Agreement. But the subject matter, *Transportation Reimbursement,* the focus of the dispute, does appear in the controverted Article III, Section 4.

Example No. 2. A grievant, a bakery sales employee, had packaged, marked, and sold bakery products; she also had prepared and handled meats, cheeses, and salads (deli work), duties that she uninterruptedly performed for two years. The union filed a grievance that alleged that the employer had violated Article 2, *Scope of the Agreement,* because the grievant "has been and is being required to perform delicatessen duties not covered by the collective bargaining agreement." The employer refused to arbitrate the grievance, and the union successfully brought suit in federal court to compel arbitration. I wrote:

The threshold, central and determining question in this arbitration is: Is the subject matter substantively arbitrable? All arguments on other questions: on procedural arbitrability, i.e., the question of timeliness, on industry-wide practice, on past practice, and on legal precedent, can have legal force only if, as the union assumed, the subject matter is substantively arbitrable. If, however, the subject matter is substantively inarbitrable, as the employer argued, there is nothing to arbitrate.

The answer to this question hinged on an interpretation and apppli-cation of Article 2(D) of the collective bargaining agreement, a strong management rights clause, and on the legal effect of Article 2(D) on Article 2(A), *Scope of the Agreement,* Schedule B.
Article 2(D) read:

The employer retains all rights not surrendered herein to manage, control, operate, or regulate his business and work force.

The strong verbs in the contract language clearly and unequivocally reserved to the employer all those rights, as residual and retained rights, that the employer had not specifically ceded to the union in the collective bargaining agreement. Therefore, I wrote:

I can arrive at only one conclusion: the employer did not and could not have violated the collective bargaining agreement when it assigned "deli" duties be-cause the employer never ceded its residual power to do so. The evidence is conclusive. The union failed to show where the agreement mentions "deli" duties and where the agreement excludes "deli" duties from the work of bakery sales employees, and Schedule B contains no job description of bakery sales employ-ees; it lists only employee classifications.

Example No. 3. A district argued that a grievance on the district's de-cision to non-renew was substantively inarbitrable because the language was clear: "Nonrenewals...shall not be subject to the grievance proce-dure" and "The decision of the Board of Directors to non-renew the contract of a provisional employee shall be final and not subject to ap-peal." The Association admitted that the grievance procedure did not apply to non-renewals but it argued that the question was not renewal, but the district's right to impose residency as a condition of employment. I decided that because the dispute was over the domicile requirement, because the domicile requirement caused the non-renewal, and because domicile is a matter specifically mentioned in the Collective Bargaining Agreement, the dispute was substantively arbitrable.

The district also argued that the dispute was procedurally inarbitrable because the agreement provided that "failure of either party to comply with the time limits set forth above will serve to declare the grievance as settled based upon the last request made or last answer provided, and no further action shall be taken." The evidence showed, and the asso-ciation admitted, that the grievant and the association did not comply with the stipulated time requirement. The association sought to be re-lieved of its contractual obligation because "it has long been a national policy to encourage arbitration of grievances as an alternative to labor strife." I rejected this argument because the matter before me "was not national policy but the domicile requirements in the Collective Bargaining Agreement." Second, the association noted that arbitrators are "generally reluctant" to deny arbitrability claims. I responded: "This preference is accorded primarily to substantive arbitrability." Third, the association argued that to have the matter resolved on the merits would "clarify the relationship between the parties." I responded: these vague, ill-defined, and dangerous assertions "would frustrate the purpose of time limits, and ultimately nullify time limits as contractual obligations." I wrote:

Parties agree to time line requirements to ensure prompt consideration of grievances, to prevent grievances from becoming stale and to obtain available and credible evidence. Time line requirements are not only procedural rights and obligations, they are also substantive rights and obligations, sacrosanct and beyond arbitral reach.

I could not relieve the union of its obligation to process the grievance within the contractually agreed to time limits. If I did I would radically alter the existing contractual relationship; I would not simply, as the parties' creature, interpret and apply the agreement, I would become the source of substantive rights and obligations. I had no choice but to hold the Association to contractual time limits; I declared the dispute to be procedurally inarbitrable.

Example No. 4. An employer urged me to dismiss a grievance becaue a grievant failed to file his grievance with his immediate supervisor "within ten working days of its alleged occurrence." The employee argued that personal reasons prevented his filing on time. He argued that he had notified and complained to the employer about the burden of work, and the employer knew of his complaint. The "burden of work" argument cannot relieve an employee from filing on time. The grievant also argued that because the grievance was a "continuing" grievance, he could file any time. In support of its assertion, the union quoted Frank Elkouri and Edna A. Elkouri, *How Arbitration Works*, to the effect that some arbitrators have permitted the filing of continuing grievances at any time. The employer quoted the same passage but concluded that the grievance was not a continuing grievance because the employer had allegedly misclassified the employee only once. I held that the grievance was not a continuing grievance; it was a single grievance because the employer assigned him out-of-classification duties only once. As the employer noted, if the grievance were a "continuing" violation, every assignment would be subject to the grievance procedure years after the assignment was made. I held that the grievant was bound by the contractual time limits because he was aware of the clear, specific, and unambiguous time requirements. I wrote:

Contractual language is sacrosanct; the arbitrator, by very office, must give the contract language its full force and effect. He has no power to vary or in any way amend, modify, or alter it.

Example No. 5. A district argued that a grievance was inarbitrable because the grievant did not file within 20 working days after he or the association "should have reasonably become aware of the occurrence." The uncontroverted record showed that the grievant knew, or should have known, and was "reasonably aware" when he signed the supplemental contract, whether or not he had a grievance. He admitted that he signed the supplemental contract because he wanted the money and because he thought "that was the way things were done." I held that, by his signature, he must have concluded that he had received his contractual rights. He, tellingly and perhaps unwittingly, knew, as he testified, "that coaches don't get paid when they are not coaching." He never contested this simple, direct, and best interpretation of his rights. He never grieved when he discussed volleyball and contract matters with the assistant coach who had signed the contract to handle the volleyball assignment. I noted that if the grievant did not feel aggrieved when he received his supplemental contract, there could be no grievance. I wrote:

If the grievant had a grievance, he was contractually obligated to file his grievance on time. But, since he failed to meet the contractual time requirements, he lost his grievance. Grievances are not filed casually or haphazardly; nor can they be resurrected or manufactured at will.

Example No. 6. A district urged me to dismiss a grievance because a grievant filed it improperly: he failed to file his grievance with his immediate administrative superior; instead he filed his grievance with the Business Manager. I held that the grievance was properly filed because in a small district where the Business Manager, the Superintendent, and employees are in constant, familiar, and informal contact, recourse first to the Business Manager for possible error and explanation is not only proper but desirable.

Example No 7. At the hearing, a district drew my attention to the following provision: "If any question arises as to arbitrability, such question will first be ruled upon by the arbitrator selected to hear the dispute." The district argued that this provision required that I rule on the question of arbitrability before I heard any argument on the merits. After argument and oral testimony on the bargaining history of this provision, I concluded that the testimony supported the district's position but I deferred my ruling on substantive arbitrability because the question of substantive arbitrability depended on the applicability of other provisions in the agreement which in turn depended on the merits of the dispute. I, therefore, heard all arguments and evidence on the merits and ruled on substantive and procedural arbitrability. In my *Opinion* I explained that my ruling "not only complied with the contractual requirement," it also arose "out of the counsel of prudence. A hasty ruling, particularly on procedural arbitrability, might deprive a party of substantive rights. Rulings on procedure must be made only after long, earnest, and careful study of written argument."

13

Illustrative Opinions on Disputes over Contract Language

EXAMPLE NO. 1

A teacher filed a grievance because the district changed one of her grades. The opinion points to the importance of following the procedures in the policy manual and illustrates the relationship that exists between state law and the collective bargaining agreement.

Facts

At the end of the semester in June, B., the grievant, a physical education teacher, gave an "E," a failing grade, to two students. Later, the grievant noticed that the grades of these two students had been changed. Upon inquiry, she found out that the vice principal had instructed the school secretary to change the grades. In the belief that this violated the collective bargaining agreement, she filed a grievance on March 3. The principle reviewed and denied the grievance. He concluded that the district had the right to change a grade because the grievant had not complied with district policy 5212.1, titled *Special Progress Reports: Secondary Schools*. The superintendent's designee also reviewed the grievance and concluded that "in such a case, the teacher's grade is not void but voidable." Therefore, "any teacher who wants to ensure that his/her grades will not be subject to change must comply with the spirit and detail of the district's rules and regulations." On further review, the School Board agreed with its school administrators. The grievance went unresolved and the parties proceeded to arbitration.

Question

The parties agreed to submit the following two questions:

1. Did the district violate the collective bargaining agreement, Article VII, Section BB, by changing the grade given by B.?
2. If so, what is the appropriate remedy.?

Relevant Contract Provision

Article VII, Section BB, *Grading Practices,* reads:

The teacher shall have the authority and responsibility to determine grades and other evaluations of students. No grade or evaluation shall be changed by anyone other than the teacher provided that:

    1. It is adequately documented, and

    2. It is based on achievement, and

    3. It is consistent with school and/or district rules.

Argument

To determine whether or not the district violated the collective bargaining agreement, I must first answer the question: Did the grievant comply with the District Regulation 5212.1? If I find that the grievant did not comply with Section BB, I would have to conclude that the district violated the collective bargaining agreement because the district readily admitted that it had no power to change a grade if the grievant complied with Section BB of the collective bargaining agreement.

Question No. 1: Did the grievant comply with District Regulation 5212.1?

District Regulation 5212.1 reads as follows:

Home and school should work as partners in the educational development of students. Teachers are encouraged to keep parents informed about the learning activities of their youngsters. Parents should be made aware at the outset of any classes having special or unique requirements which might affect the student's final grade.

In general, no student may be assigned a final grade of failure unless prior notice has been sent to the parent or guardian in sufficient time for the student to correct the deficiency. The following shall apply: 1. Grade estimates of E or U communicated to parents at the mid-term shall be considered "prior notice"; additional communication to parents via telephone or note is encouraged.

    2. Special progress reports must be issued to all students who did not receive

an E or U estimate at mid-term and are in danger of failing at the end of the term.

3. "Sufficient time" shall be determined by the class teacher, but in no event shall it be less than two weeks prior to the end of the term.

4. There may be unusual circumstances warranting a failing grade because of unsatisfactory performance during the last two weeks of the term. In such cases, there must be a parent/teacher conference prior to issuing the failing grade.

Special progress reports are available on self-carbonizing paper. The original white copies are to be given to students to take home and return signed by parent or guardian. The duplicate yellow copies are to be sent to counselors on the same day as issued. The returned signed originals are to be retained by classroom teachers for reference. Telephone communication with parents is strongly encouraged but in cases regarding potential failures, a written record must follow.

The purpose of District Regulation 5212.1 is to give a parent or guardian "prior notice," that is, to give them sufficient time to help their children avoid a failing grade. The district's promulgated Regulation 5212.1 explicitly sets forth the procedural requirements that a teacher must follow before she can issue a failing grade. Subsection 2 of the Regulation requires teachers to issue the printed and available "special progress reports" to those students who did not receive an E or U estimate at mid-term and are in danger of failing at the end of the term. The teacher must issue the original of the special progress report to students; students are to take these special reports to a parent or guardian for signature, and students are to return these special progress reports to the teacher. The teacher must send a duplicate copy of the form to the counselor on the same day it is issued; and the teacher must retain the returned, signed original in her file for reference. This signed form constitutes proof of "prior notice." If a teacher assigns a failing grade, that is, an E at mid-term, the E grade automatically constitutes "prior notice." If a student is failing or in danger of failing, but has not received prior notice within the last two weeks in the semester, the teacher must schedule a parent/teacher conference before the teacher can issue a failing grade.

Position of the District. The district's position is simple and direct: the grievant cannot substitute her own progress report form for the district's special progress report because her progress report failed to comply with "either the letter or the intent of the district's regulation." The district points to the following facts: the grievant has an obligation to use the district's special, printed, available progress report form; she has no right to use her own report form. Her progress report form is defective in form because it does not provide space for the parent to sign, that is, it does not contain the following statement that appears on the district form:

Please sign and return immediately. A conference with the teacher is always appreciated and welcomed. It would be well to telephone the office for an appointment. Any comments may be written on the reverse side.

Further, the grievant's report form does not contain the following statement that appears on the district's form:

To avoid possible failure, this record should be improved; certain ways in which work may be made more satisfactory are checked below.

The grievant also failed to follow proper procedure: she failed to obtain, keep, and file the signed original of the progress report for herself, and she failed to send a copy to the counselor.

The grievant's report form is also substantively defective; it does not meet the substantive requirement of District Regulation 5212.1, that is, she failed to indicate that the student was receiving or in danger of receiving a failing grade. The grievant gave both students a D −, which is a passing, not a failing grade. The grievant's word "unsatisfactory" on her form does not satisfy the rule's requirement because the word "unsatisfactory" did not unequivocally tell the parent that the student was failing or was in danger of failing.

Position of the Association. The association believes that the grievant complied with the District Regulation 5212.1 "on timeliness of the notice, on contact with parents and on written notification" and even "if B. did not follow the letter of the policy, she did not fail to follow its spirit." The association thought that the grievant's progress form was substantially the same as the district's form because both forms use the word "unsatisfactory." In fact, the grievant's report form was better than the district's form because it gave more specific and detailed information and anaylysis of the student's progress deficiencies.

The Arbitrator's Conclusion. The association's view of procedure derogates from its importance. Procedure, the "how" of the law, is a substantive legal obligation because the observance of procedure guarantees the substance, the "what" of the law. The grievant is bound not only by the spirit of the law but also by the "letter" of District Regulation 5212.1, that is, by its procedural requirements. District Regulation 5212.1 unequivocally and directly imposes a procedural obligation: a teacher must issue grades on the district's special progress reports. A teacher's own progress form, even if superior in all respects to the district's special progress report form, can only be an auxiliary aid, not a substitute for the district's "special" progress report form. The reasons are legally compelling: a teacher's progress report form is not equal in status, in dignity, or in validity to the district's special progress form because only the district has the authority to make and promulgate rules and regulations on progress reports. If a teacher could substitute her progress report form for the district's special progress form, a teacher would engage in an inchoate form of rule making, that is, she would first displace and then rob the district of its right to make and promulgate files on progress reports.

The grievant not only failed to use the district's special progress form, but, as the district pointed out, she also failed to meet the substantive requirements of District Regulation 5212.1, that is, to clearly, unequivocally, and unambiguously give parents or guardians prior notice that the students were failing, or that they were in danger of failing. District Regulation 5212.1 explicitly requires the teacher either to assign an E grade at mid-term or hold a parent/teacher conference within the last two weeks of the term before the teacher can assign a failing grade. The incontrovertible fact is that the grievant's evaluation of the two students was D−, a passing and not a failing grade. D− gives and can only give one message to the parent or guardian: the student is doing poorly but will pass. I can reach only one conclusion: the grievant failed, procedurally and substantively, to comply with District Regulation 5212.1

Does the grievant's failure to abide by District Regulation 5212.1 give the district the right to change the grade? The district assumed so. The district said that the administrators "may change a grade or evaluation if it has not been assigned in compliance with any one of the three enumerated requirements." Does either the collective bargaining agreement or the state law grant the district the power to change grades?

Does Section BB grant the district the right to change grades? The first sentence of Section BB unequivocally grants the teacher the authority to issue grades and makes the teacher responsible for the grades; the sentence does not confer this power on principals, superintendents, or the School Board.

Can the power be implied from the second sentence of Section BB, as the district claimed? The district said that "the second sentence reflects the parties' agreement that the district administrators may change a grade or evaluation if it has not been assigned in compliance with any of the three enumerated requirements." The district believed that this understanding is "consistent with the provision's literal language." and that "the provision recognized the district's discretionary authority to change a grade if it was not assigned in compliance with school district rules." This was the district's intent when it agreed to the language, this was and always has been the district's interpretation of Section BB, and the history of negotiation supports this interpretation. The district's Director of Employee Relations testified that in 1970 or 1971, the parties were not able to agree on grading practices when a dispute arose at a high school over the change of a grade. They were able to agree to Section BB in February 1975 after the association had made a proposal that no grade of a teacher could be changed. The district concluded: "Given the association's original proposal that no grade of a teacher could be changed, and the language ultimately agreed upon, Section BB authorized the district to change a grade if it is not assigned in compliance with School district rules."

The district's canons of contract interpretation are useful and valuable guides in interpreting contract language, but these extrinsic aids are unnecessary because the meaning of Section BB, the controverted language, can be ascertained by an internal, grammatical, and linguistic analysis of the language. The feeble, ambiguous, contorted language of the second sentence in Section BB yields a discernable, clear, and distinct meaning if a comma is inserted after the word teacher, and if the words "other than" are translated as "except." Thus: "No grade or evaluation shall be changed by anyone other than [except] the teacher." The language assumes strength, vitality, and a direct meaning if the word 'anyone" becomes 'no one' and if the language is transposed from the passive to the active voice. Thus, the expression "shall be changed by anyone" becomes "No one [only the teacher] shall change [has the power to change] a grade or evaluation." The words "no one" are strong, undiluted, and unqualified; they deny all others the right to change a grade, and they vest in the teacher, and only in the teacher, the prerogative to determine and to change a grade.

I can reach only one conclusion: the recast sentence of Section BB directly, unequivocally, and clearly gives the teacher the unique, sole, independent, and autonomous right (the prerogative), to determine and to change a grade. The second sentence does not grant the district the right to determine and to change a grade because the words "no one shall change," by deductive logic, exclude the district.

The three enumerated conditions in Section BB do not grant the district the right to change a grade. Their main purpose is to procure the district's, and ultimately the student's, abiding interest, that is, a fair grade. Condition No. 1 and Condition No. 2 are substantive requirements, and Condition No. 3 is the procedural requirement (District Regulation 5212.1) for a fair grade. If the district does not challenge the fairness of a teacher's grade, the district tacitly clothes a teacher's grade with status, dignity, and binding force; the district certifies and guarantees that the teacher has exercised her power to determine grades responsibly, that is, according to effort and ability, not arbitrarily, capriciously, or discriminatorily. In short, the district confirms that the teacher has not corrupted the power entrusted her to assign grades.

Therefore, the full extrapolated meaning of Section BB in simple, concise, and clear recast language is:

The teacher shall determine grades and other evaluations; only the teacher can determine and change the grade; the grade is valid only if the teacher (1) has adequate documents to justify the grade, (2) bases the grade on achievement, (3) complies with school and/or district policy.

Does state law empower the district to change a grade? The district believed that the *Basic Education Act of 1977* gives teachers "only the initial evaluation of students. The ultimate authority for the conduct of the school district's entire educational program rests with the Board of Directors." Indeed, the law does grant the district board the ultimate and general power to run the district, but the general power to administer the district is not the same as the power to change a grade. Neither Washington Administrative Code (WAC) 180.44.010, Revised Code of Washington (RCW) 28A.58.758, nor RCW 28A.58.760 expressly support the district's view that the teacher has only the "initial" right to evaluate students and the district has the "ultimate" authority to change a grade. WAC 180.44.010 says nothing about the district's power to determine and change a grade. WAC 180.44.010 merely repeats the substance of Section BB, that is, "Teachers shall be responsible for the evaluation of each pupil's educational growth and development." RCW 28A.58.758 only says that the district School Board is to "be held accountable for the proper operation of their district in the local community." RCW 28A.58.060 simply holds certified teachers and administrative staff "accountable for the proper and efficient conduct of classroom teaching." The whole of RCW 28A.58.760 sets forth specific instructions on how to achieve this end (Section 2a through 2g). The conclusion is ineluctable: state law does not expressly grant the district the right to change a grade.

Since neither Section BB nor state law expressly confers on the district the power to determine and to change a grade, can the power be implied from either Section BB or from state law? In other words, is a teacher's right to determine a grade only an "initial" right, as the district contended, or has the district a residual power, that is, the "ultimate" power to change a grade? A teacher's right to determine the final grade is neither a delegated right, recallable at will by the district, nor a right reserved to the district as a residual right because Section BB confers on the teacher a prerogative: an independent, exclusive, and plenary right to determine grades. Section BB recognizes the reality of the teaching context: the prerogative to determine grades inheres only in the teacher because only the teacher performs the unique, independent, and indivisible function, that is, to judge academic progress. This is, and must be so, because only the teacher can and does make assignments; only the teacher "lives" with students, only the teacher has the subject matter expertise, and only the teacher is in a position to judge a student's progress. No other person in the school district performs the same functions, is similarly situated, or has the same interests. If the district could change a grade, the teacher, robbed of her prerogative, could ultimately become a mere functionary, not the independent and responsible teacher contemplated in Section BB. The district board's abiding interest is not to judge academic progress but to insist on the observance of Section BB because the section ensures that the teachers grade fairly. The district may invalidate but not change a teacher's grade if it can show in arbitration that the teacher did not comply with the three enumerated conditions in Section BB, and that consequently the grade was unfair. If an arbitrator concludes, as I have done here, that the grade is unfair (noncompliance with District Regulation 5212.1), the teacher, not the district, must change the grade. This conclusion conforms with Section BB: it squarely and properly places the responsibility for grades directly on the teacher; it preserves the integrity of the student-teacher relationship, and it removes grading from public, parental, or other political pressures.

Conclusion

I have arrived at two conclusions. First, the grievant failed to comply with District Regulation 5212.1 Therefore, she unfairly assigned an E grade to the students. Second, the district improperly changed the grade of the students because the district had no power to change a grade.

> *Question No. 1:* Did the district violate the collective bargaining agreement, Article VII, Section BB, by changing the grade given by the grievant?
>
> *Answer:* Yes. The district has no power to change a grade.
>
> *Question No. 2:* What is the appropriate remedy?
>
> *Answer:* The appropriate remedy is the *Award.*

Award

I have already written a tentative *Award.* However, it is far better if the parties can negotiate a remedy based on my two conclusions. If the parties cannot agree on a remedy by January 23, the parties are hereby directed to reduce to writing and to submit to the arbitrator on January 24 the minutes of their negotiations on the remedy. I will then determine the remedy.

EXAMPLE NO. 2

This opinion interprets and applies a common phrase in labor-management agreements: "Where qualifications are relatively equal, seniority shall govern." In a promotion dispute, must the union show that two employees are "relatively equal," or must the employer show that seniority does not apply because the one employee is substantially superior to another employee?

Facts

On May 12, the employer posted a vacancy notice for Support Technician II in Financial Reporting. The vacancy notice read: "Please refer to the standard job description to determine the responsibilities and qualifications necessary to perform this job." S. (the grievant), P., and others applied for the position. The employer interviewed all applicants, bypassed all employees and the grievant, and selected P. On the general Notification Card, the employer told S. and the other employees that because the position requires a "working knowledge of our accounting system (OPARS), and accounting principles, strong analytical skills, and a familiarity with basic financial records and reports produced by the Financial system," they had not been selected. They had "limited or no experience in one or more of these areas." S., senior to P., thought she should have been promoted. Therefore, the union filed a grievance that alleged that the employer had violated the seniority provision of the collective bargaining agreement: the union thought that seniority governed the promotion. The grievance went unresolved and the parties proceeded to arbitration.

Question

Did the employer violate the collective bargaining agreement when it denied the grievant, S., job vacancy 1–0006 as Support Technician II? If so, what is the remedy?

Applicable Contract Provisions

Article 15, Job Bidding and Classification Changes provides:

15.2   When a permanent opening occurs in any classification . . . notice of such opening will be mailed to each exchange and posted on the bulletin boards.

15.2.3   Job descriptions will be posted on bulletin boards for the information of employees interested in submitting job bids.

15.4   Permanent job openings in the classifications named in Article 26 of this Agreement shall be filled only after each interested employee has been considered in accordance with the job bidding procedures provided for in this Agreement, or in accordance with Sections 15.10, 16.2, 16.3 or 17.4 and the Company agrees to fill such opening with such interested employees whenever they are qualified and available.

Article 14, Credit Service and Seniority, provides:

14.2.6(1) It is understood and agreed that in all cases of transfer, promotion and demotion, consideration shall be given to seniority, knowledge, training, ability, performance, skill, adaptability, and efficiency, and where qualifications are relatively equal, seniority shall govern.

Article 26, Compensation, provides:

26.2.3 Job descriptions for all classifications except "Laborer" and "General Clerk" have been established. . . . Job descriptions and the duties of any classifications may be established by the Company. Provided, however, that the position of new or substantially revised job classification in the wage schedule shall be mutually agreed to by the Company and the union.

Argument

The employer thought that the union had the burden of proof to show that the employer either had violated the agreement or acted unjustly, arbitrarily, or discriminatorily because the union brought the grievance. The union took the position that the burden of proof fell on the employer to show that P., the junior employee, was "substantially" more qualified than S., the senior employee.

The proper question in arbitration is not who has the "burden of proof" but who must "convince the arbitrator"? Must the employer convince the arbitrator that P. is substantially more qualified than S., or must the union convince the arbitrator that S. and P. are relatively equal? It is the employer who must "convince the arbitrator." The employer must defend its judgment because the employer committed an affirmative act: it bypassed the clear contractual requirement: "Where qualifications are relatively equal, seniority shall govern."

Article 14.2.6(1), a qualified seniority clause, obligates the employer to consider seniority, knowledge, training, ability, performance, skill, adaptability, and efficiency when it exercises its discretionary right to promote an employee. If the employer finds that the competing employees are not "relatively equal," the employer may promote a junior employee, but only if it adjudges that the junior employee is "substantially" more qualified than the senior employee. Here, the employer concluded that P.'s qualifications to do the work of Support Technician II are "substantially" greater than S.'s qualifications; S. and P. are not "relatively equal." The logic is ineluctable. If P. is, in fact, "substantially" more qualified that S., the employer did not violate the agreement, but if, as the union contends, P. is not "substantially" more qualified than the senior S., the employer did violate the agreement.

The contract language imposes a difficult task on the employer. The expression "seniority shall govern" is clear, unequivocal, strong language in the imperative mood. Its intent cannot be diluted because it protects a vital union interest. The thrust, spirit, and intent of the language require that the employer always prefer, and ultimately select, a senior employee if at all possible; doubt favors a senior employee; seniority is more than a "tie breaker": it is clear preference for the senior employee. Therefore, the employer must adduce specific, tangible, and real (not abstract or speculative) evidence, to convince the arbitrator that P., the junior employee, is (not will be), definitely, evidently, unmistakably, undoubtedly, manifestly, distinctly, patently, significantly, discernibly, and unequivocally superior to S.; that P. is "head and shoulders" above S.; that P. is truly "exceptional," not simply "the most qualified" employee. The junior employee cannot simply "look" superior, be "nearly," "almost," "possibly," "probably," "arguably" superior; the junior employee must actually "be" recognizably superior.

The evidence does not support the employer's conclusion that P. was "substantially" more qualified than S. to perform the job functions of Support Technician II. The employer selected P. primarily because P. had formal education in business administration and accounting, education that would enable him to master the job functions of Support Technician II in a short time. S. lacked formal accounting education and training in accounting; she had graduated from high school but she did not possess the "requisite credentials," and it would take her about one and a half years to learn all the job functions. Further, the employer did not promote her to the job when it created the position.

Undoubtedly, formal education is valuable: it can affect and contribute to increased job performance; and, it is true that P. surpasses S. in formal education. However, formal education does not necessarily translate into improved job performance. Formal accounting education exposes a student to broad, theoretical knowledge, to those principles, ideas and concepts which help a student understand accounting. Nonetheless, formal education has limitations: it does not confer training, experience, specific "know-how," or the practical knowledge necessary to do a specific job. Training may not confer theoretical knowledge, but it does confer a different and specific kind of knowledge: experience and skill. P.'s formal education, by itself, does not make him "substantially" more qualified than S. for the position of Support Technician II. In fact, the employer failed to establish the assumed causal link between P.'s formal education and his job performance. The evidence shows that P.'s formal education in accounting, completed in 1979, did not improve his job performance. The employer's evaluation of P. was a modest "meets expectations," . . . "P. needs to develop his analytical skills." "Deficiencies in attention to detail" is damaging and decisive evidence. The evidence argues not for a promotion but for needed improvement in the very skills which are needed for the position. Furthermore, his absenteeism, an important indicator of job interest and performance, was 5.3 percent. In sharp contrast, the employer rated S. "above expectations" in ability, performance, skill, adaptability, and efficiency; S. had "excellent attendance": tangible and objective evidence of her performance. P. is superior to S. only in formal education; S. is superior in training, in greater work experience obtained by performing many of the functions currently done by the Support Technician II. S. is more qualified in ability, performance, skill, adaptability, and efficiency.

The job Support Technician II requires a trained and experienced employee, not an educated employee. The job title so indicates. The word "support" indicates that a Support Technician II works under supervision. The word "technician" denotes a trained person who performs routine, mechanical tasks learned after a period of time. A technician does not exercise independent judgment or address himself to analytical or theoretical questions. The job requires a trained person like S., not an educated person like P. Not only has S. greater work experience than P., she also has performed many of the job functions required for the position of Support Technician II. As an "Analytic Assistant," she must have some analysis. She prepared parts of the Monthly Operations Report and Toll Reports, and she reconciled accounts with other departments. S., an excellent and productive employee for many years, can gain the necessary accounting knowledge and training on the job. Accounting clerks, other Analytical Assistants, and the Operations Manual for the Reports Department are available to train and help her. The employer is obligated to perform the job functions because the posted job descriptions for Support Technician II specifically says that "Classroom and on-the-job training is provided." S. is willing to learn; she can learn; she has taken classes in management orientation and computers.

The employer's statement that S. would not be able to perform the job or that P. could do the job better is speculative, unsupported evidence.

The employer has not convinced me that P. is an exceptionally qualified employee or that he is substantially more qualified than S. to perform the job functions of Support Technician II. Therefore, I can only conclude that the employer violated the seniority provision of the collective bargaining agreement when it bypassed S: the employer should have promoted S., the senior, and not P., the junior employee.

The employer not only violated the agreement, it also acted unfairly against S. because it added a new and different requirement, accounting, to the posted job description. It is evident that the new and non-posted job description favors P. and excludes S. The objective evidence shows that the employer disregarded its own negative comments against P. on critical matters, disregarded P.'s analytical and accounting skills, and ignored its own highly favorable appraisal of S's excellent, continuous, and experienced work performance.

Questions

(*1*): Did the employer violate the collective bargaining agreement when it denied the grievant, S., job vacancy 1–006 as Support Technician II?

Answer: Yes.

(2): If so, what is the proper remedy?

Answer: The proper remedy is in the Award.

Award

1. The employer is hereby ordered to promote S. to the position of Support Technician II.

2. The employer is hereby ordered to promote S. to the job of Support Technician II with all back pay and benefits, from the date that P. assumed the position to the date of her promotion, which she would have earned had she been promoted. The parties are hereby directed to work out the details of this Order. If the parties cannot agree on the specifics of back pay and benefits, the union is hereby directed to so inform me no later than May 21.

3. The employer is hereby ordered to promote S. at its administrative convenience, but no later than April 21.

I hereby retain jurisdiction over this *Opinion and Award* until (date).

EXAMPLE NO. 3

This federal sector dispute over a suspension discusses criteria that mitigate discipline. It is arbitration at its best because the parties proceeded expeditiously and asked for a summary opinion.

At the request of the parties, I have written a *Summary Opinion*.

Opinion and Award

Question No. 1: Was the grievant, C., AWOL as specified in the suspension letter?

Answer: The grievant, C., was AWOL as specified in the suspension letter?

The grievant was AWOL because management neither authorized nor approved the leave that he took. The *ABSENT WITHOUT LEAVE*

(AWOL) provision is clear and unequivocal: an employee is AWOL if his request for leave is not authorized or not approved. The grievant cannot assume that his request was approved because his supervisor did not deny his leave. A supervisor's failure to act upon (that is, to sign) a leave request, is not approval, because to authorize and to approve are affirmative acts, not negative acts. Even if the grievant's assumption were correct (it is not), his assumption would be inapplicable because his original leave request was for other dates. After the agency preempted these leave dates, the grievant had the affirmative obligation to submit other dates; he failed to do so. Further, the supervisor, not the grievant, has the power to determine when leave will be taken. The grievant may suggest dates, but he cannot contractually go on leave without his supervisor's explicit and written approval. Could the grievant determine his own dates at will, the grievant, not the agency, would determine the leave schedule, a conclusion at variance with administrative rules and regulations.

Question No. 2: Was the five (5) day suspension appropriate?

Answer: The five (5) day suspension is not appropriate.

The five day suspension is not appropriate for three reasons. First, the five day suspension includes two offenses: "unauthorized absence and failure to complete work assignment," but only one offense is before me, the AWOL offense. Therefore, the five day suspension necessarily is an excessive penalty. Second, the five day suspension denies the grievant the progressive discipline he is entitled to under Article 20, *DISCIPLINE,* of the Collective Bargaining Agreement, and under the agency's own *TABLE OF OFFENSES AND PENALTIES.* Article 20 says that "the objective of discipline is to correct and improve employee behavior." The *TABLE OF OFFENSES AND PENALTIES* provides guidelines to management "for constructive and rehabilitative discipline," that is, to "correct offending conduct, attitudes, or work habits." Third, the discipline is too severe. The agency's guidelines specify that the imposed discipline must "be reasonable in its degree of severity" and not "out of proportion to the offense." Here, there are many mitigating circumstances all recognized by the *TABLE:* the grievant's offense was not a repeated offense, his offense was not intentional nor was it committed maliciously or for gain; his past record is exemplary and he is a longtime employee; and, his position and experience make it unlikely that he will repeat the offense. The agency could have imposed the minimal discipline, that is, a reprimand; or the maximum discipline, the five day suspension, for a first AWOL offense. However, the agency chose the harshest penalty (a punitive penalty, rather than the minimum discipline required by the just cause provision) to correct the grievant. The penalty is too harsh because the grievant did not flout a rule or regulation; he exercised poor judgment, remediable by a lesser penalty.

Therefore, the appropriate remedy is a written reprimand to be kept in the grievant's official Personnel Folder, removable in less than three years if the agency concludes that the reprimand has had its desired effect. This discipline accords with the initial judgment of his supervisor who thought that a written reprimand was the appropriate discipline.

Award

The agency is ordered to lift the five day suspension and to make the grievant whole for all losses he may have incurred.

I retain complete jurisdiction over the interpretation and application of this *Opinion and Award* until (date).

EXAMPLE NO. 4

The city denied a union steward paid leave to conduct union business. The opinion points to the supremacy of clear language over bargaining history and past practice, and gives the work "meeting" its usual, common, ordinary meaning.

Facts

W., the grievant, an equipment operator with the Wastewater Treatment Division of the city and the chief steward of the union, works approximately five miles north of the city's Civic Center. In December, he asked D., his immediate supervisor, to take off the last hour of his work shift on paid union leave to file a Step II grievance with an appropriate city official in the Civic Center. M., the superintendent at the plant, told the grievant that he was not entitled to paid union leave. M. told the grievant that unless he had set a meeting with someone at the Civic Center in connection with the grievance, he could not grant him paid union leave. The grievant asked for and the city granted him one-half hour personal leave to file the grievance at Step II. In the belief that the grievant was entitled to paid union leave, the union filed a grievance. The city denied the grievance and the parties proceeded to arbitration.

Question

The parties agreed to submit the following questions: Did the city violate the collective bargaining contract between the parties, specifically Articles 4.3(a), 4.3(c), 4.3(d) and Articles 18.5(a), 18.11 and 19.1 when the city refused to allow W. to leave his work station one hour early in December for the purpose of completing and filing a union grievance? If so, what is the appropriate remedy?

Argument

Simply stated, the main question is: Can a steward legally leave his work station to conduct union business on city time independent of the city? The answer to this question hinges on the interpretation and application of Article 4.3(d) and Article 18.11, *Absence from Work Station;* all other Articles are irrelevant to the issue.

The Revelant Contract Provisions. Before I interpret and apply Article 4.3(d) and Article 18.11, I have recast the language to extrapolate its meaning.

1(a)   *The Language of Article 4.3(d) reads:*

Duties required by the union of its stewards excepting attendance at meetings with the city supervisory personnel and aggrieved employees arising out of a grievance already initiated by an employee, shall not interfere with their or other employee's regular work assignments as employees of the city.

1(b)   *The Recast Language of Article 4.3(d) reads:*

[The] duties [that are] required by the union of its stewards ... shall not interfere with their or other employee's regular work assignments as employees of the city. [There is one exception: a steward may interfere ... when he attends] meetings with the city, [with] supervisory personnel, and [with] aggrieved employees arising out of a grievance already initiated by an employee.

2(b)   *The Language of Article 18.11, entitled Absence from Work Station, reads:*

Union Stewards representing employees or the union at the meetings or hearings provided for in this Article shall be permitted, after notice to the immediate supervisor, to leave their assigned work areas without loss of pay during their attendance at such meetings or hearings.

2(c)   *The Recast Language of 18.11 reads:*

Union stewards shall be permitted to leave work areas without loss of pay [to represent] employees or the union at meetings and [at] the hearings provided for in this Article. [The steward shall give] notice to his immediate supervisor.

Interpretation of Article 4.3(d) and Article 18.11. As the union pointed out, the word "shall" in Article 18.11 unequivocally grants a steward the right to leave his work station to conduct union business on city paid time (*Brief,* p. 7). The city did not deny the existence of the right. The city argued that the right can be exercised only in certain restricted circumstances.

Three Articles, Article 18.11, Article 4.3(d), and Article 4.3(g), circumscribe the right granted in Article 18.11. Article 18.11 itself imposes a condition: a steward must give notice to his immediate supervisor that he intends to leave his work station. Article 4.3(g) requires more than notice: it requires specific city approval because it reads:

No steward shall leave his duty or work station for purposes connected with his or her office of steward without the specific approval of his or her supervisor or other authorized management official.

The legal and practical effect of the clear, specific and unequivocal language of Article 4.3(g) is enormous and far-reaching. Legally, the city has retained full and complete control over a steward's work time. Practically Article 4.3(g) reduces the power granted a steward in Article 18.11 to a nullity because a steward cannot exercise his right independently of the city's will.

Article 4.3(d) further qualifies a steward's right: a steward may not leave his work station if his union activity interferes with his work assignment or with the work assignment of an employee. It is here and only here that a steward may legally exercise the right granted in Article 18.11 independently of the city: a steward may interfere with his own and an employee's work assignment only "when he attends meetings with the city [and] with supervisory personnel" (recast language of Article 4.3(d)).

To summarize: a steward's right to conduct union business on paid city time is a very narrow and restricted right. A steward must first obtain specific approval from the city to leave his work station; then he may conduct union business on paid city time but only for a very specific and limited purpose, which is to attend meetings with the city and with supervisors.

Although it is true, as the union says, that bargaining history does not determine the interpretation of Article 4.3(d) and Article 18.11, the above, and now the authoritative, interpretation of Article 18.11 and Article 4.3(d) accords with bargaining history. The city's chief negotiator testified that the union never objected to the city's interpretation of Article 4.3(d) and Article 18.11, an interpretation that carried through the negotiations of 1981–1982. More persuasive, however, is the fact that in negotiations, the union unsuccessfully sought to expand a steward's right to include the filing of a grievance at Step II on city time. I can only conclude that the city's intent to exclude the expanded right prevailed over the union's intent to include the expanded right.

Application of Article 4.3(d) and Article 18.11. Was the grievant going to a "meeting" on December 23? Does the filing of a grievance at Step II constitute a "meeting" under Article 18.11 and Article 4.3(d)? The simple and direct answer is: the grievant was not going to a meeting as defined in the contract, and the filing of a Step II grievance is not a meeting. It is a well-known and long established principle of contract construction that words be given their ordinary meeting: a common usage meaning, a meaning generally understood by all. The union thought that "the validation of the grievance by a signature . . . constitutes a meeting." However, this definition is contrary to the common and usual meaning given the word "meeting." A meeting is markedly different from a perfunctory ministerial act, the simple signing of a grievance form. The word "meeting" always implies a conversation, a discussion, and an exchange of views. The undisputed evidence is that the grievant had no scheduled meeting. As he testified, he had to "hunt up" a city official, and, in many instances, stewards simply obtained signatures from functionaries, not from city officials.

All other union arguments are legally insufficient. The union's past practice argument from Article 19.1, *Maintenance of Standards,* has and can have no legal force because the past practice argument has and can have legal cogency only if the contract is silent or if the language is ambiguous. Here, the language is clear and unequivocal. Clear language not only controls practice, but also directs and determines it. Even if, as the union says, "The city practice previously has always been to allow stewards time when necessary or insisted upon by supervisors," and even if the grievant "had always been able to meet and validate grievances" the union failed to show that stewards exercised this right independently of the city, and that stewards could interfere at will with their work assignments if they did not attend a meeting as defined above. Further, and finally, the union's own understanding of its contractual rights is not authoritative; it does not determine legal rights. Whether the period of time was "substantial" is immaterial to the issue.

Conclusion

The city acted within its legal rights when it refused the grievant permission to file a Step II grievance on paid city time.

> *Question:* Did the city violate the collective bargaining contract between
> the parties, specifically Articles 4.3(a), 4.3(c), 4.3(d), and Articles
> 18.5(a), 18.11, and 19.1, when D. refused to allow W. to leave his

work station one hour early on December 23 for the purpose of completing and filing a union grievance?

Answer: No.

Question: If so, what is the appropriate remedy?

Answer: No remedy is necessary.

Award

The union's grievance is hereby denied.

EXAMPLE NO. 5

The employer refused to pay employees travel pay. The question before me was: Does "miles" mean "road miles" or "radius miles"? The opinion illustrates four criteria parties commonly use to interpret and apply ambiguous contract language: the context of the disputed language, the history of the language, past practice, and industry wide practice.

Facts

The employer, located in a large city within the geographical work jurisdiction of the union local, began work at a paint hangar located about 30 miles away. The job site was within the geographical jurisdiction of a different union local, whose offices and dispatch point are 60 miles from the large city. The employer assigned a crew from his own shop, and he employed painters dispatched from the union local 60 miles away.

A dispute arose when the employer refused travel pay to those employees who were dispatched from the local 60 miles away and who lived more than 25 miles from the job site because the employer believed that these employees were working within the free travel area created by Article 22.3. The union disputed the employer's interpretation of Article 22.3 and filed a grievance. The grievance went unresolved and the parties proceeded to arbitration.

Questions

At the hearing, the parties agreed to submit the following questions:

1. Did the employer violate Article 22 of the collective bargaining agreement when it failed to pay travel pay on the job at the airfield? If so, what is the proper remedy?
2. Is the free travel zone measured by road miles or by radius miles?

Relevant Contract Language

Section 22.3. On work in nearby towns employees shall not leave the shop's free travel area (25 miles free travel) before regular working hours from the contractor's starting point of record, and shall be back at regular quitting time, except that traveling time may be paid at twenty-one ($0.21) cents per mile in the first year of the Agreement ($0.24 in the second and $0.26 in the third year) to enable the working of a full shift. An additional twenty-five cents ($0.25) per mile traveled in the first year of the agreement (28 cents in the second and 30 cents in the third) will be paid if transportation is not provided. An employee, living in an outlying area where travel time is concerned, shall not receive same if not required to report to the employer's shop. This will be treated as a local area. Regular employees who live outside the 25 mile free travel time area and within 25 road miles of the job site shall not be paid travel time.

Argument

The resolution of this dispute depends on the answer to the two questions discussed below.

Question No. 1: Is the free travel area (not "zone") in Article 22.3 to be measured by road or by radius miles?

If the measurement of the 25 miles free travel area is by radius miles, the employer is not legally obligated to pay travel pay because the job site is within the 25 mile radius of the starting point, whether the starting point is the county court house or the employer's workshop. However, if the 25 miles free travel area is measured in road miles, the employer would have to pay travel pay because the job site would be outside the free travel area: it is 31 plus road miles from the employer's shop to the job site and it is 26 miles from the county court house to the job site.

In support of their positions, the parties advanced arguments from the history of the language, from an analysis of the contract language, from past practice, and from industry practice.

The History of Article 22.3

Before 1971 each of the seven locals that comprised the District Council defined the free travel area in different ways. These arrangements became supplements identified as "Schedule A's" and attached to the main agreement with the District Council. When in 1971 the employers requested a "free flow" of their men into as many other jurisdictions as possible, the parties replaced the old Schedule A's with the new Article

22.3 which created the 25 mile free travel area applicable to all of the locals in the District Council.

The union contended that the negotiating history of the travel pay position supports its position that the word "miles" means road miles for two reasons. First, N., the present executive secretary and a business agent of the union since 1969, testified that H., the executive secretary and chief union negotiator, stated in 1971 that the "free flow of men" concept "would not work" on the radius basis. However, according to the president of the Company, H told L. only a few weeks after the 1971 negotiations that to compute travel pay all he would have to do was to draw a 25 mile radius on a map with a compass. This argument is inconclusive. What H. said or did not say is hearsay; hence, it is doubtful evidence because the deceased H. cannot be called on to testify.

Second, the union argued that because the word "radius" does not appear in the 1971 contract or in any subsequent contracts the measurement must be by road miles. The union has determinedly, continually, and successfully resisted every employer effort, particularly in the 1980 negotiations, to include the word "radius" in the contract.

The employer countered that the parties must have intended a radius, not a road measurement. The word "road" does not appear in Article 22.3 and because in 1971 the parties substituted Article 22.3 for the earlier free travel arrangements in the various Schedule A's, which contained boundary measurements by street and road miles as the old Schedule A did. The parties must have specifically rejected the road mile measurement because they referred to and specified a road mile measurement in the last sentence of the Article that provides that regular employees who live outside the 25 miles free travel time area and within the 25 road miles of the job site shall not be paid travel time.

Furthermore, the employer disputes N.'s testimony. Employer's witnesses L., G., R., and S., who attended the 1980 negotiations, testified that in the 1980 negotiations they did not seek to define the free travel area in terms of radius miles. Their proposal was to extend the free travel area to 30 miles, and the union's response was: "thirty radius miles is too far."

The argument from putative intent is also inconclusive: its very subjectivity robs it of legal force. Parties can argue forever that they intended to write or thought they had written "road" or "radius" miles. In addition, the logic is doubtful: it does not necessarily follow that because the word "radius" or the word "road" does not appear in the contract that either one or the other can be read into the contract.

Arguments from the history of the contract language and deductions from that history are legally insufficient. The contract language, past practice, and industry practice provide sufficient, compelling, and objective criteria to determine whether "miles" means road miles or radius miles.

An Analysis of the Language of Article 22.3

The Employer's Analysis of the Language of Article 22.3. The employer believed that Article 22.3 created a free travel area that must be determined by a "radius" and not a "road" measurement because the word "area" as defined by Webster necessarily implies a radius boundary measurement. To measure the free travel area by road miles, as the union suggested, would be both impractical and impossible: an employer could not accurately determine travel costs in bidding jobs or computer travel pay.

The Union's Analysis of the Language of Article 22.3. The union believed that Article 22.3 created a free travel area that must be measured in road miles, not radius miles. No other meaning but a common sense and common usage meaning should be read into the contract unless the labor contract clearly states to the contrary. The commonsense meaning of the word "miles" in the travel pay provision of construction labor contracts means "road" miles, not "radius" miles because "miles" are ordinarily driven by ground transportation.

The Arbitrator's Analysis of the Language of Article 22.3. The union's sound and well-known principle of contract construction paraphrased above, would be the applicable and determining principle if the contract language were simply "25 miles free travel," and not "25 miles free travel area." The union's analysis of the language is incomplete and insufficient because it fails to give the word "area" its full legal force and effect. The word "area" in the controverted language must be given its legal effect because it is axiomatic in the construction of labor contracts that no contract word can ever be ignored, no word can be considered superfluous to the text.

The meaning of the disputed "25 mile free travel area" must be ascertained by examination of the entire text. The text must be given its confluent and natural meaning, a meaning that accords with the common understanding of the language.

Taken by itself, the word "miles" does mean, as the union said, road miles, but as the employer properly noted, the union's own principle of contract construction leads to the same notion because "area" in common usage means the extent of space. Hence, we commonly say "the space of a rectangle," "the space of a triangle," and "the space of a square,": all measurements of space enclosed by lines. Only a radius measurement can enclose and measure a 25 mile area equidistant from a starting point. Thus, a radius begins at point zero, goes in every direction for 25 miles, and becomes a circle that encloses and thus defines, the 25 mile free travel area. Therefore, I must and do conclude that the "25 mile free travel area" must be measured in radius, not road miles.

This interpretation of the language of Article 22.3 (now the authoritative interpretation), though legally sufficient, is supported by two employer arguments, past practice and industry wide practice. These two arguments are far more persuasive and compelling than any language analysis because they show how the parties have substantively interpreted and applied the cold, inanimate contract language.

The Employer's Past Practice Argument

The employer's uniform, consistent, and uninterrupted practice has been to assign his regular employees; other employees would be dispatched from the local that had geographic jurisdiction over the job site. The employer has never paid travel pay to non-regular employees dispatched from another local if the work was within the free travel area and if those employees were not required to report to L.'s shop. The practice has developed a uniform, undisturbed, and continuous pattern of action for the past ten years. Furthermore, critically, employees continually relied on and profited from the practice. The union must have accepted the employer's interpretation because neither the union nor any of its locals ever filed a grievance that challenged the ten year practice. Whatever grievances were filed, were not over the principle of measurement but over the distance traveled.

Industry-wide Practice

The practice of other employers, never contested by the union, supports my interpretation of the contract langue. Company G. has used, and still uses a map similar to L.'s, which is marked with a 25 miles radius to define the free travel area. G., present at the 1971 negotiations, testified that he prepared his map with a radius to define the free travel area immediately after and as a result of the agreement reached in the 1971 negotiations. Like L., G. uses and has used his map to estimate jobs and to pay travel pay, and also to explain to all employees how travel pay is paid. G. has consistently defined the free travel area by radius miles since 1971.

Q., president of the Q. Painting Co. (who has been working under the area agreement for a number of years), testified that he, too, has consistently used a map posted at his shop that measures the free travel area in radius miles.

Question No. 2: Does Article 22.3 limit the free travel area to the county of the specific local union that dispatches employees within that area?

If the job site is in a particular local's jurisdiction, an employer must employ a certain percentage of employees from that local union (Article 13.6). Here, L. employed employees from the local 60 miles away because the job site was within another local's jurisdiction.

The employer argued that Article 22.3 should not be limited to the county of the specific local union that dispatched employees within that area because Article 22.3 specifically provides that "any employee living in an outlying area where travel time is concerned shall not receive same if not required to report to the employer's shop."

The union argued that "since it was 43 miles from the local 60 miles from the large city's dispatch point to the job site, those employees who lived more than 25 miles from the job site are entitled to travel pay from the dispatch point."

I must, and do reject the union's contention because it assumes what is legally incorrect, namely, that the free travel area is to be measured by road miles, not radius miles, and that the job site was outside the employer's free travel area. The union's interpretation would limit the employer's free travel area to the geographic jurisdiction of the local union within which the employer's shop is located, an interpretation of contract language that would rob the free travel area of its substantive contractual value.

Conclusion

The language of the agreement, the past practice of the parties, and the industry practice conclusively show that the employer's interpretation of the agreement is the correct interpretation. The employer is not legally obligated to pay travel pay to those employees dispatched from the dispatch point 60 miles away because they worked within the employer's free travel area, and because they were not required to report to L.'s shop.

Question No. 1: Did the employer violate Article 22.3 of the collective bargaining agreement when it failed to pay travel pay on the hangar job.?

Answer: No.

Question No. 1a: What is the proper remedy?

Answer: No remedy is necessary because the employer did not violate Article 22.3.

Question No. 2: Is the free travel zone measured by road miles or by radius miles?

Answer: The free travel area is to be measured in radius miles.

Award

The union's grievance is hereby denied.

EXAMPLE NO. 6

A teacher objected to the district's deduction of emergency leave and family leave from accumulated sick leave. The opinion discusses the effect the incorporation of state law has on the collective bargaining agreement.

Facts

The parties' collective bargaining agreement provided for 10 days per year for illness and injury, 3 days emergency leave, and an unspecified number of days for family illness leave to be deducted from the employee's emergency leave. However, the state legislature established an unused sick leave cash out, which limited the allowable leave for illness, injury, and emergency leave to 12 days per year, and removed the 180 day maximum unused leave accumulation. To comply with state law, the parties reopened their agreement and signed an *Addendum.*

The amended Article IV, Section I, *Absences and Leaves,* reads:

An employee may be properly absent from duty only with authorization. Absence from duty may be authorized by the School Board or by the Superintendent of Schools or by his representative, and only as provided by these rules and regulations and within the provisions of the law governing such absences. Partial or full compensation during a period of unauthorized absence may be paid within the limitations of these rules and regulations and/or the law governing such absence. Absence without pay may also be authorized.

Absence from duty not authorized by the School Board or by the Superintendent of Schools under these rules and regulations and/or by the law governing absence of employees shall be considered unauthorized absence. No payment of a salary will be made for unauthorized absence.

When an employee will be absent from work due to illness he/she shall give notice to the principal or the person designated by the Superintendent to receive such notice, not later than 7:00 A.M. or as soon as possible in cases of emergencies on the first day of illness. If an absence is for consecutive days, the principal should be notified of the probable date of return.

Annual leave with compensation for illness and injury is as follows:

(a)   For such employees under contract with the School district as full-time employees, twelve days per contract year.

(b)   For such employees under contract with the School district as part-time employees, at least that portion of twelve days as the total number of days contracted for, bears to the regular employee's contract days;

(c) Compensation for leave for illness or injury actually taken shall be the same as the compensation such person would have received had such person not taken the accumulated leave provided for in this provision.

(d) Accumulated leave under this provison shall be transferred from one district to another within the state;

(e) Leave accumulated by a person in a district prior to leaving said district may, under the rules and regulations of the Board, be granted to such person when he returns to employment of the district;

(f) After an illness of five (5) days or more consecutive employment days, the employee shall present a doctor's statement attesting to the inability of the employee to meet his contractual obligations. However, on other occasions a doctor's statement may be required by the Superintendent if such request is made during the illness.

Section 5, *Emergency Leave for Abnormal and Unusual Circumstances,* reads:

Emergency leave of three (3) days shall be granted with pay. Such leave is non-accumulative. Emergency leave may be taken at the teacher's discretion, due to a problem that has been suddenly precipitated or is unplanned, or where preplanning could not relieve the necessity for the teacher's absence. Teachers shall give prior notification to the Superintendent or his designee unless circumstances make prior notification impossible. Teachers are subject to loss of pay or other penalities in cases where leave is obtained under false pretenses.

The Superintendent may grant requests for non-emergency circumstances if in his judgment such absence is in the best interest of the school district and the employee. The Superintendent shall have 3 options in unusual and abnormal absences:

1. Grant absence with pay.
2. Grant absence with deduction of substitute pay.
3. Grant absence without pay.

Section 6, *Leave for Family Illness,* reads:

In the event of accidents or illness in the immediate family requiring the contact of a doctor and/or hospitalization, refer to Article IV, Section 5, Emergency Leave/Leave for Abnormal or Unusual Circumstances.

In its December 22 checks, the district notified the teacher employees that:

Due to State Law RCW 28A.58.100, emergency leave and family illnesses must be subtracted from your accumulated sick leave balance. Your sick leave balance reflects a reduction for the above leaves you have taken.

The association objected to the district's deduction of emergency and family leave from the accumulated sick leave and filed a formal grievance that alleged that the district had violated the agreement by deducting family illness leave from the accumulated sick/injury leave of some employees. The association asked the district to "cease and desist" and to reinstate the accumulated sick/injury leave days of any bargaining unit employees deducted for family illness and to deduct instead from the employees' emergency/abnormal and unusual circumstances leave.

The district denied the grievance, because the legislature had passed a sick leave buy-back law and because the district had agreed to increase the number of days to be granted annually from 10 to 12. The district said that it had no choice but to comply with state law, which states:

> For certificated and noncertificated employees, annual leave with compensation for illness, injury, and emergencies shall be granted and accrued at a rate not to exceed twelve days per year; provisions for any contract in force on June 12, 1980, which conflict with requirements of this subsection shall continue in effect until contract expiration; after expiration, any new contract executed between parties shall be consistent with this subsection.

Unable to resolve the dispute, the parties proceeded to arbitration.

Question

In its pre-hearing statement, the association submitted the following questions as the arbitrable questions:

(1) Did the district violate the parties' Collective Bargaining Agreement (CBA), or state law, or otherwise act inappropriately by deducting emergency leave from employees' accumulated sick/injury leave and/or by deducting family illness leave from employees' accumulated sick/injury leave instead of from employees' emergency/abnormal and unusual circumstances leave?

(2) If so, what is an appropriate remedy?

In its pre-hearing statement, the district formulated the following question as the arbitrable question:

Has the district administered the CBA in conformity with state law as interpreted by the Attorney General?

At the hearing, the parties could not agree on the formulation of the question. After some discussion, they agreed to submit the dispute over the formulation of the question to the arbitrator. Therefore, my first task is to answer the question: Which formulation of the question is the proper?

The association proposed the following language:

Did the district violate the CBA when the district deducted emergency and family illness leave from the employee's accumulted sick leave?

The district proposed the following language:

Did the district administer the leave provisions according to the CBA, and/or state law?

The association's formulation of the question is the proper formulation because it addresses itself to the grievance, that is, to an alleged violation of the collective bargaining agreement; the district's word "administer," a neutral word, does not connote an alleged violation of the CBA, the substance of the association's grievance.

Jurisdiction of the Arbitrator

The main question, "Did the district violate the collective bargaining agreement?" limits my jurisdiction to the collective bargaining agreement. Therefore, I have no jurisdiction over the legal effect of state law on the collective bargaining agreement, unless the collective bargaining agreement incorporates state law. Two provisions of the collective bargaining agreement incorporate state law: Article IV, Section 1, contains an incorporation provision: "Absences from duty may be authorized . . . only as provided by these rules and regulations, and within the provisions of the law governing such absences;" and Article I, Section 3, *The Savings Clause*, acknowledges that the collective bargaining agreement must cede to statutes by the language: "If any provision of this agreement is held invalid by the operation of law." Therefore, I have jurisdiction and authority to interpret and apply state law because this portion of state law has become part of the parties' collective bargaining agreement.

Position of the Parties

The district's position is: the parties had reopened the collective bargaining agreement and negotiated a new agreement on leaves (the *Addendum*) to accommodate the changes prescribed in state law. Therefore, the exclusion provided for in state law was invalidated but the remainder of the section was in force. The agreement must be administered in accordance with the 12 day maximum for illness, injury and *emergencies* as limited by the statute. In short, the 12 day maximum in state law nullified the 3 day emergency leave in the agreement. Since employees are entitled to only 12 days paid leave, emergency leave must be deducted from the maximum 12 day annual leave.

The association's position is: the *Addendum* changed only the *Illness/*

Injury Section of the agreement; the *Addendum* left intact the two sections on *Emergencies,* which are independent from the *Illness/Injury* Section 1. Therefore, emergency leave and family illness leave must be deducted from the *Emergency Leave* provision, not from the 12 day illness/injury leave. In short, an employee is entitled to 12 annual illness/injury paid leave days and 3 additional emergency paid leave days.

Argument

The district's argument fails for two reasons. First, the reopening and modifying of a collective bargaining agreement does not, and cannot of itself, invalidate any part of state law. Second, parties must incorporate all of state law, not just one part of the statute.

Since the parties must incorporate, and have incorporated, the whole of state law, the interpretation and the application of state law determines the legal rights of the parties. The spirit and intent of the law is conservative and prospective: to maintain the status quo, and at the same time to prepare for the future. The law is conservative: the language, "provisions for any contract in force which conflict with requirements of this subsection shall continue until contract expiration" seeks to protect existing rights and to leave the legal status quo undisturbed. The law is also prospective, it prescribes a rule for the future: the 12 day maximum accrual for paid leave for illness, injury, and emergencies becomes operative only "after expiration" of the old contract, that is, "any new contract . . . shall be consistent with this subsection." A simple and succinct restatement of the language would be: the 12 day maximum accrual of all leaves is effective immediately unless the collective bargaining agreement stipulates to the contrary. Collective bargaining provisions that are contrary to state law shall remain in force until the collective bargaining agreement expires and until the parties sign a *new agreement.* After the contract expires, the district cannot grant more than 12 days of paid annual leave for illness, injury, and emergencies.

The practical effect of this interpretation of the incorporated state law on leaves is as follows. At present, since the parties have not yet signed a *new agreement,* district employees are entitled to 10 days paid annual leave, not 12, for illness and injury (Article IV, Section 1) and to 3 days for emergency leave (Article IV, Section 5 and Section 6). Therefore, deductions for emergency leave and for family illness must be taken from the 3 day emergency leave (Section 5 and Section 6). After the parties sign a new collective bargaining agreement, district employees are entitled to only 12 leave days with compensation for illness, injury, and emergencies. After the new agreement is signed, emergency leave for both emergencies and family illness must be deducted from the 12 days maximum annual leave.

Conclusion

The district improperly deducted emergency leave and family illness leave from illness/injury leave because the parties have not yet signed a new collective bargaining agreement.

Award

The district is hereby ordered to rectify all deductions in accordance with this *Opinion and Award,* that is, all emergency and family illness leave deducted from the 10 day illness/injury leave must be deducted from the 3 day emergency leave.

I hereby retain jurisdiction over any dispute that might arise over the interpretation and application of this *Opinion and Award* until (date).

EXAMPLE NO. 7

A teacher alleged that transfer from one building to another violated the collective bargaining agreement. The opinion discusses the importance of the formulation of the questions, the admissibility of post-hearing evidence, the jurisdiction of the arbitrator, notice and timely filing, management rights, and past practice.

Facts

In October, the director of education, R., and B., the grievant (a psychologist), discussed a possible change in the grievant's building assignment. The grievant expressed a reluctant willingness to be reassigned if the director felt she was no longer appropriately serving the needs of the junior high school. The director decided to change her building assignment and met with the grievant to discuss the change and the reasons for the change. He notified her in writing that on January 5, she would serve at an elementary school. The grievant requested the director to acknowledge in writing that the change in building assignment was an involuntary change. The director complied with her request. In February, she filed a grievance that alleged that the director had violated Article 34 and Article 6 of the collective bargaining agreement. The district denied the grievance and the parties proceeded to arbitration.

Questions

In the *Briefs,* the parties formulated the questions differently from the agreed to formulation of the questions at the hearing.

The District's Formulation

1.   Does the arbitrator have jurisdiction over Article 34.3 of the collective bargaining agreement between the association and the district?

2.   Is the district to comply with the notice requirements of Article 34.1 of the agreement?

3.   If so, did the district comply with the notice requirements of Article 34 of the agreement?

4.   Did the district violate Article 6, the Maintenance of Standards provision of the agreement?

The Association's Formulation

1.   Has the arbitrator jurisidiction over Article 34.3?

2.   Is the district required to comply with the notice requirements of Article 34.1? If so, did the district comply?

3.   Is the district required to comply with consent language in Article 34.3? If so, did the district comply?

4.   Did the district violate the Maintenance of Standards of Article 6?

I must, and do, reject each party's formulation of the questions because neither of these formulations of the questions is identical to the agreed upon formulation at the hearing. I can address myself only to the agreed upon formulation of the questions because only this formulation specifies and determines my jurisdiction. Were I to answer any other or different questions, I would exceed my authority and I would furnish grounds for a vacation of the *Award*. The agreed upon formulation of the questions, read back to the parties at the hearing to ensure accuracy and copied verbatim from my notes, is now the authoritative and only formulation of the questions before me.

The Agreed Upon Formulation

1.   Has the arbitrator jurisdiction over Article 34.3?

2.   Is the district required to comply with the notice requirements of Article 34.3?

3.   If so, did the district comply with Article 34.3?

4.   Did the district violate Article 6, *Maintenance of Standards?*

Argument

Before I answer these four questions, I must answer the district's question:

Question: Is the association's post-hearing evidence admissible?

Answer: The association's post-hearing evidence is inadmissible.

On December 21, the district formally objected to the association's inclusion of certain testamentary and documentary evidence in its *Brief*. The district believed that the matter was improperly introduced because the evidence was not introduced at the hearing. The association responded that the evidence was not new evidence but "supportive information for a premise" advanced at the hearing.

When the parties proceed to arbitration, the terminal point of the grievance process, the arbitrator must assume that they have exhausted the discovery process and that they will present their arguments and all their supporting facts at the hearing. I cannot allow the association to introduce supporting evidence after the hearing because I would extend the discovery process beyond the grievance procedure, and because I would frustrate one of the major ends of arbitration: the speedy resolution of the dispute.

Question No. 1: Has the arbitrator jurisdiction over Article 34.3?

Answer: The arbitrator has jurisdiction over Article 34.3.

The district believed that the arbitrator had no jurisdiction over Article 34.3 because the association had never raised the substantive question in Article 34.3, that is, whether the transfer/reassignment was necessary "to prevent undue disruptions of instructional programs, in cases of emergency, or change in staff requirement due to student distribution." The association never raised this issue in its request for arbitration to the American Arbitration Association or in its statement of the issues to the arbitrator before the hearing. In its formulation to the arbitrator, the association made the issue "consent" and "the number of days notice" under Article 34.1, not the substantive matter in Article 34.3. The association cannot expand the arbitrator's jurisdiction because Rule 7(b) of the AAA rules, incorporated into the agreement, states that "after the arbitrator is appointed, no new or different claim may be submitted." Further, because the district never agreed to arbitrate this substantive matter, the arbitrator has no jurisdiction over 34.3 because Article 46.1.3(c) specifically states that "the arbitrator shall have no power to alter, add to, or subtract from the terms of this agreement."

The association argued that the arbitrator had jurisdiction over Article 34.3 because the association had alleged that the district violated the whole of Article 34 through all the steps of the grievance procedure. The association has always contended first, that the district had no cause to reassign the grievant, and second, even if it did have cause, the district failed to give adequate notice. Further, at no time did the association agree to withdraw any portion of Article 34 from its grievance, nor did the district ever challenge the association's *Submission Statement* prior to the arbitration hearing. The district cannot raise the arbitrability question.

The arbitrator has jurisdiction over Article 34.3 because the original grievance at Step 1 specifically alleges a violation of all of Article 34, not a violation of only Article 34.3. Further, the language of Article 34.3, "no transfer/reassignment as defined above"—a reference to Article 34.1—contractually connects Article 34.3 to Article 34.1. It is axiomtic that contract language must be examined in toto; each part must be given its intended effect in order to give the text its intended confluence and unity. It is also axiomatic that the meaning of each part of a controverted text, whether Article 34.1 or Article 34.3, be ascertained by an analysis of its textual companions.

Question No. 2: Is the district required to comply with the notice requirements of Article 34.3?

Article 34.3 reads:

In the event that the district considers a transfer/reassignment for an education employee for the ensuing school term due to a change in program, student enrollment, building staff needs, etc., the educational employee shall be notified in writing at least thirty (30) days prior to the proposed transfer/reassignment, provided that this thirty (30) day notice may be waived following consultation with the association and the employee.

The obvious answer to this question is "yes": the district must comply with Article 34.1 because the district must comply with every Article in the collective bargaining agreement. However, this question requires more than the obvious answer. It requires an answer to the two disputed subquestions below:

Sub-question 2a: Does the language "educational employee" in Article 34.1 apply to psychologists, as the association contended, or only to teachers, as the district contended?

Answer: The phrase "educational employee" includes and applies to psychologists.

The district advanced several reasons to show that Article 34.1 is not applicable to psychologists. First, psychologists are district-wide employees; they belong to one district-wide special education department under the supervision of the Director of Special Education who hires, assigns, and evaluates them. Past practice and present procedure show that psychologists are district-wide employees. Second, Article 34.1 applies only to classroom teachers because teachers are not district-wide employees. Teachers' duties are limited to one school, and they are transferred from one school to another. Third, G., the Administrative Assistant to the Superintendent for Personnel and a member of the bargaining team, testified that Article 34.1 was applicable only to teachers. Fourth, teachers and psychologists are hired and supervised differently: the building principal assigns and supervises teachers, but the director of Special Education hires, assigns, and supervises psychologists. The reassignment of the grievant did not affect this relationship in any way. Fifth, and finally, Article 34.1 does not mention psychologists.

The association argued that the language "educational employee" applied to psychologists because first, psychologists, like teachers, receive assignments in specific buildings; second, psychologists have schedules as teachers do; third, the language does not exclude psychologists; and fourth, practice does not exclude them. G.'s testimony must be discounted because the parties did not discuss the inclusion or exclusion of psychologists in the controverted language.

None of these arguments is conclusive. The application of a well-known and widely recognized axiom in the construction of labor contracts decides the issue: general language must be broadly construed to include all categories. Exceptions or exclusions to general language can be read into general language only if other language clearly and unequivocally excepts or excludes a particular category from the general language.

Sub-Question 2b: Did the district comply with the notice requirement of Article 34.1?

Answer: The district did comply with the notice requirement of Article 34.1

The contractual procedural time requirement in Article 34.1 is clear and direct: if the district decides to transfer/reassign an educational employee, the educational employee "shall be notified in writing at least thirty (30) days prior to the proposed transfer/reassignment."

The district cannot dismiss this obligation to notify as a "technical" requirement. The procedural requirement to notify formally is a substantive obligation even if, in the words of the district, it "would place serious restraints on his [the director's] ability to comply with the mandates of these [federal and state] laws." The district must be held to its contractual bargain in spite of its doubtful and hypothetical legal view that state and federal laws "might necessarily supersede any notice requirements of a bargaining agreement."

The district argued that the director complied with the time requirement of Article 34.1 because the change was a voluntary change, that is, the grievant, not the director, suggested the change in building assignment. As early as the end of September, the grievant said that she would be willing to accept a change in her building assignment. When the grievant and the director discussed the change in October, he told her that he had decided to change part of her building assignment. It was only at the request of the grievant in December that the director formally acknowledged that the transfer was involuntary. Therefore, the district complied with the time line requirements of Article 34.1: the grievant had actual notice a full three months before January 5, and she received formal oral notice on December 3, that is, over one month before the effective date, January 5.

The association disputed the district's testimony: the grievant testified that she recalled some discussion of a building change, but she did not recall ever meeting with the director to request a transfer. In fact, she had consistently resisted any such transfer. In any event, the district did not give timely notice because the district gave official notice in writing on December 12, and the transfer became effective on January 5. Clearly, the grievant was not given 30 days notice.

It is plain, as the association pointed out and the district admitted, that if time began to run on December 12, the date of the district's formal notification, the district did not meet the contractual 30 days notice requirement. However, for the reasons below, time did not begin to run on December 12, because the grievant relieved the district of its obligation to formally notify.

To support my conclusion, I have first recast and then interpreted the contract language to give the language its clear, precise, integral, and intended meaning. Thus, the recast language:

If the district decides to transfer/reassign an educational employee...the district must notify the educational employee in writing at least thirty (30) days prior to the proposed transfer/reassignment...the association and/or the employee may waive this thirty (30) days requirement notice.

The language says that when the district decides to transfer/reassign an educational employee, the district must give the employee 30 days notice prior to the transfer/reassignment. After notice, the employee/association may or may not relieve (may waive) the district of its obligation to formally notify. If the employee/association waives the requirement, the transfer/reassignment becomes a voluntary transfer/reassignment: the district need not formally notify. If, however, the employee/association does not waive the formal requirement to notify the transfer/reassignment becomes involuntary: the district must then give 30 days notice in writing before it transfer/reassigns.

The evidence is conclusive that, on September 30, the grievant relieved the district of its obligation. The grievant's *Letter* of December 23 to the director, her own written account of events, clearly, unequivocally, and conclusively shows that the grievant was willing to accept a transfer/reassignment from one building to another. She wrote:

On September 30...I stated that if you felt I was not properly serving that school and was perhaps too ego-involved with it, you might consider switching me to another Jr. High and having the psychologist from that school serve here ...I express a willingness to switch Jr. Highs if you felt I was no longer serving their needs appropriately.

When, on September 30, the grievant told the director she was willing to be transferred/reassigned, she entered into an oral agreement with the director, which relieved the director of his obligation to notify her formally. In short, the director properly made a good faith assumption, an assumption inherent in personal relations and in contracts, that he could rely on the grievant's word. He properly concluded that he need not issue an official notice because the transfer/reassignment was voluntary. Therefore, the grievant's request of December 16 to convert a voluntary transfer/reassignment into an involuntary transfer/reassignment is neither fair nor legally tenable because she broke her oral agreement with the director. The grievant must be held to her word. She cannot legally hold the director hostage to her will: to relieve him of his obligation on September 30 and then to reimpose the obligation on December 16. For the employee/association to waive the notice requirement and then to reimpose the requirement would subject the director to the changing and arbitrary will of the educational employee, a result at variance with the contract language.

Question No. 3: Did the district comply with Article 34.3?

Answer: The district did comply with Article 34.3. Article 34.3 reads:

No transfer/reassignment as defined above shall be made without the consent of the educational employee except to prevent undue disruptions of the instructional program, in case of emergency, or change in staff requirement due to student distribution.

The association interpreted Article 34.3 to mean that in cases of involuntary transfer/reassignment, the district can transfer/reassign only for cause, that is, "to prevent undue disruption of the educational program, in case of emergency, or change in staff requirement due to student distribution." Even if the district had "cause," the district must formally notify because its practice had been "first, to show cause," and then "to give thirty (30) days notice or reach agreement with the employee and the association that the notice will be waived." The association pointed out that it was the district's practice to assign psychologists to particular buildings for a full school year. The district changed assignments only with the full agreement of those involved. The district always has been careful "to involve the effected [sic] educational employees as well as the association". When the district transferred/reassigned 28 employees this year, "the employees and the association were apprised and agreed each time."

The association misconstrues Article 34.3, and its past notice argument is legally insufficient. First, the language of Article 34.3 "without the consent of the educational employee" refers only to involuntary transfer/reassignments. Therefore, Article 34.3 is inapplicable to the 28 transfers/reassignments in which the district informed, consulted with, and sought the approval of the asociation because the association failed to show that these tranfers/reassignments were involuntary transfers/reassignments.

Second, Article 34.1, not Article 34.3 obligated the district to give formal notice of involuntary transfer/reassignments. Article 34.3 has no formal notice requirement.

Article 34.3 not only preserves the district's prerogative to transfer/reassign but it also creates exceptions to Article 34.1, that is, Article 34.3 relieved the district of the formal notice requirement found in Article 34.1 when in the judgment of the district, not in the judgment of the association, there is "cause" to disregard the formal notice requirement. I have recast the language of Article 34.3 from its passive voice to active voice to extrapolate its meaning.

The district shall make no transfer/reassignment without the consent of the educational employee as in Article 34.1 ... but the district may transfer/reassign, if in its judgment, three conditions arise: if there are undue disruptions of the educational program, if there is an emergency, and if the student distribution requires a change of staff.

The language, as recast, retains to the district its residual and reserved management rights unimpaired and protected by Article 13, *DISTRICT RIGHTS*, which reads:

Except as otherwise specifically limited by provisions of this agreement, the district has the exclusive right to exercise all the rights and functions of management ... and the use of judgment and discretion ... in the exercise of district rights.

The association's argument that the district's unilateral action did not improve the program is faulty. The association thought that "the abrupt change without notice impacted working conditions of the grievant and fellow employees ... the action could have been avoided ... undue disruption ensued to the programs" and the program was "negatively impacted by the quick change." This argument fails because only the district, in the exercise of its discretionary administrative powers, has the legal right to judge consequences of transfer/reassign decisions.

Question No. 4: Did the district violate the *Maintenance of Standards* of Article 6?

Answer: No. Article 6 reads:

While this agreement is in force, the district shall maintain those written School Board policies and procedures which affect educational employee wages, hours, and terms and conditions of employment directly related hereto, unless the district communicates to the association that in order to conform with legislation, regulations, or other legal authority it is required to change such policies and procedures.

Article 6 guarantees that all School Board policies and procedures shall remain in force for the duration of the agreement.

The association alleged that the district violated Article 6 because the district changed the grievant's working conditions. The grievant knew every year what her assignment and responsibilities were: building changes were always "agreed to by her supervisor" and only under "extraordinary circumstances," that is, when a new psychologist was hired. Then, "new assignments were issued with the same expectations of being answerable to specific buildings and schedules."

The district believed that it did not violate Article 6 because it exercised its exclusive right to manage under Article 13, *DISTRICT RIGHTS*. The director had always followed the same procedure in the past: he had changed building assignments of school psychologists, and he continues to maintain this practice.

These arguments from past practice have no legal force because the meaning of the language in its recast form is clear. The district did not and could not have violated Article 6 because the district properly exercised the administrative prerogative to transfer/reassign retained in Article 34.3 and protected by Article 13.

Award

The grievance is hereby denied.

EXAMPLE NO. 8

The union alleged that the district violated the agreement when it issued supplemental contracts. The *Opinion* discusses three commonly disputed matters: the arbitrator's jurisdiction, management's residual rights, and past practice.

Facts

During negotiations for a successor agreement and just before the opening of school, the district sent each bargaining unit employee a copy of his contract for the school year. The district stipulated that the contract would be valid only if the employee returned the contract to the district's personnel office by a certain date in August. In protest, the association filed an unfair labor practice charge with the Public Employment Relations Commission (PERC). Mediation failed, and the association voted to strike. On the first strike day, 18 members of the bargaining unit crossed the picket lines and reported to work; 3 other bargaining unit employees on various assignments away from the district also reported to work. On the evening of the same day, the district postponed opening of school and authorized the Superintendent to hire replacements for striking employees. On September 3, the district issued supplemental contracts to the 21 employees for each day of service at the rate of pay established by the agreement for supplemental contracts. The association objected to the issuance of these supplemental contracts and filed a formal grievance. The district denied the grievance, and the parties proceeded to arbitration.

Questions

The parties agreed to submit the following questions:

1. Did the district violate the terms of the new collective bargaining agreement by compensating certain employees through the issuance of supplemental contracts for services which the employees are said to have performed on September 2 and/or September 3?

2. If so, what is the appropriate remedy?

Relevant Contract Provisions

ARTICLE I—*RECOGNITION AND JURISDICTION*

Section 1. *Recognition*

The school district recognizes the education association as the exclusive representative for the purpose of collective bargaining of all certificated employees of the district. The district agrees not to bargain with or recognize any certificated employee organization other than the association for the duration of this recognition. Such bargaining and recognition shall extend to the maximum period allowed by law.

In addition to the foregoing and subject to the limitation provided for in (c) below, the district recognized the association as the exclusive representative for the purpose of collective bargaining for the following employees:

a) Substituted certificated employees employed by the district for more than thirty (30) days of work within any twelve (12) month period ending during the current or immediately preceding school year and who continue to be available for employment as substitute teachers.

b) Substitute certificated employees employed by the district in positions where it is anticipated or comes to pass that a member of the bargaining unit will be replaced in such assignment for a period in excess of twenty (20) consecutive work days.

c) If the court of competent jurisdiction rules that pursuant to RCW 41.59 substitutes as defined herein are not appropriate for inclusion in the bargaining unit identified in this provision or if such court rules that a showing of majority support is required for inclusion in the bargaining unit, then this recognition of substitutes and Article XXVII shall be stayed until a proper showing of majority support is forthcoming in the latter instance.

ARTICLE II—*STATUS OF AGREEMENT*

Section 1. *Responsibility and Bargaining Procedures*

The district and the association recognize that under this agreement each has a responsibility for the welfare and security of the employees. Agreement reached between authorized negotiators for the association and the district shall become effective only when appropriately ratified by the association and the Board of Directors of the district.

The parties acknowledge that during negotiations resulting in this agreement, each had the unlimited right and opportunity to make demands and proposals with respect to any and all subjects or matters not removed by law from the area of collective bargaining and that the understanding and agreement arrived by the parties after exercise of that right and opportunity are set forth in this agreement.

This agreement shall supersede any rules, regulations, policies, resolutions, or practices of the district which shall be contrary to or inconsistent with its terms.

This agreement constitutes the entire agreement between the parties and concludes the collective bargaining for its term; subject only to a desire by both parties to amend or modify at any time.

During the term of this contract, there may be agreement between the parties that this contract needs amendment or modification. In the event that both parties agree that amendment or modification is needed, collective bargaining will commence on said subjects.

In any bargaining between the association and the district, neither party shall have any control over the selection of the bargaining representative of the other party. During such bargaining, the parties pledge that representatives selected by each shall have all necessary power to make proposals, consider proposals, and modify positions during the course of bargaining subject only to ultimate ratification by the governing bodies of each party.

ARTICLE IV—*MANAGEMENT RIGHTS AND RESPONSIBILITIES*

Section 1. *General Rights*

Management rights and functions except as limited by this agreement, shall remain with the district as employer. It is recognized, by way of illustration, that such rights and functions include but are not limited to:

a) control of the management of the district; the supervision of all operations; the methods, process, and means of performing any and all work; the control of property; the composition, assignment, direction and determination of the size of its working forces; the establishment of educational programs, services, and staffing in accordance with district educational policies and goals; and the right to maintain and protect all property and equipment;

b) the right to determine the work to be done by employees in the unit;

c) the right to introduce new or improved operations, methods, programs, means, or facilities;

d) the right to hire, schedule, promote, demote, transfer, release, and lay off employees; and the right to suspend, and discharge employees according to state statutes and district policy, and otherwise, to maintain an orderly, effective, and efficient operation.

The district shall adhere strictly to all federal and state statutes and regulations and the Constitution of the state of Washington.

The district will issue such rules and regulations necessary to properly manage the district consistent with this agreement.

The exercise of the district's rights stated herein does not modify the right of an employee to appeal through established grievance procedures when an act of the district is construed to violate this agreement.

The exercise of the district's rights stated herein is a function of management. However, the district shall announce proposed changes in policies reasonably in advance of making changes.

ARTICLE V—WORKDAY AND WORKYEAR

Section 1. *Workday*

Each full time employee shall work eight (8) hours per day. The on-site starting and ending times for each employee shall be determined by the employee and his/her immediate supervisor, whose ultimate decision shall prevail based on the program and the schedule. All work need not be performed at the school site.

Employees who are required in the course of their employment to travel between buildings will be scheduled by their supervisors to provide reasonable time for travel and preparation.

The district may require employees to perform extra duties related to the functioning of the total school and/or educational program, which are not covered by the activity salary schedule, which on occasion may extend or add to the on-site workday. Extra duties shall be assigned in such a manner that no one employee shall have an undue share of such duties.

Section 2. *Workyear*

The contracted workyear for regular employees shall be one hundred eighty-three (183) days. The contracted workyear for 1980–81 shall be consistent with the calendar as provided in Appendix 3. Beginning with the 1981–82 school year, calendars shall be established using the following criteria:

a) When Labor Day falls on 1, 2, or 3 September, school will start on the Thursday following Labor Day. Tuesday and Wednesday following Labor Day will be contracted preparation and secondary school registration days.

b) When Labor Day falls on 4, 5, 6, or 7 September, school will start on the Wednesday following Labor Day. Friday preceding Labor Day and the Tuesday following Labor Day will be contracted preparation and secondary school registration days.

c) One hundred and eighty (180) instructional days for students.

d) March 4 is inservice staff day for staff and noncontracted days for students.

e) Winter vacation will be on two (2) weeks and three (3) weekends, with spring vacation immediately following the completion of third quarter.

f) One (1) secondary staff evaluation day, as contracted day, the second Friday preceding the last school day. Secondary schools to be in session.

h) Emergency school makeup days designated, in order of selection, as follows:

1. March inservice day providing determination of need made prior to 1 March.

2. Days of week immediately following calendared last day of school, as needed.

ARTICLE XXIII—*BASIC SALARY SCHEDULE AND PAY*

Section 5. *Pay for Extended Work*

Pay for added time beyond the 183-day contract will be paid according to the schedule below:

a) Extended workyear in summer school or basic assignment—(1/200th per day).

b) All other extended work—($10.00 per hour).

ARTICLE XXVIII—*GRIEVANCE PROCEDURE*

Section 1. *Purpose*

The purpose of this procedure is to provide a means for the orderly and expeditious adjustment of grievance of individual or groups of employees of the district. The procedure, excluding provisions for binding arbitration, shall also be used to process complaints of alleged non-compliance with Title IX of the Education Amendments of 1972, which prohibits sex discrimintaion in employment.

Section 2. *Definition*

As used in this procedure, a "grievance" is a claim by an individual employee, group of employees, or the association that an agreement between the district and the association, an existing school policy, or an established practice has been violated, misinterpreted, misapplied, or applied unevenly or unfairly, or a claim that there has been unfair, inequitable, or unwise treatment of the grievant by the employer. A "grievant" is an employee or group of employees having a grievance. A "Grievance Review Request Form" is a printed form utilized in the process of adjusting grievances under this procedure. As used herein, "established practice" shall mean a method of dealing with or course of conduct in regard to a reoccurring event or situation which is of general application in the conduct of such events or situations as carried out by the district, the Board, the Superintendent or administrative staff of the recognized employee organization. Such practices may be written or unwritten and the burden of proof regarding their established existence shall be the responsibility of the party claiming their existence.

The Jurisdiction of the Arbitrator

The many *Exhibits* and the many diverse contentions and arguments in the parties' lengthy *Briefs* tended to, and for a time did obfuscate the main issue before me. The polemic *Briefs* contained political and legal arguments that touched every facet of the strike, from the onset of negotiations, to the district's issuance of contracts, mediation, the filing of unfair labor practice, the work stoppage, the conclusion of a collective bargaining agreement, and the issuance of supplemental contracts. To disengage myself from the multitude of conflicting considerations and arguments, I asked myself two preliminary but central and critical questions: first, what is my jurisdiction, and second, what articles in the collective bargaining agreement are germane to the issue before me? The answer to these preliminary questions simplified my task, gave focus and perspective to the issue, and made possible a certain coherence, unity, and emphasis in my *Opinion and Award*.

Preliminary Question No. 1: What is my jurisdiction?

The parties saw fit to incorporate a well-known and long established axiom of labor arbitration in step three (a) of Article XXVIII, *GRIEVANCE PROCEDURE,* which limits the arbitrator's jurisdiction. Thus,

> The arbitrator shall limit his/her decision strictly to disputes involving the application or interpretation of the express terms of this agreement. The arbitrator shall have no power to change, alter, detract from, or add to the provisions of this agreement.

The clear intent of this provision is to narrow the arbitrator's jurisdiction and to confine that jurisdiction to those matters specifically mentioned in the *Submission Agreement.* Here, the *Submission Agreement* clearly confines my jurisdiction to one issue: supplemental contracts.

Therefore, in accordance with the limiting principle in Article XXVIII quoted above, I must, and do, declare the following matters, some discussed at length by the parties, beyond my jurisdiction: first, the district's argument that the district had a contractual and statutory duty to bargain "to consider" September 2 as a workday; second, the district's argument that the district properly issued continuing contracts to members of the bargaining unit on August 13, because it had the duty to bargain; third, the district's argument that it had no duty to respond to a work stoppage; fourth, the district's argument that it is appropriate for the district to compensate employees who work during the strike. I also must and do declare two association arguments beyond my jurisdiction. First, that the district's unilateral issuance of individual contracts on August 13 is improper because the district did not "bargain in good faith," and second, that the district did not comply with the emergency rules established by the PERC.

Preliminary Question No. 2: What Articles are germane to the issue before me?

The association alleged that the district violated the articles reproduced in Part III of this *Opinion and Award*. However, I find the following Articles irrelevant to the issue of supplemental contracts: first Article I, *RECOGNITION AND JURISDICTION*, because Article I does not mention supplemental contracts; and second Article III, *STATUS OF THE AGREEMENT*, because Article III discussed bargaining procedures, not supplemental contracts. Therefore, my task is to determine only two questions: first, whether the district violated Article XXIII, *BASIC SALARY SCHEDULE*, Section 5, *Pay for Extended Work;* and if so, did the district violate the *BACK TO WORK AGREEMENT?*

Argument

Question No. 1: Did the district violate Article XXVIII, *BASIC SALARY SCHEDULE AND PAY*, Section 5, *Pay for Extended Work?* Section 5 reads:

Pay for added time beyond the basic 183-day contract will be paid according to the schedule below:

a) Extended workyear in summer school or basic assignment (1/200th per day)

b) All other extended work ($10.00 per hour)

This grievance pertains only to the 18 employees who reported to work on September 2 or September 3, not to the 3 employees (the exchange teacher in Hawaii, the one at the Educational Service district in the County, and the one on a special project at a University) who were assigned outside the district. The association believed that these 3 employees were properly paid under Article XXIII because they did extended work.

Therefore, why does the association object to compensation by the issuance of supplemental contracts? The objection is neither to the compensation itself nor to the work done because the association admitted that the 18 employees performed "some type of service" for which the district must pay. One principal testified that the 18 employees were "ready to teach" and the district said that they performed a "normal day of work." The association clearly and unequivocally objected to the compensation of the 18 employees because the compensation "was not the result of actual services . . . but rather the mere fact that they showed up at the work site."

Is the association's allegation legally valid? The answer to this question depends on the interpretation and application of Section 5 of Article XXIII. The language of Article XXIII is clear, simple, and direct; it needs no interpretation. In contrast to the basic contract issued to regular classroom teachers on a contracted workyear of 183 days, a supplemental contract is issued to bargaining unit employees for "added time beyond the basic 183-day contract." Typically, the district issues supplemental contracts for expanded work to counselors, librarians, home economics teachers, and industrial arts teachers.

The language, "management rights and functions, except as limited by this agreement, shall remain with the district as employer," in Article IV, *MANAGEMENT RIGHTS AND RESPONSIBILITIES*, clearly and explicitly reserves to the district, as residually retained rights, all those rights not specifically ceded or limited by the agreement. The legal right to assign and to issue supplemental contracts is an inherent, plenary, residual, and retained right, legally exercisable at will and at the district's administrative convenience circumscribed only by the stipulated wage rate.

Since the district can issue supplemental contracts at will, can the district properly issue supplemental contracts for the work done on September 2 or September 3? To be paid for work done, bargaining unit employees must hold either a basic contract or a supplemental contract. The association persuasively and cogently argued that September 2 is not a contracted workday for regular classroom bargaining unit employees because the district cannot unilaterally declare it to be so, and because September 22, not September 2, became the first contracted workday for regular classroom teachers. Since September 2 is not a contracted workday but a day beyond the contracted 183 days, September 2 can only be an extended workday for which the district must pay for the work done.

Therefore, since the district properly issued supplemental contracts under Article IV, and since September 2 was not a contracted workday but an extended workday, the district properly paid the eighteen employees at the extended rate.

The association alleged that the district violated Section 2, the "established practice" section of Article XXVIII *GRIEVANCE PROCEDURE*, because the district violated its own established practice, a practice in existence for the past four years.

Article XXVIII, Section 2, defines "established practice":

A method of dealing or course of conduct in regard to a reoccurring event or situation which is of general application in the conduct of such events or situations as carried out by the district, the Board, the Superintendent, or administrative staff, or the recognized employee organization.

In defense, the district argued that "established practice" is grievable but not arbitrable because Article XXVIII, Section 2, specifies grievable matter, not arbitrable matter, that is, existing school policy, established practice, or unfair, unequitable, or unwise treatment of employees. Therefore, the district has no obligation to arbitrate "established practice," a matter beyond the arbitrator's jurisdiction, because the "arbitrator shall have no power to change, alter, detract from, or add to the provisions of the agreement." Even if the matter were arbitrable, the district did not violate "established practice."

The expression "established practice" is arbitrable because, as the association pointed out, the expression "established practice" is undeniably and expressly written into the agreement. Therefore, it is arbitrable, because, like any other provision of the contract, it is subject to arbitral review when a question arises over its interpretation and application. Even so, the district's actions support this conclusion: the district submitted a dispute on this very phrase to arbitral review without protesting its arbitrability.

Did the district violate its own "established practice"? The association argument that an establishsed practice had developed over four years and that the district had violated its own established practice cannot have, and does not have legal force because a legally binding established practice can only arise if the contract language is ambiguous and only if there is a lacuna in the contract. As I said above, Article XXIII is clear and unambiguous; it does not limit the district's residual and reserved right to issue and to pay for supplemental contracts. The district's residual and reserved right, exercisable at will, contains an inherent discretionary power to determine the means to accomplish the ends. Hence, the practice follows the will of the district: today, one practice, tomorrow, another practice.

There can be only one conclusion: since the district properly issued supplemental contracts, since September 2 and September 3 were not contracted workdays but extended workdays, since the district properly paid 18 employees at the rate established for extended work, and since the district did not and could not violate its own established practice, the district did not violate Article XXIII.

Question No. 2: Did the district violate Section 3 of the *BACK TO WORK AGREEMENT* when it issued supplemental contracts on September 30 to bargaining unit employees for work done on September 2 and/or September 3? Section 3 of the *BACK TO WORK AGREE-MENT* provides:

The agreement reached on September 21 puts an end to the issues raised in connection with or generated by the work stoppage which commenced on September 2. It is agreed that there shall be no reprisals or recriminations by or against the district, association, or any employee, student, or other person as a result of said work stoppage.

The association contended that the district violated Section 3 because the purpose of the agreement was to forget the issues "raised in connection with or generated by" the work stoppage which commenced on September 2. Payment to the eighteen (18) employees rekindled the animosities of the strike and violates the spirit of the *BACK TO WORK AGREEMENT*. Further, the district paid the eighteen employees more than other employees, i.e., for 182 days, but the agreement stipulates that all employees be paid for 181 days. And these eighteen employees were paid not for the actual service rendered but merely because "they showed up at the worksite."

I must reject the association's first argument because I cannot inquire into the district's motives or into the association's perception of these motives. The association's second argument also fails because there can be no reprisal or discrimination in the proper exercise of a legal right. Therefore, the district did not invidiously discriminate against the other employees because the district properly exercised its legal right to issue supplemental contracts under Article XXIII.

In conclusion, the district did not violate Section of the *BACK TO WORK AGREEMENT*.

Conclusion

Question No. 1: Did the district violate the terms of the new Collective Bargaining agreement by compensating certain employees through the issuance of supplemental contracts for services which the employees are said to have performed on September 2 and/or September 3?

Answer: No. The district did not violate Article XXIII, nor did the district violate the *BACK TO WORK AGREEMENT*

The association can have no legal complaint against the district. Its genuine but political complaint is against the 18 bargaining unit employees who reported to work because they obeyed the district but not the association.

Question No. 2: What is the appropriate remedy?

Answer: No remedy is necessary.

EXAMPLE NO. 9

A union alleged that the city denied an employee her right to union representation, that it discriminated against her, and that it disciplined her unfairly. The opinion interprets a provision that gives an employee the right to union representation, and discusses insubordination and progressive discipline.

Facts

The maintenance manager told the grievant, a staff employee, in the presence of the staff supervisor and the shop steward for the union, that "your actions are disturbing the work force.... I cannot tolerate your irrational and disturbing behavior.... I expect you to accept and follow orders and directions from your supervisors." He also pointed out that she had failed to complete assignments on time and that her work required numerous corrections. He could no longer tolerate her behavior. She had to improve her attitude and become part of the office team.

One month later while the construction supervisor was talking with a telephone repair person in his office, the grievant stormed into his office and, "in an antagonistic way" interrupted the conversation. She asked what he wanted her to do with a work authorization agreement. He told the grievant to return the work authorization to its originator. The grievant then said that she had never done that before and "stormed" out of his office. The supervisor described the incident as a "confrontation," "highly inappropriate," "disruptive," "counterproductive," "insolent," and intolerable." As he followed the grievant who was returning the authorization form, she said in a loud voice, "I don't know where they should go." The supervisor reported the incident to his immediate supervisor who then went to the grievant's desk. The grievant then declared in a loud voice that she would not talk to him unless her union representative were present. The supervisor testified at the hearing that he told the grievant that he wanted to discuss only the work authorization process, that she "screamed" at him and that she said she was sick and tired of the stress he had caused her and was causing her.

Two weeks later, the city formally suspended her for one day without pay "for insubordination and work force disruptions." The suspension letter specified the offenses: she had refused to discuss and follow work procedures, she had spoken in a "loud voice," and she had "screamed" at her supervisor.

The union grieved the suspension at step two and alleged that the grievant had been disciplined "without cause" and the disciplinary letter was "unreasonable and inaccurate." The union also alleged that the city had violated the agreement because the city had denied the grievant union representation. Further, the union also alleged that the city was discriminating and retaliating against the grievant because the grievant had actively supported a human rights complaint recently filed against the city. Specifically, the union alleged that the employer had violated:

1. Article I, Section 1 (Nondiscrimination)
2. Article IV, Section 2, 3, 4 (Employee Rights)
3. Article VI, Section 2 (Grievance Procedure)
4. Article XXI, Sections 1, 2, 3 (Disciplinary Actions)

The union asked the city to rescind all disciplinary actions taken against the grievant and to agree that it would not retaliate against employees who seek adjudication of their grievances and that it would inform members of the union of their right to representation when employees are called into meetings that may result in discipline. The city denied that "a standard of conduct has been established for the grievant that is different from that allowed to male employees." For the city, "the only issue" was her "clear act of insubordination," her refusal to discuss a work procedure without union representation in spite of his assurance that the discussion was job related.

Unable to resolve the dispute at step three, the union demanded arbitration.

Questions

Although the city continued to object to the grievant's office disruptions, the city unequivocally stated that the main issue was her "clear act of insubordination.'

Question No. 1: Did the city's refusal to allow the grievant union representation at the June 10 meeting called by her supervisor violate Article IV, Section 3 of the Agreement? *Article IV,* Employee Rights, reads:

Section 3. The city agrees that when an employee covered by this Agreement attends a meeting for the purpose of discussing an incident which may lead to suspension, demotion, or termination of that employee because of that particular incident, the employee shall be advised of his/her right to be accompanied by a representative of the union. If the employee desires union representation in said matter, he/she shall so notify the city at that time and shall be provided reasonable time to arrange for union representation.

Article IV, Section 3 guarantees an employee the "Weingarten" right, that is, the right to request union representation if the employee reasonably believes that an investigatory interview with an employer might lead to discipline. Article IV, Section 3, also imposes the "Miranda" obligation: the employer has the duty to inform an employee that he is entitled to exercise the Weingarten right (*NLRB v. Weingarten,* 1975).

This dispute raises two questions. First: Did the grievant have a right to union representation? Second: Did the city have the affirmative obligation to advise the grievant of her Weingarten right under the circumstances prevailing on June 10? The logic is ineluctable. If, as the union contended, the grievant had a right to union representation, the suspension for insubordination would be improper; and the city would have had the affirmative obligation to inform the grievant of her Weingarten right. However, if, as the city contended, the grievant had no right to union representation, the suspension for insubordination was proper, and the city had no affirmative obligation to inform her of her Weingarten right.

The Union's Interpretation and Application of Article IV, Section 3. The union believed that the grievant was entitled to her Weingarten right under the circumstances of June 10 because the meeting was "designed to elicit answers to *work related questions* which might affect the employee." Here, the grievant reasonably feared that the meeting would result in discipline. Therefore, the grievant was entitled to union representation because, in the words of the union, an employee's Weingarten right turns upon "reasonableness of potential disciplinary action as perceived by the employee and not supervisory intent.... Weingarten rights would be empty rights if supervisory intent triggered them." Management not only denied the grievant her Weingarten right; management also failed in its Miranda obligation because management did not allow her reasonable time to arrange for union representation.

The union argued that the circumstances before the June 10 meeting and the circumstances on June 10 were "replete with potential disciplinary implications." Previously, management had reprimanded the grievant verbally for her disruptive activity at the work site, for her failure to follow orders, and for her poor work performance. Management had told her that her irrational and disturbing behavior would no longer be tolerated. The events of June 10 were also fraught with disciplinary implications. The supervisors sought to elicit answers from the grievant to discipline her. It is "exactly this type of work related question for which a supervisor wants answers that trigger Weingarten rights where the employee has reasonable fears of resulting discipline." The grievant's fears of possible discipline were well founded.

The City's Interpretation and Application of Article IV, Section 3. The city believed that Article IV, Section 3, did not entitle the grievant to union representation on June 10 because "The facts of the instant grievance establish that the actions necessary to trigger the guarantee of Article IV, Section 3, never occurred." Weingarten rights do not attach to "run-of-the-mill" conversations, that is, to a discussion of procedures. "No provision of the Agreement requires that an employer accede to an employee's demand for union representation where the only subject to be discussed is work related." The city's affirmative duty arises *"only* when the purpose of the meeting is to address an incident which may lead to certain types of discipline."

The city did not violate Article IV, Section 3, on June 10 because the supervisor had approached the grievant's desk to explain work procedures. He testified that he told the grievant, before and after the grievant demanded union representation, that the purpose of the meeting was to discuss work procedures and that he had no intention to discipline her, that the grievant failed to mention the subject matter, and, that even if the grievant feared discipline, the grievant failed to state her fears or show that her fear was reasonably related to the events of June 10. Weingarten rights do not attach to an employee whenever an employee feels he would like to have a representative present. The city believed that the grievant had demanded the presence of a shop steward not because she reasonably feared discipline but because she had resolved not to talk to her supervisor for any reason.

The Arbitrator's Interpretation and Application of Article IV, Section 3. When does an employee enjoy the Weingarten right? When does the city have the affirmative obligation to advise an employee of that right?

The union's criterion that an employee's Weingarten right arises when an employee reasonably fears that discipline would result from an interview is contractually deficient, because subjective feelings, emotional states, and personal needs are neither sufficient nor practical guides to determine legal right. The language in Weingarten is "reasonably fears," not "fears." If the language were "fears," an employee's mere declaration of his subjective fears would trigger Weingarten rights. The language "reasonably" fears requires that an employee have reasons: real, tangible, and objective evidence to show that a particular interview might possibly lead to discipline. The very subjectivity of the criterion "fears" makes it unacceptable as an objective and practical rule to determine a contractual right. If it were, the employer would be hostage to each and every demand of every employee for union representation at all times: an impractical and harmful consequence.

At the hearing, the city asserted that the Weingarten right arises when a meeting with an agenda is held in an office. This criterion is practical and essential but incomplete. To give the parties an objective, definitive, complete, and practical interpretation and application of Article IV, Section 3, I have analyzed the disputed language. I have first inserted the words implied in the controverted paragraph, and second, I have recast some of the language from the passive voice to the active voice.

The expanded and recast language gives the language the needed clarity, strength, vitality, and thrust. The recast language appears in parentheses, thus:

The city agrees that when an employee covered by this Agreement attends (will attend) a meeting (a formal meeting) for the purpose of discussing an incident (a past incident) which (an employee reasonably fears) may (might) lead to a suspension, demotion, or termination of that employee because of that particular incident, (the city shall advise that employee that he/she has a right to union representation). If the employee desires union representation, he/she shall so notify the city at that time (after he/she receives notice) and (then the city shall give that employee) reasonable time to arrange for union representation.

The explicated and recast language has two characteristics: the meeting must be held in the future and the meeting must be a formal meeting. The meeting must be held in the future because the contract language is future language. Although the word "attends" is in the present tense, the meaning is "will attend" because the present tense can, and here, does grammatically signify the future. To discuss an incident necessarily means to discuss a past incident sometime in the future. The city's obligation to advise an employee of his/her rights entails an obligation in the future: to give an employee adequate time to prepare a defense and to arrange for union representation. Therefore, Weingarten rights do not attach to impromptu, informal, on-the-spot, usual, or daily contacts between employer and employee.

The contract language also calls for a formal meeting. What is a formal meeting? A meeting is a formal meeting when the employer gives formal notice. A notice is a formal notice only if it contains all of the following elements: the notice must be in writing; it must specify the time and place of the meeting; it must specify the agenda, that is, the employee's conduct to be discussed; and, the employer must unequivocally state that the discussion/interview is pre-disciplinary action. Only formal notice triggers the Weingarten right and the Miranda obligation. Formal notice unequivocally and objectively alerts an employee to the possibility that discipline might ensue; formal notice obligates the employer to advise the employee that he has a right to union representation because the employer might discipline; and formal notice gives an employee the necessary objective evidence to conclude that he might "reasonably fear" that the interview might lead to discipline. Formal notice also achieves the purpose of Article IV, Section 3: to give an employee the time and the opportunity to explain his conduct and to defend himself against the possible discriminatory action, and to prohibit, or ultimately eliminate, unreasonable and inaccurate materials in an employee's personnel file.

Question No. 2: Did the employer violate the agreement when it denied the grievant union representation at the June 10 meeting called by her supervisor?

The employer did not violate Article IV, Section 3, because the grievant was not entitled to union representation on June 10 nor was the city obligated to advise the grievant of her right to union representation because the June 10 meeting was not a formal meeting. The employer had not given the grievant formal notice that the city would review her past conduct for disciplinary purposes.

Question No. 3: Did the employer's actions of suspending the grievant for alleged insubordination and disruptive conduct occurring on June 10 constitute prohibited discrimination in violation of Article I, Section 1, of the Agreement? *Article I, Section 1,* reads:

The city and the union agree that they will not discriminate against any employee by reason of race, color, age, sex, marital status, sexual orientation, political ideology, creed, religion, ancestry, national origin, or the presence of any sensory, mental or physical handicap unless based on bona fide occupational qualification reasonably necessary to the normal operation of the city or union activities.

The city's suspension of the grievant for insubordination did not constitute discrimination under Article I, Section 1, because the grievant did not have the right to union representation on June 10. The city's exercise of its legal right to discipline the grievant is not, and cannot be, arbitrary, capricious, or discriminatory.

Question No. 4: Did the employer's actions of placing a written reprimand in the grievant's personnel file violate the reasonableness and accuracy requirements of Article IV, Section 2, of the Agreement? *Article IV, Section 2,* reads:

The employees covered by this Agreement may examine their personnel files in the departmental Personnel Office in the presence of the Personnel Officer or a designated supervisor. In matters of dispute regarding this section, no other personnel files will be recognized by the city or the union except that supportive documents from other files may be used. Materials to be placed in an employee's personnel file relating to job performance or personal conduct or any other material that may have an adverse effect on the employee's employment shall be reasonable and accurate and brought to his or her attention with copies provided to the employee upon request. Employees who challenge material included in their personnel files are permitted to insert material relating to the charge.

It is reasonable for the city to place the notice of suspension in the grievant's personnel file because the city properly suspended the grievant for insubordination. The record of the suspension is an accurate account of the grievant's action: the grievant, the union, and the arbitrator have scrutinized the facts for accuracy.

> *Question No. 5:* Did the employer's actions of disciplining the grievant for conduct normally accepted constitute promulgation of unreasonable performance standards in violation of Article IV, Section 4 of the Agreement? *Article IV, Section 4,* reads:

Any performance standards used to measure the performance of employees shall be reasonable.

The union argued that the city violated Article IV, Section 4, because the the city allowed male employees to emote, to swear, to pound on desks, to throw silverware, and to pass obscene materials "without negative evaluations being forthcoming." The union thought it unfair and unreasonable to allow male displays of emotion and at the same time reprimand the grievant for acting emotionally.

The union's contention fails for two reasons. First, the city does not and did not approve of the "shop talk." In step three the city said that the shop talk is "nothing to brag about and we are attempting to clean it up." Second, the issue is not the grievant's display of emotions or the display of "male" emotions. The city unequivocally said that "the only issue involved in P.'s suspension was her clear act of insubordination" (step two), not "her disagreeable attitude or her productivity" (step three). The grievant's refusal to obey, not her display of emotion, prompted the discipline.

> *Question No. 6:* Did the employer's actions of disciplining the grievant for alleged activities occurring on June 10 constitute restraint, interference, coercion, discrimination, or reprisal for the grievant's having sought union assistance on May 10 and previous occasions for having sought redress for problems on the job?

The city did not "restrain, interfere, coerce, discriminate, or take reprisal action" against the grievant when she attempted to exercise her Weingarten right because on June 10 the grievant did not have the right to union representation. There is no evidence to show that the city interfered with the grievant's exercise of her Weingarten right on May 10.

On the contrary, the grievant's shop steward was present at the May 10 meeting at the employer's direction. The record is silent on the grievant's efforts to seek legal redress for job problems before May 10.

> *Question No. 7:* Did the employer's actions of suspending the grievant constitute disciplinary action without cause in violation of Article XXI, Section 1, of the Agreement? *Article XXI—Disciplinary Actions, Section 1* reads:

The city may suspend, demote or discharge an employee for just cause.

The city suspended the grievant for just cause, that is, for insubordination, because the grievant had no Weingarten right to union representation on June 10 and there was no obligation to advise the grievant of her Weingarten right.

Question No. 8: Was the employer's action of disciplining P. in violation of Article XXI, Section 2, inasmuch as progressive discipline was not utilized? *Article XXI, Section 2,* reads:

The parties agree that in their respective roles primary emphasis shall be placed on preventing situations requiring disciplinary actions through effective employee-management relations. The primary objective of discipline shall be to correct and rehabilitate, not to punish or penalize. To this end, in order of increasing severity, the disciplinary actions which the city may take against an employee include: 1. verbal warning, 2. written reprimand, 3. suspension, 4. demotion, 5. termination. Which disciplinary action is taken depends upon the seriousness of the affected employee's conduct.

PERSONNEL RULES

Chapter 8   Employee Relations

Section 1. *Discipline and Termination*

8.1.100 *General Provisions:*

In order of increasing severity, the disciplinary actions which his/her supervisor may take against an employee for inappropriate behavior or performance include:

(1) a verbal warning, which should be accompanied by a notation written in the employee's personnel file; (2) a written reprimand, a copy of which must be placed in the employee's file; (3) suspension up to thirty (30) days for a single occurrence; (4) demotion; (5) termination.

Which disciplinary action is taken, depends on the appointing authority's judgment upon the seriousness of the affected employee's conduct.

Upon suspension, demotion or termination of a regular employee, a written statement of the reasons for the action, signed by the appointing authority, shall be delivered to the employee and shall be filed with the Civil Service Commission concurrently or prior to the effective date of the action.

Suspension, demotion or termination shall be immediately reported by the appointing authority to the Personnel Director for records purposes.

The following is a nonexclusive list of grounds for discipline or termination of an employee.

* * *

c. Intentional violation of a regulation, order or direction given by one's supervisor, in the absence of exonerating circumstances.

8.1.200 *Suspension:*

A regular employee may be suspended for cause by the appointing authority for a period up to thirty (30) days for a single occurrence. A written statement of the reasons for such suspension, signed by the appointing authority shall be delivered to the employee and shall be filed with the Civil Service Commission concurrently or prior to the effective date of suspension; except, an employee may be suspended up to one day without the appointing authority's approval for emergency situations.

The city had no legal obligation to follow the progressive discipline steps outlined in Article XXI, Section 2, and in the *PERSONNEL RULES* because these rules give the city broad discretionary power to determine the discipline, that is, "which disciplinary action is taken depends upon the seriousness of the affected employee's conduct." Here, the city adjudged that the grievant's insubordination on June 10 was a serious offense: she adamantly and unequivocally refused to speak with her supervisor. The city did not act hastily, arbitrarily, or capriciously: the city gave adequate and due consideration to the severity of the discipline. At first, the city thought to impose a five day suspension, but, upon consideration of the grievant's health, the city reduced the suspension to one day. Therefore, the city properly suspended the grievant for her insubordination.

> *Question No. 9:* Did the employer violate *Article* XXI, Section 3, of the Agreement because it failed to notify the grievant of the nature of the disciplinary action taken against her within one day of its effective date? *Article XXI, Section 3,* reads:

> In cases of suspension or discharge the specified charges and duration, where applicable, of the action shall be furnished to the employee in writing not later than one (1) working day after the action becomes effective. An employee may be suspended for just cause pending demotion or discharge action.

The city did not violate Article XXI, Section 3, because the city notified the grievant of the nature, the effective date, and the duration of her discipline on June 24; the suspension became effective on June 29.

Conclusion and Award

The city acted properly in all respects. Therefore, the union's grievance is hereby denied.

14
Discipline and Discharge

Employees are keenly aware of and have definite and strong opinions about management's disciplinary actions. Unions recognize an employer's inherent and residual right to discipline and to discharge an employee but unions insist, and agreements overwhemingly require, that an employer discipline an employee only for "just" cause, "proper" cause, "sufficient" cause, or simply for "cause." The "just cause" standard seeks to protect an employee from an employer who might use its enormous economic, psychological, and political advantage to unfairly, arbitrarily, or capriciously discipline, punish, or "get rid of" an employee. Unions also generally seek to include a provision in the agreement that specifies, as much as possible, those offenses for which an employer might discipline or discharge an employee.

THE NOTION OF JUST CAUSE

During the early days of industrial capitalism, courts applied the master-servant notion to labor relations: either party could terminate the employment relationship for any or no reason. *Adair v. United States* (1908) held that an employer could discharge an employee at will, "for good reason, for bad reason, or for no reason at all." This view allowed an employer to legally discharge an employee without notice, without a hearing, arbitrarily, capriciously, or maliciously. Today, both labor and management reject the old notions that the employee is a "servant" subject to flogging or other punishment, or that the employer is "sovereign" and morally superior or competent, simply because he is an employer.

Congress has restricted the "termination at will" doctrine. The Taft-Hartley Act prohibits an employer from discharging an employee for participating in union activity; the Civil Rights Act of 1964 prohibits an employer from disciplining or discharging an employee because of his race, color, religion, sex, or national origin; the Rehabilitation Act of 1973 forbids an employer from disciplining or discharging an employee for non-job related handicap and disability; the Age Discrimination Act of 1967 prohibits an employer from disciplining or discharging an employee because of age; and the Occupational Safety and Health Act protects workers who refuse to carry out dangerous asssignments. Civil Service laws also require that civil service employees can be disciplined or discharged only in accordance with civil service tenure provisions.

Today, some courts accept the "employment at will" doctrine. Other courts reject the doctrine and hold that the agreement to employ implies and requires good faith on the part of an employer not to discipline or discharge an employee if his conduct and work are satisfactory. Courts also have held that an employer's oral statements or stated policies in employee manuals constitute an implied agreement not to discipline or discharge an employee unjustly, or they hold that an employee is terminable only for just cause because he has earned some kind of property rights in his employment.

The "at will employment" doctrine is not only outmoded, it is patently and manifestly unjust. All employees are entitled to the just cause protection independent of a collective bargaining agreement for three reasons. First, an employer, as a person, must always act justly and for good reason: it is morally offensive and politically unwise for an employer to act for a bad reason, capriciously, arbitrarily, or with animus, hate, spite, or other reprehensible motive. Second, an employer's agreement to employ assumes a continuing relationship between an employer and an employee. As long as the employee keeps his part of the bargain, the employer is bound to keep his part of the bargain. Third, an employee develops unspecified but real, vested, and prescriptive rights as soon as he begins his employment: it is manifestly unjust to deprive an employee of these rights without sufficient or just cause. Only one reason justifies a discharge, "the capital punishment" of labor relations: whereby an employee, by his conduct or performance, irretrievably breaks the employment relationship.

To guarantee non-unionized employees the same just cause protection enjoyed by unionized employees, writers propose that Congress pass a statute similar to the British Industrial Relations Act (1972) which provides public law protection against unjust discharge to all employees. The proposed statute would subject all employer discipline and discharge actions to review by either an arbitrator or a court. If an employee were protected by a just cause provision in a collective bargaining agreement, an arbitrator would decide the issue; if an employee were not protected by a just cause provision, a court would decide the issue. Writers also suggest the federal or state government establish arbitral tribunals to adjudicate discharge or discipline disputes or pass a law that allows damage actions against an employer for unjust disciplinary or discharge actions; other writers suggest that Congress empower the NLRB to review an employer's discipline or discharge action.

FORMULATIONS OF THE JUST CAUSE STANDARD

The following is a very simple formulation of the just cause standard: "No employee shall be disciplined or discharged except for just cause." Another simple formulation is: "The Employer retains the right to discharge a permanent employee for just cause such as incompetence, unsatisfactory performance of duties, and unexcused absenteeism."

The following just cause provision specifies those acts for which an employee cannot be discharged.

The Employer shall be the judge of the competency and qualifications of his/ her employees; provided however, that no employee shall be discharged or discriminated against for any lawful Union activity, or for performing service on a Union committee outside of business hours, or for reporting to the Union the violation of any provisions of this Agreement.

PROCEDURAL AND SUBSTANTIVE CRITERIA FOR JUST CAUSE

The just cause standard imposes two obligations on the employer. The employer must, first, give an employee procedural due process, and second, convince an arbitrator that the reason for the discipline or discharge is sufficient. Procedural due process obligates an employer to specify the offense in writing, give written notice, provide an open and formal hearing, assert the reason for the discipline, provide all available information to the employee and the union, and provide time and opportunity for the employee to protest and appeal the discipline or discharge in the presence of the union. A clear, well defined procedure with specific time limits is critical because it guarantees a free exchange of views between accuser and accused, guarantees review and reconsideration at every step of the procedure, and uncovers possible arbitrary and capricious treatment of employees. However, procedure by itself does not ensure fair treatment, nor does it eliminate personal animosities or labor-management antagonism. Procedure must be supported by fair dealing, mutual trust, and certainty of enforcement.

The following principles specify the procedural and substantive criteria inherent in the just cause standard.

- An employer must comply with the procedure in the collective bargaining agreement.

The following examples illustrate this paramount obligation. One agreement set forth very specific conditions which an employer must fulfill before he can discharge an employee:

An employee shall not be discharged immediately, but shall first be suspended for a period of five working days by issuance of a "Suspension Prior-to-Discharge" Notice.

In all cases of suspension, the Company shall notify the Union by personally giving such notice in writing or by mailing such notification by certified mail to the Chief Grievance Committeeman or, in his absence, to his designee, with a copy to the Local Union President.

Similarly, an employer must give an employee "a formal warning in the supervisor's office of the employee involved"; an employer cannot act "until the matter has been discussed with the Chief Steward"; the employer must notify the union "immediately by copy of the written notice to the employee giving the reason(s) for such discharge". Other agreements provided that the employer "must give the employee two (2) weeks notice or two (2) weeks pay prior to discharge"; or, if an employer must reprimand a public employee, the employer must do so "in a manner that will not embarrass the employee before other employees or the public." Alternatively, the employer must allow an employee "to have the union representative present at an interview with supervisor when the employee has a reasonable belief that the interview is part of an investigation which could result in disciplinary action."

- An employer must make the work rules known to employees.

An employee has the right to know what the employer expects. An employer gives adequate notice when it gives a new employee any document (for example, the collective bargaining agreement, the company manual, or rules of procedure) which contains the work rules. If the employer promulgates a new rule, the employer must disseminate the new work rule widely and post it in conspicuous and customary places, such as bulletin boards. It is wise for an employer to make a new employee sign a receipt for the documents and a statement that he understands and will obey work rules.

- An employer cannot discharge or discipline an employee summarily or before it investigates the incident.

The employer must investigate the incident fairly, objectively, and immediately after the offense. After its investigation, the employer must give an employee, in writing, timely notice of the time and place for a disciplinary meeting. The employer must conduct a full, fair, and impartial hearing in the presence of a union representative and make known to the employee the reason for the discipline and all available facts related to the discipline. The employer must furnish minutes of the disciplinary hearing to the employee's union representative. An employer must not intimidate the employee either during the investigation or at the investigatory hearing.

• An employer must apply discipline consistently and uniformly to all employees.

The employer cannot single out one employee with the deliberate intent to harm that employee. An employer cannot show favoritism or treat employees disparately. If an employer has been lax in imposing discipline for a particular offense, the employer cannot discipline an employee for the same offense without a clear, unequivocal, and well publicized announcement that the particular offense will be punished in the future. An employer cannot, by delay, give employees the impression either that the rule is insignificant or that a violation of the rule is acceptable to the employer. The employer cannot "make book" against only one employee and record his every infraction in order to justify discipline or discharge.

For many years, an employer had a published grooming code policy which prohibited all facial hair. The employer had advised the grievant of the prohibition at the time of his employment. At the arbitration hearing, the grievant acknowledged that he had read and understood the policy in the Personnel Handbook. At the time of his employment and thereafter, the grievant had a moustache and sideburns in violation of the grooming code, and the employer took no action against him when his moustache and sideburns grew together to form a full beard. The employer considered him an excellent meat cutter, his full beard did not affect his work as a meat cutter, and he had attended several negotiation sessions with full beard, as a member of the union's negotiating committee in the presence of the personnel manager. After negotiations, the Vice President of Operations sent a memo to all store managers which restated the prohibition against beards. The memo directed managers to advise employees that from then on facial hair standards of the grooming code would be strictly enforced.

The question before me was: Did the employer violate the collective bargaining agreement when it sought to strictly enforce its previously published "no beard" policy? The employer believed that it could properly enforce its grooming code because the grievant was aware of the rule, he was advised of the "no beard" policy when he was hired, and the employer's recent memo made it very clear that the employer intended to strictly enforce the policy. I wrote:

The Employer's attempt to enforce its grooming code is unfair because the Employer failed to enforce its own grooming code consistently over an extended period of time. The Grievant rightly assumed that the Employer's non-enforcement of its own grooming code was tantamount to acquiesence and acceptance of beards, possibly a modification of its stated policy. It is intrinsically unfair and arbitrary to seek to impose strict observance of the grooming code after the Employer acquiesced in its non-observance, and tacitly tolerated and accepted the violations of its own grooming code. It is unfair to condone non-observance today and insist on strict observance by fiat tomorrow. The undisputed facts are: the Grievant had facial hair during his employment; he participated in negotiations with the beard fully evident to the Employer, but the Employer never objected to his beard.

• An employer must apply progressive, corrective discipline.

Progressive discipline inheres in the just cause standard even if progressive discipline is not spelled out in the agreement, because an offending employee has the right to be put on notice to explain and correct his behavior.

The following is a simple statement on progressive discipline: "Discipline may include oral reprimand, written reprimand, suspension without pay, demotion, and discharge."

The following is a detailed provision on progressive discipline.

The parties agree that in their respective roles primary emphasis be placed on preventing situations requiring disciplinary actions through effective employee-management relations. The primary objective of discipline shall be to correct and rehabilitate, not to punish or penalize. To this end, in order of increasing severity, the disciplinary actions which the City may take against an employee include: 1. verbal warning 2. written reprimand 3. suspension 4. demotion 5. termination.

Some provisions on progressive discipline distinguish between major and minor infractions, specify the discipline for each infraction, divide the infractions into major and minor infractions, and set forth the conditions for removal of the record of the infraction from the personnel file.

Many agreements enumerate those serious offenses for which an employer may discharge an employee immediately. Thus,

No warning notice need be given to an employee before that person is suspended or discharged if the cause of such suspension or discharge is (a) Dishonesty; (b) Drunkenness; (c) Recklessness resulting in a serious accident while on duty; (d) The carrying of unauthorized passengers; (e) Unprovoked physical assault on a supervisory employee; (f) Selling, transporting, or use of illegal narcotics while in the employment of the Employer; (g) Willful, wanton, or malicious damage to the Employer's property; (h) Failure to report an accident to Employer immediately; (i) Unauthorized personal use of company vehicle.

- An Employer must take into account mitigating circumstances when it imposes discipline.

An agreement between a federal agency and its union lists the mitigating circumstances that a supervisor must consider before he recommends or imposes discipline or orders discharge.

1. The nature and seriousness of the offense, and its relation to the employee's duties, position, and responsibilities, including whether the offense was intentional, technical, or inadvertent, or was committed maliciously or for gain, or was frequently repeated;

2. The employee's job level and type of employment, including supervisory or fiduciary role, contacts with the public, and prominence of the position;

3. The employee's disciplinary record within the past three years or longer in more serious cases;

4. The employee's past work record, including length of service, performance on the job, ability to get along with fellow workers, and dependability;

5. The effect of the offense upon the employee's ability to perform at a satisfactory level and its effect upon the supervisor's confidence in the employee's ability to perform assigned duties;

6. Consistency of the penalty with those imposed upon other employees for the same or similar offenses;

7. The notoriety of the offense or its impact upon the reputation of the Department;

8. The clarity with which the employee was on notice of any rules were violated in committing the offense, or had been harmed about the conduct in question;

9. Potential for the employees's rehabilitation;

10. Mitigating circumstances surrounding the offense such as unusual job tensions, personality problems, mental impairment, harassment or bad faith, malice, or provocation on the part of others involved in the matter; and

11. The adequacy and effectiveness of alternative sanctions to deter such conduct in the future by the employees or others.

- An employer cannot change the reason for the discharge or use unrelated offenses to justify the discipline or discharge.

The following discharge case illustrates the principle. I wrote:

It is manifestly unfair to change or to expand the reasons for the discharge. The employer can discharge an offending employee only for the reason stated in the original letter of discharge. Here, the original reason for the discharge was for "abusive conduct, physical and verbal, toward a fellow employee."

The employer could not use "fighting" or "horsing around" or "poor performance" as a reason for discharge because the employer did not mention these two offenses in its original letter of termination.

• The discipline must be proportionate to the offense.

A federal agency had imposed a five day suspension on a federal employee because the employee was AWOL. I thought the five day suspension was not appropriate for three reasons. First, the employer imposed the five day suspension for two offenses: "unauthorized absence and failure to complete work assignment," but the agency disciplined him for one offense, the AWOL offense. Therefore, the five day suspension necessarily was excessive discipline. Second, the five day suspension denied the grievant the progressive discipline to which he was entitled under Article 20, *DISCIPLINE,* of the Collective Bargaining Agreement, and under the agency's own *TABLE OF OFFENSES AND PENALTIES*, which says that "the objective of discipline is to correct and improve employee behavior." The *TABLE OF OFFENSES AND PENALTIES* also provided guidelines to management "for constructive and rehabilitative discipline," to "correct offending conduct, attitude, or work habits." Third, the discipline was too severe. The agency's guidelines specifically stipulate that the imposed discipline "must be reasonable in its degree of severity" and not "out of proportion to the offense." I found many mitigating circumstances, all recognized by the *TABLE*. I wrote:

The Grievant's offense was not a repeated offense, his offense was not intentional nor was it committed maliciously or for gain; his past record is exemplary and he is a long time employee; and, his position and experience make it unlikely that he will repeat the offense. The agency could have imposed the minimal discipline, i.e., a reprimand, or the maximum discipline, the five day suspension for the AWOL offense. But the Agency chose the hardest penalty, a punitive penalty, not the minimum discipline required by the just cause provision, as the corrective and rehabilitative discipline. The penalty is too harsh because the Grievant did not flout a rule or regulation; he exercised poor judgment, easily remediable by a lesser penalty.

• An employer must adduce substantial not speculative or hypothetical evidence to sustain the discipline or discharge.

The employer at an aluminum plant had discharged an employee after he pled guilty before a court to one count of unlawful delivery of marijuana. Rule 9 of the collective bargaining agreement clearly said that the commission of a crime was a major and serious offense and that it was a just cause for discharge when the offense "is harmful to the interests of the Company or other employees." The only evidence of direct and actual injury to either the company or employees was the statement of the Industrial Director who testified that some employees "didn't want to work with him." However, the union rebutted this evidence on cross-examination when the Industrial Director admitted that "no employee had refused to work with him." I found all other employer arguments either hypothetical or speculative. The employer said that it was "concerned that [the grievant] could be a destructive influence on the other employees"; that there is a "reasonable basis for the inference" that [the grievant] uses drugs; reinstatement "may cause other problems such as absenteeism and tardiness"; . . . "continued employment would be damaging to the employer's reputation" especially in a small community; "the drug problem threatens to reach acute proportions"; and "there is a drug problem in the plant." I found all of these statements unverified and hypothetical conclusions, unsubstantiated by evidence.

- An employer must show that the employee actually committed the offense.

An employer had discharged a truck driver for the "willful, wanton, or malicious damage" of the company's property. I wrote:

The undiluted, strong, and unequivocal contract language imposes more than "an extremely difficult burden of proof on the Employer" (the Union's criterion); the language imposes an almost impossible burden of proof on the Employer because the Employer must prove that the Grievant caused actual damage, and then show that the Grievant caused the damage "willfully, wantonly, and maliciously."

I considered the evidence and concluded that the employer did not show how or that the grievant actually fractured the drive shaft: the employer did not x-ray the parts alleged to be damaged; no mechanic examined the truck for actual damage to the clutch, to the frame, or to other parts of the truck. The record conclusively showed that the employer failed to adduce hard, specific evidence that the grievant actually damaged the employer's property. The employer only showed that the grievant might or could have caused damage. I wrote:

Speculative, hypothetical assertions of damage do not constitute damage. Damage to be damage must be actual, real, evident, and tangible. Further, elementary notions of justice and equity also demand that the Employer must show actual, not speculative damage.... The words "willfully," "wantonly," "maliciously" are also strong, powerful, undiluted words. They impose an enormously difficult burden on the employer. The employer must show that the Grievant acted out of spite, ill will, or some other reprehensible motive. The employer must show that the Grievant deliberately and by design intended, planned, and sought to damage the Employer's property. The Employer failed to meet its difficult burden of proof.

KINDS OF EMPLOYEE OFFENSES

I have compiled the following (an incomplete list), of the kinds of behavior for which an employer might discipline or discharge. They are: intoxication on the job, insubordination, violation of work rules, deliberate destruction of company property, sleeping on the job, absenteeism, dishonesty, continued tardiness, dangerous "horseplay" in the plant, failure to observe safety rules and regulations, incompetence, selling goods in the plant, defective work, restricting production, and falsifying work records. Here are some others: stealing the employer's property, gambling, the use of drugs, immoral conduct, improper language, political activity in the plant, distributing literature or spreading rumors, failure to report communicable diseases, negligence on the job, disorderly conduct, or giving or taking bribes to get a job. A few more are: failure to meet work standards, subversive activity, quitting early, loitering, carrying weapons, throwing objects outside of windows, and violation of sanitation rules. Still more are: reading books or magazines not required in the line of duty, failure to immediately report accidents or persosnal injury to proper authorities, falsifying or refusing to testify when accidents are being investigated, receiving outside visitors or phone calls, leaving job, department, or plant, or unauthorized use of the employer's property. In addition, punching the time clock for another employee, lending or borrowing a badge of authority, disclosure of confidential information to a competitor, false or malicious statements about a company, or off-duty conduct that injures an employer's reputation.

DISCHARGE AND QUIT

An employee who quits is not entitled to the "just cause" protection standard because the employer has not discharged the employee; it is the employee, not the employer, who has broken the employment relationship. In a dispute concerning whether an employee has or has not quit, management cannot assume that he has quit. Management must show that the employee by official notice or by some recognizable, clear, unequivocal, and deliberate act has quit. To prevent a dispute parties define quit as "an absence for three working days without notification to the employer" or as "accepting employment elsewhere when on leave of the employer"; or as "failing to report on the first working day after the expiration of the leave of absence or vacation" or as "failing to return within a specified time when recalled from layoff."

To illustrate: In one case, I wrote,

What is a quit? An employee contractually quits when his actions accord with the definition of a quit in the collective bargaining agreement. Here, neither the collective bargaining agreement nor the *RULES OF CONDUCT* defines those specific acts that constitute a quit. Absent a clear, specific contractual definition of a quit the following identifiable, ascertainable, objective and specific acts constitute a quit. An employee quits when he openly, unequivocally, clearly, deliberately declares that he quits and then reduces his declaration to writing. Both acts are necessary because quit, an act unique in labor relations, has specific and serious consequences: it irretrievably breaks the assumed continuing employer-employee relationship, the ultimate criterion in labor relations.

PROOF IN DISCIPLINE AND DISCHARGE

Some writers state that in a dispute over a discharge an arbitrator should apply the level of proof required in criminal law, that is, "beyond a reasonable doubt," because discharge (a severe measure, sometimes called industrial "capital punishment") deprives an employee of a livelihood. These writers suggest that in other cases an arbitrator should apply either the "preponderance of evidence" or the "clear and convincing evidence" level of proof, the proof required in civil cases. I find court criteria vague and inapplicable to arbitration because court proceedings and arbitral proceedings are only superficially similar. An arbitrator interprets and applies a labor agreement, not criminal statutes. An advocate's task is not to reach a particular level of proof but a simple and direct one: convince the arbitrator that the employer had just cause to discipline or discharge an employee.

In a discharge case I ask myself the ultimate question: "Did the employee irretrievably break the employer-employee relationship?" In a discipline case I ask myself: "How serious was the offense and how does the offense affect the employer-employee relationship?"

REMEDIES IN DISCHARGE AND DISCIPLINE

An Arbitrator's Remedy Power

In *United Steelworkers v. Enterprise Wheel and Car Corporation*, the Supreme Court said the arbitrator must have wide latitude in the formulation of remedies.

When an arbitrator is commissioned to interpret and apply the collective bargaining agreement, he is to bring his informed judgment to bear in order to reach a fair solution of a problem. This is especially true when it comes to formulating the remedies. There is need for flexibility in meeting a wide variety of situations. The draftsmen may never have thought of what specific remedy should be awarded a particular contingency. Nevertheless, an arbitrator is confined to the interpretation and application of the collective bargaining agreement; he does not sit to dispense his own brand of industrial justice. He may, of course, look for guidance from many sources, yet his award is legitimate only so long as it draws its essence from the collective bargaining statement.

An arbitrator's "great flexibility" may be limited by the collective bargaining agreement or the submission agreement. If an agreement specifies the remedy, an arbitrator must order the remedy specified in the agreement no matter what he thinks of the remedy because the agreement binds not only the parties but also the arbitrator. An arbitrator must order reinstatement with full back pay if the agreement stipulates that the employer must "reinstate the aggrieved employee to his former position and pay full compensation for lost time." An arbitrator has no discretionary power to order a remedy if the agreement says that an unjustly discharged employee "shall be reinstated to his former position with like seniority and pay for all time lost." Similar provisions impose limits on an arbitrator's remedy power. For example: "Any back pay award shall not be in excess of 60 days or to the date of discharge or disciplinary suspension, whichever is less" or "Back pay shall be retroactive to the date of wrongful discharge." Additionally, if an arbitrator awards back pay, "the amount so awarded shall be less any unemployment compensation received or compensation which the employee would not have earned had he not been suspended or discharged."

If an agreement does not circumscribe the arbitrator's power, or if an agreement is silent on the remedy, an arbitrator may order the remedy he deems appropriate. Some writers assert that an arbitrator should not substitute his judgment for management's judgment on the proper discipline. Of course, an arbitrator has no superior wisdom or special insight on what constitutes appropriate discipline, but if he could not review management's judgment, the arbitrator would not dispense justice. Management, one of the parties, would determine whether the discipline is commensurate with the offense: whether the discipline is "too severe," "not fair," "not appropriate," "not just," "not even-handed," "not reasonable," or "too harsh." It is the arbitrator's function to determine not only whether an employee was guilty of the infraction but also whether management's reasons or the discipline itself was sufficient, fair and just.

Kinds of Remedies in Discharge and Discipline

Remedies in the private sector are as diverse as arbitrators; CSRA governs remedies in the federal sector. In March 1977 the Comptroller General published a *Manual of Remedies Available to Third Parties in Adjudicating Federal Employee Grievances* to help arbitrators fashion remedies consistent with federal statutes and regulations, and in particular under the Back Pay Act. Under the Back Pay Act, a wronged employee is entitled to receive an amount equal to all or part of the employee's pay, allowances, differentials, and leave reaccreditation that he would have earned "but for" the employer's wrongful action. The arbitrator may also award reasonable attorney fees "in the interest of justice."

In general, punitive damages are foreign to arbitration. "Cease and desist" orders are ineffectual because they do not remedy, but they can lay the basis for punitive damages if a union can show that an employer willfully, deliberately, and maliciously intended to or actually did injure an employee. The following are examples of the remedies I have ordered in discipline and discharge disputes.

Unconditional Reinstatement. Unconditional reinstatement, sometimes called the "make whole" remedy, reinstates a grievant with full back pay, without loss of seniority or benefits. The "make whole" remedy seeks to restore a grievant as much as possible to his original position, and no more or no less; the grievant is not entitled to windfall gain or unjust enrichment.

Here is an example of the "make whole" order.

The Employer is hereby ordered (1) to make the Grievant whole for all lost wages and benefits minus all the money he has earned from date of his discharge to the date of this *Award;* (2) the Employer is hereby ordered to reinstate the Grievant at its earliest administrative convenience but no later than (date).

It is easy for an arbitrator to order the "make whole" remedy, but it is difficult for the parties or the arbitrator to fashion it. Often, parties or the arbitrator must answer the following questions.

1. What would the grievant have earned had he worked or had he been offered work? Is the "probable" overtime he would have worked to be included?

2. Should the grievant be paid a lump sum or should he be paid quarterly, yearly, or on any other time basis?

3. What adjustments, if any, should be made for a grievant's absences, bonuses, insurance, pensions, vacations, holiday pay, overtime, and time spent looking for another job?

4. Should interest be paid on back pay? I might award interest but only if the

union asked for it and only if the Union can prove that the grievant would have saved or invested the money.

5. If the grievant had worked during the discharge period, should interim earnings and unemployment compensation benefits be subtracted from his back pay? Is unemployment compensation a collateral benefit or earnings?

6. Why should an unjustly discharged employee mitigate damages for the employer?

7. Should the "make whole" remedy seek to repair psychological damage and take into account increased interest payments, lost opportunities, injury due to a default in meeting financial obligations, and the need to borrow money?

The following case illustrates the difficulties. An employer had suspended a contract miner for absenteeism. I ordered the employer to reinstate the grievant and ordered the parties to determine the specifics on what would make the grievant "whole." However, the parties could not agree on the amount of back pay, on vacation credit, on holiday pay, and on insurance benefits. The parties did agree that the grievant's interim earnings should be deducted from the amount he would have earned had he not been discharged, but they disagreed on the applicable hourly rate and on whether contract rates should be included in the calculation of back pay. The employer was willing to pay a certain hourly rate, but the union contended that the hourly rate was too low: the union wanted to add a shift differential to the hourly rate because the grievant had worked a uniformly rotating schedule of a two weeks of day shift followed by two weeks of night shift. The union also would add quarterly cost-of-living adjustments (COLA) adjustments to the hourly rate. The union sought and the employer strongly objected to the inclusion of contract rates because the agreement guaranteed only the straight time rate. Furthermore, the union wanted to add a shift differential and a COLA adjustment to the contract rate. The parties also disagreed on the applicable vacation pay factor, the calculation of vacation pay, and the number of holidays, insurance, and non-occupational disability pay. I set forth the principles I used to decide each issue.

The make whole remedy, the equity principle, attempts to restore to the extent possible and practicable to the Grievant all that he probably would have earned had he not been discharged. Equity abhors all "windfall" gain. Two specific equitable postulates follow: first, the grievant should profit, not from honest error, but only from personal effort; and second, the Company should be held financially liable for its legal obligations.

Reinstatement with Full Back Pay. An employer had discharged a retail clerk stocker for off-duty conduct. I ordered the employer to reinstate him and to make the grievant whole for all lost wages and benefits, minus all the money he had earned from the date of his discharge to the date of the *Award*. I recognized that it might be difficult for the parties to negotiate a mutually acceptable remedy. Therefore, I wrote:

If the parties cannot agree on the specifics of reinstatement on or before (date), the Union must so notify the arbitrator. In this case, each party is hereby directed to submit its negotiation notes and offers and to propose to the arbitrator not later than (date), an equitable solution. I hereby retain complete jurisdiction over any question that might arise over this *OPINION AND AWARD* until (date).

The employer reinstated the grievant. The parties agreed on the total gross back pay, the grievant's interim earnings, and on the principle that the grievant had an obligation to mitigate damages, but the parties disagreed on whether or not the grievant made a reasonable and diligent effort to mitigate damages and on the benefits the grievant would have accrued had he not been wrongfully discharged by the employer.

The employer had argued that the grievant had failed to mitigate damages because he did not make diligent, reasonable, and sufficient efforts to obtain other employment. Specifically, he quit an interim job at a pizza parlor without justification, he never registered for work with the Employment Security Department, and he did not apply for unemployment benefits. The employer asked that the arbitrator not award any back pay to the grievant for his periods of unemployment because he failed to mitigate damages.

The union believed that the grievant sought to mitigate damages because he applied for a job at the main post office, he took and passed two tests, and he checked for openings every week at the Employment Agency office (no positions were vacant). He applied for work at an airline company, and he continually checked the company for openings by phone and personally at least once a week until the arbitration. He applied at a department store and he checked there at least once a week. He applied at a floral shop and he checked there every two weeks for approximately two months. He applied at other florists, but no florist needed drivers. He applied at a telephone company four times but the company was not hiring. He continually checked the classified listings for jobs; he did apply for a number of them although he did not keep a record of the names of the companies. He checked the College Job Center at least twice a week, and he personally checked the Employment Security Department once a week and the department at least once a week.

The grievant explained why he did not register with the Employment Security Department: he believed he would not receive unemployment compensation; if he had applied and received unemployment benefits, he would have had to reimburse the state if the employer then had to pay full back pay. I wrote:

Whether the Grievant made a "diligent, reasonable, and sufficient effort" to seek employment is forever arguable and difficult to judge because subjective interests color the parties' perception of the sufficiency of the effort. The Company's argument that the Grievant's quit at the pizza parlor constitutes failure to make a "diligent, reasonable, and sufficient effort" fails because it assumes that the Grievant was obliged to remain at the pizza parlor and that his quit was unjustified. The Grievant's interim work record evinces a minimal but satisfactory effort to make a "diligent, reasonable and sufficient effort" to obtain employment.

The parties could not agree on benefits that the grievant would have accrued had he not been unjustly discharged. The union asked that the grievant, a junior apprentice clerk, be reclassified a journeyman because the number of hours he would have worked by the time he was reinstated would have qualified him as a journeyman. The company argued that the grievant should not be classified as a journeyman because he did not have the necessary actual experience to qualify. I ruled that "merit and experience, not the mere passage of time determine journeyman status. The Union produced no evidence to show that the Grievant qualified as a journeyman." The union asked that I award the grievant interest on the gross back pay. I denied interest on back pay because the union failed to show that the grievant would have either borrowed or saved money at the current rate of interest.

Conditional Reinstatement. An employer had improperly discharged a grievant for off-duty falsification of unemployment forms. I ordered the employer to reinstate the grievant but the reinstatement was conditional and probationary. I wrote:

(a) The Grievant must pay the Employer, no later than (date), an equitable sum, either in a lump sum or in installments, for all the time the Employer spent on the investigations and on the trial. The Employer and the Union are hereby ordered to negotiate the amount of the sum payable to the Employer. If the Employer and the Union cannot agree on the equitable sum by (date), the parties are hereby directed to so inform the arbitrator and to set forth in writing to the arbitrator their specific proposals no later than (date). Then, I will determine the amount payable to the Employer.

(b) The Grievant is hereby ordered to handwrite a letter of apology to the Employer which contains a statement of apology, and a statement of his appreciation for the opportunity to work for the Employer.

(c) The Grievant is hereby ordered to handwrite a letter of thanks to his Union to express his appreciation for its defense of his interests.

(d) The Grievant is on probation for two years, from (date) to (date). During this probationary period, the Grievant cannot avail himself of the protection afforded him by the just cause provision of the contract in all matters of honesty, whether on duty or off duty. If a court finds the Grievant guilty of any off-duty dishonesty, the Employer may discharge him at will. In a future arbitration on the Grievant's on-duty dishonesty of the smallest sum, time, materials, or equipment, the arbitrator's jurisdiction shall be limited to a question of fact.

(e) The Union is hereby ordered to apprise the insurance carrier no later than (date) that the Grievant is able and willing to work, and that for purposes of employment, I have found him to be contractually honest. Therefore, the Employer is hereby ordered to seek reinstatement of the Grievant's insurance policy no later than (date). If the insurance carrier refuses to insure the Grievant, the Employer is hereby ordered to so notify the arbitrator no later than (date). I will then order a remedy.

(f) If the Grievant refuses reinstatement on these terms, or if the Grievant refuses to work for the Employer for three months, the Grievant must pay full Union arbitration costs.

(g) The Union is hereby ordered to read this *Opinion and Award* aloud to the Grievant, particularly the *Award,* to make sure he understands its terms.

(h) The Union shall certify to the Employer no later than (date) that both the Grievant and the Union have complied with all these *Orders.* If either the Union or the Grievant fail to comply with any one of these *Orders,* the Employer may discharge the Grievant at will.

(i) The Employer is hereby ordered to retain the complete record of this arbitration in the Grievant's file for the two year probationary period.

A "Last Chance" Remedy: Conditional and Probationary Reinstatement. An employer had improperly discharged a grievant for absenteeism. The employer had argued that I had no authority to reverse the employer's policy on absenteeism: I had to sustain the discharge because the employer terminated the grievant in accordance with its policy. I ruled that discharge was not the appropriate remedy because the employer's application of its policy did not sufficiently consider mitigating circumstances. I also rejected the union's remedy, probation for six months, as the proper remedy because probation did not fully take into account either the employer's overwhelming interest and right to reliable employees, or the disruptive effect of the grievant's long record of absences. Further, probation was an insufficient remedy because it neither disciplined nor remedied; it merely prolonged the grievant's employment.

To arrive at the proper remedy, I gave relative weight to the following employer contentions: the grievant, an adult, had seriously disturbed the employer-employee relation; he must be held responsible for his tardiness and for his absences; he was hired to work, but he caused problems for the employer; he violated the employer's clear, specific, and well-known policy; the employer implemented its policy without animus; and the employer had a legitimate and abiding interest to retain only reliable employees. However, the record showed that the grievant had been an acceptable employee for eight years, although he had had many personal problems aggravated by his physical problems, which adversely affected his emotional life and, consequently, his reliability.

Therefore, I sought to devise a remedy that sought to reach that "attainable, perhaps imperfect justice which embraced not only the letter of the law [the employer's policy], the grievant's frailty [the union's progressive discipline], but also the mystery of human behavior." My remedy sought to restore the original employer-employee relation and to take into account the grievant's weaknesses, needs, and hopes for the future. The remedy sought reconciliation and possibly a congruence of interests, and above all, the remedy sought to protect the employer from an unreliable employee. I wrote:

I think the proper remedy is to give the Grievant another chance, a last chance. The Grievant must now prove by strict and faithful observance to the *Order* that his problems are indeed behind him and that he genuinely wants to work for the employer.

The spirit and intent of my remedy is to compel the Grievant to comply scrupulously with the conditions on tardiness and absences as set forth in the *Order*. If the Grievant does not comply with any one of the *Orders,* he will have discharged himself. Then, he cannot claim that he was discharged without just cause.

A. *Specific Orders for the Company*

1. The Company is hereby ordered to reinstate the Grievant at its administrative discretion, but no later than (date) without loss of seniority and without backpay. Reinstatement shall be conditional and for two years from (date) to (date).

2. During the probationary period, the Grievant cannot avail himself of the protection inherent in the "just cause" provision of the contract to contest any employer disciplinary actions against him for tardiness and for absences.

3. During the probationary period, the Grievant shall observe the following rules:

a) For all doctor and dental appointments, he shall give his supervisors no less than two weeks' notice. Only evident emergencies excuse the Grievant from this rule. If the Grievant claims an emergency, the attending doctor must concur by written statement that an emergency actually existed.

b) If the Grievant calls in sick, he must prove to the employer on the day of his return by written evidence or by outside oral testimony that he was indeed sick and that he stayed at home.

c) If the Grievant fails to notify the Company twice during any one of the probationary years that he will be absent, the Company may discharge him at will. The first absence will be considered unexcused, the second absence, a sufficient and just cause for termination.

d) The Grievant shall be considered tardy if he arrives after the posted time. By this order, the Grievant loses the three minute grace period. Two unexcused tardies shall constitute one unexcused absence.

4. The Company is ordered to keep this *Opinion and Award* and all documents that pertain to it in the Grievant's file only for the two year probationary period.

B. *Specific Orders for the Grievant*

1. The Grievant, no later than (date) shall hand write a letter of apology to the Employer, addressed to the Manager, which states (a) that he is sorry for all the trouble and inconvenience he has caused; (b) that he promises faithfully to obey the rules set down in this *Award*; (c) that he appreciated the efforts the Employer has made on his behalf, particularly for the leave of absence; and (d) that he appreciates the opportunity to work for the Employer.

2. The Grievant, no later than (date) shall hand write a letter to the President of his Union to express his appreciation for the time and money spent on his defense. The Grievant must furnish a copy of this letter to the employer.

C. *Specific Order for the Union*

The Union is ordered to review the entire *Award* with the Grievant, particularly the *Orders*, no later than (date) to make sure that he understands his tenuous position and the specifics of the *Orders*. The Union shall certify by written letter to the employer that the Union has compiled with this *Order*.

If the Union fails to comply with this *Order*, the employer may discharge the Grievant at will.

Reinstatement without Back Pay. An employer had discharged an employee for off-duty criminal conduct, the possession of marijuana. I ordered the employer to reinstate the employee because the employer had no jurisdiction over his off-duty conduct. However, his employment record showed seven unexcused absences, seven unexcused tardies, and two neglects of duty. The work record plus the crime was not good. I wrote:

1. The employer is ordered to reinstate the Grievant at its administrative convenience on or before but not later than (date).

2. The reinstatement is without back pay.

3. The Grievant accumulates no seniority from the date of his discharge to the date of his reinstatement.

4. The reinstatement is conditional:

a) if the Grievant is found to possess marijuana on the employer's property, the employer is free to discharge him at will.

b) if the Grievant is again found guilty by a court of selling or buying marijuana outside the employer's premises, the employer is free to discharge at will.

c) for the next three calendar years the Grievant's absenteeism and lateness are subject to the following rules. Each calendar year is defined as the period from 17 January of one year to 17 January of the next year. The Company may discipline the Grievant as follows: 1. for a second lateness, a suspension of five work days; for a fourth lateness, an additional suspension of 10 work days; for a sixth lateness, discharge. 2. after two unexcused absences, the Company is free to discharge at will. 3. the Grievant hereby loses all further protection under the just cause provision of the contract in criminal matters, absenteeism, and tardiness.

Conditional Reinstatement and Specific Performance. I ordered conditional reinstatement and specific performance in another discharge because the grievant's offense, "fighting on the job," was not a dischargeable offense. However, I ordered specific performance for the reasons set forth below.

1. The Employer is hereby ordered to reinstate the Grievant at its earliest convenience but no later than (date).

2. The parties are hereby directed to negotiate the amount of back pay due the Grievant. To determine the amount, the Union must consider the following: the Employer had cause to discipline the Grievant, and the Employer made a good faith effort to resolve the grievance. The Employer has a financial and abiding interest in well-behaved employees, the Grievant has caused the Employer much expense, he lied to the Employer, he has family ties with the Employer's family, he has committed similar acts in the past, and some employees are reluctant to work with him. The Grievant is an adult, at age 54 he must be held responsible for his actions. The Employer must consider the following mitigating circumstances: the Grievant did not assault W.; he grabbed W. momentarily by the shirt, he then let go; the Grievant's actions were not premeditated or malicious; he lost his temper and he offended and manhandled W., but he did not injure W. The Grievant is 54 years old; he has been an acceptable employee for 22 years, and, as his interim unemployment shows, he is unlikely to get a similar or better job. He wants to return to work, he wants and intends to get along with his fellow employees, and he has agreed to and has had beneficial counseling sessions.

If the parties cannot agree on the amount of back pay by (date), the Union is hereby directed to so inform the arbitrator no later than (date). I will then determine the amount of back pay based on the record of the negotiations.

3. The Grievant is hereby ordered to hand-write a letter of apology to the president of the company and in the same letter to express his gratitude for the opportunity to work at the company. The Grievant is hereby ordered to hand-write a letter to the president of his Union to express his appreciation for its efforts in his defense. If the Grievant does not write these two letters on or before (date), the Employer can discharge him at will.

4. The Employer may keep a copy of this *Opinion and Award* and a copy of the two letters in the Grievant's file but only for two years after the date of this *Opinion and Award.* I hereby retain jurisdiction over the interpretation and application of this *Opinion and Award* until (date).

Formal Warning. A school principal had rated a grievant, a certificated teacher, as "satisfactory in his general art classes but unsatisfactory in his yearbook class" because the principal thought the grievant had run up a $3,000 deficit in the yearbook. The grievant rejected the principal's findings, filed a grievance, and asserted that the "deficit amount is not true." Later in the year, the principal ordered the grievant to meet with him after school to discuss the management of the yearbook accounts. The grievant appeared before the principal, but the principal refused to meet with the grievant because the grievant insisted that a union witness be present at the meeting. The principal issued the grievant a letter of insubordination because "You refused to meet with [an administrator] me to discuss how you could find our current balance in the annual account." The grievant filed another grievance on the letter of insubordination in the belief that the principal had no contractual right to force him "to meet with him [the principal] alone behind closed doors."

I found that the district had violated the collective bargaining agreement because the principal failed to investigate fully and diligently, and because the Superintendent and the Board improperly and unfairly changed the basis for the evaluation. I also found that the district's unsatisfactory evaluation of the grievant was not disciplinary action, as the association alleged and that the grievant was insubordinate because he refused to obey his principal's clear, direct, unequivocal, and repeated order to attend the meeting scheduled for (date). I ordered the following remedy:

The District is hereby ordered (1) to remove from the Grievant's personnel file, in the presence of the Association, and no later than (date), any and all references to the two grievances; (2) to keep a copy of this *Opinion and Award* in the Grievant's personnel file and in the principal's personnel file until (date). On (date), the District shall remove this *Opinion and Award* from the Grievant's file and from the principal's file.

The *Opinion and Award* serves as adequate and sufficient notice to the Grievant that he must first obey and then grieve his principal's direct, unequivocal order.

The *Opinion and Award* serves as a clear and direct warning to the Grievant that the District has the contractual right to discharge him for insubordination.

This *Opinion and Award* is sufficient notice to the District and to its agents, and in particular to the Grievant's present principal, that the Grievant, and by extension, all employees, has a right to an Association witness at any and all scheduled grievances and disciplinary meetings.

This *Opinion and Award* directs the District to grant all employees their right to an Association witness at all grievance and disciplinary meetings. If an arbitrator finds that a District agent has willfully and purposely denied the right to Union representation to any employee, the arbitrator may impose punitive damages, payable to the Union, against the District. This *Opinion and Award* directs the District to make known to all its agents, in writing, no later than (date) and in a manner of its own choosing, the District's obligation to provide Union representation at grievance and disciplinary meetings.

I retain jurisdiction over the interpretation and application of this *Opinion and Award* until (date).

REQUEST FOR A REMEDY

The AAA *Demand for Arbitration* form and other grievance forms require the moving party to specify the *Remedy Sought*. The union and the employer should present their views on the remedy either in the pre-hearing statement or in a brief. The employer's statement of an appropriate remedy is not an admission of legal weakness but a precautionary statement to modify, to limit, or to deny the union's particular remedy.

Here is an example of a requet for a remedy.

The Union respectfully asks the arbitrator to rescind the disciplinary action taken against the Grievant, to make the Grievant whole, and to order the employer not to harass employees when they seek to avail themselves of the grievance procedure.

If I find that an employer has violated the collective bargaining agreement, it is my practice to ask the parties to work out a remedy because parties know the circumstances better than I do and because a negotiated remedy is more acceptable than an imposed remedy. If parties fail to agree on the remedy within specified time limits, I scrutinize their record of the negotiations on the remedy to determine the remedy.

15
Illustrative Opinions on Discipline and Discharge

The following opinions on discipline and discharge illustrate how I have applied the just cause criteria and what remedies I have ordered on a variety of alleged employee offenses.

EXAMPLE NO. 1

The employer discharged the employee for stealing the employer's time.

Facts

On January 10, the employer dispatched some movers to an office at 11:30 A.M. At 12:30 P.M., R., and other crew members to the same job. When the grievant filled out his time card on the following day, he wrote 11:30 A.M. as the starting time, not 12.30 P.M., his actual starting time. The employer noticed the discrepancy. When the grievant appeared for work on January 14, the employer told the grievant that he was discharged for "time stealing." On January 15, the employer sent him his formal letter of termination. The union grieved the discharge, and the parties proceeded to arbitration.

Questions

Did the employer discharge its employee, R., for just cause? If not, what is the appropriate remedy?

Relevant Contract Provisions

Section 10, Discharge or Suspension:

19.1　Warnings, suspensions, or discharges not in accord with the provisions of this Section are null and void.

19.2　No employee(s) shall be warned or suffer suspension or discharge except for just cause and in strict accord with the provisions of this Section, and such must be in writing and dated.

19.3　As a condition precedent to any suspensions or discharges the employer must have given the employee a written warning notice wherein the facts forming the grounds of employer dissatisfaction are clearly set forth. The facts therein set forth must be of the same type as those upon which the suspension or discharge is founded. Warnings, suspensions or discharges must be given by registered or certified mail or personally with a written acknowledgement of receipt.

19.4　Copies of all warning notices, suspensions or discharges shall be immediately forwarded to the union.

19.5　Warning notices not given and suspensions and discharges, except as hereinafter provided, not executed within ten (10) days of any given incident shall be null and void and incompetent evidence under the provisions of this agreement after nine (9) months.

19.6　EXCEPTION: Warning notices not necessary if the grounds are dishonesty, recklessness, carrying unauthorized passengers while operating employer's vehicles, possession, sale or use of dangerous drugs or narcotics or drinking related to employment. Discharges or suspensions under these exceptions must be executed within five (5) days of the time the employer acquires knowledge of the incident if not immediate, a discharge or suspension founded thereon must be executed within five (5) days of the time the employer acquires knowledge of the same, but in no event more than sixty (60) days following the incident, except for dishonesty. Dishonesty is defined as the theft or false statements of time worked, miles driven or other dishonest matters giving rise to a money obligation for the employer or its customers; provided further, no warning notice is required for suspension and/or discharge on the ground of striker misconduct (i.e., threats of harm to person or infliction of harm to person or property).

19.7　Any employee(s) has the right to request an investigation, by the union, of any warning notice, suspension or discharge provided such request is made within ten (10) working days of receipt of same; otherwise the right to request an investigation is waived. The day of receipt of warning notice, suspension or discharge shall be excluded in figuring time. If the tenth (10th) day falls on a Saturday, Sunday or holiday, the next following normal day of work shall be considered the tenth (10th) and last day.

19.8　Grievances arising as a result of any such investigation shall be settled in accordance with the provisions of Section 22.

Argument

The union believed that the discharge was unjust because the employer did not afford the grievant procedural due process, and because the employer discharged the grievant for an improper motive, namely, he joined the union.

Procedural Due Process Questions. The union asserted that the discharge was procedurally defective because the employer failed to apply progressive discipline, to investigate properly, and to counsel the grievant. All these allegations are unfounded.

First, the grievant is not entitled to progressive discipline, that is, to a warning notice before discharge because the employer discharged the grievant for "time stealing" on January 11 and for "your past history of time stealing" (Letter of Termination), and not because he had "the temerity to join the union in defiance of the employer's wishes." Article 19.6 clearly says "Warning notices are not necessary if the grounds are dishonesty, recklessness. . . . " The agreement defines dishonesty as "theft or false statements of time worked. . . . "

Second, the employer did investigate objectively and fairly: the employer did examine all card entries of January 10. The employer found that the grievant had written in 11:30 A.M. as his starting time, not 12:30 P.M., his actual starting time on his card. There was no need to inquire any further. Third, there was no need to counsel the grievant on January 14. The grievant knew, or should have known, that these false entries constituted dishonesty. The collective bargaining agreement forbids it, and the employer had counseled him twice.

The Substantive Question. The central and substantive question before me is: Did the grievant attempt to steal one hour of the employer's time when he claimed that he started work at 11:30 A.M. although he actually began work at 12:30 P.M.? The union contended that the grievant did not intend to steal; he made an inadvertent error, a "routine mistake." The union explained: the grievant, who can neither read nor write, asked L. and C., two fellow employees, "for assistance." The crew leader, T., "apparently forgetting" that he started an hour earlier than the crew, told the grievant "just copy mine." That is how and why the grievant made the error.

The grievant's explanation is neither plausible nor convincing. First, L. testified that the grievant had asked him and C. not for the start time but for the job number of the job. Both L. and C. told him to check their cards to get the job number, not the start time. Second, all other crew members recorded their starting time accurately. Third, I find it hard to believe that the grievant forgot his starting time; he routinely had entered his starting time many other times. It is the grievant's obligation to remember and record his starting time. The grievant is an adult; he should not rely on either L. or C., nor can he shift responsibility onto them. Fourth, the grievant cannot claim ignorance of numbers. A witness for the employer testified that the grievant knows about number entries: he diligently and always checked all the number entries of the employer.

Three incidents support my conclusion that the grievant probably intended to steal the employer's time on January 11.

The October 15 Incident. After the grievant had worked on a house move, he entered a claim for 8.5 hours pay. The dispatcher reduced the grievant's claim from 8.5 hours pay to 8 hours pay and reprimanded him for false entry. The grievant filed no complaint or grievance for the loss of pay or the reprimand. At the hearing, the dispatcher testified that he had reduced the pay and he had reprimanded the grievant because he had seen the grievant and employee T. eating lunch on the job between 11.30 A.M. and noon. The dispatcher's testimony conflicts with the grievant's and T.'s testimony. The grievant testified that he did not take any lunch; he said that he worked through the lunch period, and T. testified that he went to a restaurant to eat lunch.

The October 18 Incident. On October 18, the grievant had entered a claim on his time card that showed he had worked until 6:00 P.M. The dispatcher changed the grievant's end of work time from 6:00 P.M. to 5:00 P.M. He told the grievant that the entry was false and he again warned the grievant to stop entering false time claims. The grievant filed no grievance nor did he dispute the loss of pay or the warning. The dispatcher's testimony conflicts with the testimony of B., another employee. The dispatcher testified that he saw the grievant return from work at 5:00 P.M. B. testified that he and the grievant actually worked until 6:00 P.M. The union said that the dispatcher (P.) confused the October 18 incident with an October 12 incident when he had dispatched the grievant to a different job.

I credit the dispatcher's testimony: P. had no compelling interest to falsely testify. I am convinced that the grievant made false entries on October 15 and on October 18. The entries must be false because the grievant, in self-interest, would have, and should have protested the dispatcher's reprimand and unfair loss of pay as unwarranted.

The Grievant's Application for Unemployment Benefits. On January 17, the grievant applied to the Employment Security Department for unemployment benefits. The uncontested evidence shows that the grievant falsely asserted on the application form that the reason for his unemployment was "lack of work." The real reason for his unemployment was discharge.

This incident, independent of the incidents of October 15, October 18, and January 10, conclusively support my judgment and the employer's judgment that the grievant has the proclivity to falsify and has falsified records to achieve his purposes.

Conclusion

I am convinced that the grievant intentionally falsified records on October 15, on October 18, on January 10, and on January 17 of the next year. These four false entries constitute a clear and discernible pattern: the grievant not only tends to, but he actually does, falsify records.

Question: Did the employer discharge the grievant for just cause?

Answer: Yes. Discharge is proper because the collective bargaining agreement makes stealing the employer's time a dischargeable offense.

EXAMPLE NO. 2

The employer properly discharged the employee for just cause: reprehensible conduct and unsatisfactory work performance.

Facts

The employer, managed by a general manager and a chief engineer, employs three installers and a chief technician. In May, the employer terminated the grievant, M., an installer. The employer dismissed the grievant for lying, for violating the employer's policy on fifteen minute breaks, for "goofing off" and for not performing his job properly (Company Exh. 10). The grievant grieved the dismissal, the matter went unresolved, and the parties proceeded to arbitration.

Questions

At the hearing, the parties agreed to submit the following two questions:

1. Was the grievant, M., discharged for just cause?

2. If not, what is the proper remedy?

What Constitutes Just Cause for Discharge?

Article XVII, *Discharges, Suspensions, and Demotion for Cause*, limits the employer's right to discharge for "proper" cause, that is, for those offenses specified in the *Employee's Handbook*. The *Employee's Handbook* divides the *RULES OF CONDUCT* into two categories. The first category catalogues and specifies those employee offenses that subject an employee to immediate termination, and the second category specifies those other employee offenses ("lesser offenses") that might result in suspension, or, if repeated, discharge. Therefore, to sustain the discharge, the employer must adduce sufficient concrete evidence to show that the grievant actually committed those offenses that violate the first category of work rules, or that he has repeatedly committed acts that violate the second category of work rules.

The Scope of the Grievances

The union argued that the arbitrator should consider only those offenses listed in the letter of termination, and not the grievant's employment history "minutiae," because the discharge "must stand or fall on the reasons given at the time of discharge." The employer argued that the arbitrator must consider the grievant's total work record because his other misconduct has a "cumulative" effect that compounds the discipline problem.

Ruling: The Grievant's total work record is subject to arbitral scrutiny.

First, equity, a broad and all-inclusive term, requires that I consider the grievant's total work record because only a consideration of the total record can lead to a determination of the central issue, namely, whether the employer had "proper" cause to discharge, that is, whether the grievant had made himself an undesirable employee. Second, the union's argument does not address itself to the substantive issue, that is, just cause, but rather to an easily correctable procedure. Tomorrow, the employer could easily correct the procedure: it can "make book" on the grievant by reducing every bit of the grievant's misconduct to writing and then proceed to discharge him. Third, nothing in the *Agreement* or in the *Employee's Handbook* obliges the employer to list each and every incident that led to the discharge.

Application of the Contract Language and the Employee's Handbook

Reasons for the Discharge

Offense No. 1: The employer discharged the grievant for lying. In April, the grievant asked for and received permission to go home on sick leave. He left work at 10:30 A.M., reappeared briefly at the job site, but left again shortly thereafter. At 2:30 P.M. and again at 3:00 P.M. the manager and the supervisor saw the grievant's company truck parked in front of the grievant's lawyer's office.

The employer did not believe the grievant's story that he went to the doctor, got a perscription near his lawyer's office, and then went home. The employer pointed to the discrepancy in the grievant's testimony: at first he denied that he saw his lawyer, but at the arbitration hearing, he changed his story: he admitted that he saw his lawyer but "only for five minutes" and that he spent "45 minutes" at the pharmacy. The employer admitted that it had no way of knowing how long the grievant actually spent with his attorney on employer's sick time, or whether or not he even went to the pharmacy. However, the employer believed that the grievant "contrived to take advantage of the employer to take care of a personal legal problem."

When the grievant was asked why his letter of May 29 stated that he went to see his doctor after leaving work, the grievant explained that when he wrote the May 29 letter, "he was unaware of the date the employer was concerned about, and thus he may have in his May 29 letter confused the two dates and two visits." The employer rejected the grievant's explanation that he confused the two dates, April 21 and April 28, and the two days he parked in front of his lawyer's office. The employer never referred to April 28 but to the incident of April 21, the date in the termination letter and the date on Employer Exhibit 10. Further, the employer dismissed the grievant's testimony that he confused the dates because "I was never even given a copy of the letter terminating me" as a patent lie because the manager handed the grievant a copy of his termination letter in the presence of witnesses. The attestations of D. and S. (other installers) appear on the face of the termination letter itself. The employer concluded that the grievant "changed his story when it became obvious that he had been at his lawyer's office, and attempted at the hearing to minimize the length of time involved."

I am convinced that the grievant lied to the employer. Here, lying is more than a moral delict, it is also a form of robbery because the grievant used employer sick leave time for personal purposes. Lying is a serious offense: it erodes trust and good faith, indispensable ingredients in any notion of just cause, and it fractures workable and cooperative relations between labor and management.

Offense No. 2: The employer discharged the grievant because he violated the employer policy on 15 minute breaks and he falsified the route sheets. The employer charged that the grievant deliberately took and concealed an unauthorized 45 minute break on May 5, and that he deliberately falsified the route sheet at the end of the day. The grievant knew the employer's policy, yet he left his job partially finished, went to the home of another installer, and spent at least 45 minutes there. At the end of the day, he concealed the break and filed a route sheet that listed no break whatsoever.

The grievant admitted that he took an unauthorized 45 minute break. He justified this violation of the work rule: he was having extreme emotional problems; he was recently separated from his wife and his divorce was pending; he did not feel that he could meet customers on that day, so he went to a co-worker's house to recuperate. The union sought to justify the falsification on the route sheets: "only later that day did he realize he had for most of the day forgotten to prepare his route sheet entries"..."he did not deliberately try to cover up his taking a long break" and he "normally did not even take a break." If the employer had warned him that falsification of a route sheet was a terminable offense, the grievant "probably would have made a greater effort to do it exactly right" because he thought that "the purpose of the route sheet was to give the employer an idea of the jobs performed, not to record the time accurately."

The employer found the grievant's "didn't remember" testimony incredible: that at 4 o'clock he "didn't remember" starting a job; that he "didn't remember" spending 45 minutes there. Nonetheless, the grievant did remember to enter his "lunch" break on the route sheet. (The employer noted the discrepancy in the grievant's "lunch" entry. At first he testified that he just "made up" for the entry for lunch; then that he had lunch from 12:00 to 12:30 P.M.; and later that he did not have lunch at all, but simply ate a sandwich.) The employer concluded that the grievant's explanation, like other explanations, was improvised at the hearing: "It makes no sense, and casts even further doubt on the grievant's credibility, both as to the route sheet and as to his testimony regarding his actions."

The employer rejected the grievant's divorce as an explanation: divorce is too easy and too ready an explanation. Divorce cannot explain, much less justify, an unauthorized break of 45 minutes, which violated the employer's rules.

The union's defense of the grievant claiming that the prolonged break was not taken as a "lark" but rather to recover from divorce-wrenched emotion, and that "his failure to record the break cannot be seen as unusual" is utterly inadequate. The grievant's misconduct is reprehensible and cannot be justified. On this count alone, the employer had "proper" cause to discharge the grievant because he violated Article VII, Section 3, of the collective bargaining agreement, which reads:

Fifteen (15) minutes relief period shall be allowed employees during each session of the day's work. This relief shall not interfere with the completion or the continuity of an assigned job. (Joint Exh. 1).

The grievant compounded this violation of the *Agreement*, a serious offense in itself, by violating a clear and unambiguous work rule in the *Employee's Handbook*, which lists "falsifying employer's records or reports" as an offense "subject to immediate termination" and by violating another specific work rule "reporting time inaccurately," which, though a "lesser" offense, if repeated can result in discharge.

Offense No. 3: The employer discharged the grievant because he was "goofing off" and not doing his job properly. The grievant's route sheets show that on April 7 and April 8 he quit at 4:00 P.M. and on April 10 he took nearly an hour for lunch. On April 13, the chief engineer spot-checked four of the grievant's jobs; three needed to be done again. After he reviewed the grievant's route sheets and inspected the work, the chief engineer concluded that "I just couldn't see eight hours' work there." On April 14, the grievant quit at 4:10 P.M. On April 27, he turned in a route sheet which showed that he quit work at 2:15 P.M., 2 1/4 hours before quitting time. He did not call in and he did not notify the employer of his whereabouts, nor did he tell his supervisor that he felt unable to continue. On May 6, he quit at 4:10 P.M. Hence, the employer concluded, and the grievant's co-workers agreed, that the grievant was a "goof-off" (a slur for an unwilling worker): he wasted time and he often did not complete the work, nor was he particularly careful about his work. The grievant's fellow installers complained that, because the grievant was a "goof-off", they had to carry his load.

The union sought to exculpate the grievant, and to blame the employer for procedural error: the employer failed to train the grievant; the training program was "ill-conceived"; there were no standard training procedures; "retraining [was] perfunctory, if anything"; retraining efforts omitted trouble-shooting; and performance expectations were vaguely based on the day-to-day opinions of one manager and on unfair comparisons between the grievant and experienced employees of higher job classifications. The employer has no written standards on the exact number of jobs per day required of employees. The employer should have reprimanded, warned, and disciplined the grievant on his work performance. The grievant is competent: he had taken two courses. The grievant was never given an opportunity to improve his performance. Hence, the employer's discharge leads "inexorably" to the conclusion that the discharge was arbitrary and unreasonable.

The objective evidence leads "inexorably" not to the union's subjective conclusion, but to the opposiste conclusion, that the grievant was trained sufficiently. A union witness so testified: the grievant received the same training as others, he held to the same standards of performance as other installers, and new installers all handled the same kinds of trouble calls. The senior technician handled the difficult trouble calls. Furthermore, it was the employer who suggested that and paid for the grievant's course.

However, the union's view of the grievant's training and the employer's training program are immaterial because the employer is the sole judge of competence, that is, what the *Employee's Handbook* lists as "failure to do your job in accordance with the recognized standards, both as to quality and quantity." Unsatisfactory job performance is not only a "proper" cause to discharge the grievant, but it is a compelling reason to discharge because equity, the essence of the "proper" cause, minimally demands that an employee work willingly, competently, and efficiently in return for remuneration. Further, the grievant's training is unrelated to his many other dischargeable offenses.

Other Reasons for the Discharge

The Grievant used the Company Vehicle without Authorization. The *Employee's Handbook* lists "using employer tools, vehicles, or other equipment without authorization" as an offense subject to "immediate termination." On January 27, the employer warned the grievant about his use of the company truck for his personal use without authorization. On April 3, the grievant returned his company truck to the shop at about 8:00 P.M., 3 1/2 hours after quitting time.

The grievant admitted this violation of employer policy, which he attributed to his divorce. In his defense, the union pointed out that the grievant never committed this offense again. Neither the grievant nor the union can justify the grievant's misconduct. The employer discharged the grievant for "proper" cause because the *Employee's Handbook* clearly states that an employee is subject to immediate discharge if he uses a company vehicle without authorization.

The Grievant Was Insubordinate. The *Employee's Handbook* lists "refusing to obey the valid order of your supervisor" as an offense subject to immediate termination. On February 25, the employer issued a letter of reprimand to the grievant for insubordination: he had failed to follow direct orders to remove personal equipment from employer property and to return a radio part purchased without authorization.

The union sought to exculpate the grievant: the grievant took to heart the letter of reprimand because he was no longer insubordinate, and he did return the radio part, but the store mistakenly failed to credit the employer account.

The employer had "proper" cause to discharge the grievant because the *Employee's Handbook* clearly states that insubordination subjects an employee to immediate termination.

The Grievant Was Habitually Late. The *Employee's Handbook* lists "repeated tardiness or early quitting without proper authorization" as a lesser offense but its repetition might result in discharge.

The employer detailed the grievant's habitual lateness. The uncontroverted record shows that the employer warned the grievant about his lateness on January 21; he was warned again in February, and again in March. He continued to be late in April immediately preceding his termination. The grievant admitted that, in spite of his supervisor's warning, he continued to report late for work. He was on time for only four work days in May.

The union sought to blame the employer for procedural error: the employer never gave the grievant a written reprimand on the tardies, the employer never told the grievant that he would be disciplined if the tardies continued, the employer never showed the grievant the record of the tardies, and the employer never placed the record in his personnel file. Finally, the grievant did not come late after March 13, when he was warned about his tardies.

The Grievant Was Not Accessible on his Radio for Three Hours.

The Grievant Did Not Clean the Company Vehicle Properly. The *Employee's Handbook* specifies that "failure to maintain your assigned company vehicle or equipment in neat and orderly condition" is one of the "lesser" offenses, which, if repeated, could result in discharge.

These last three "lesser" offenses are inexcusable: they violate the *Employee's Handbook* and they contribute substantially to the grievant's misconduct.

I can arrive at only one conclusion: the employer had "proper" cause to terminate the grievant: for continuing misconduct and for unsatisfactory work performance. The grievant knew the rules, he received many warnings, but he ignored both the rules and the warning. The grievant broke his contractual bargain: he broke his promise to work diligently and cooperatively and to abide by the rules in the *Employee's Handbook*. He made himself an undesirable employee. He cannot be excused for his intolerable behavior which has caused the employer much trouble.

The grievant's offenses are many and serious. The three offenses specified in the letter of termination, sufficient by themselves to warrant the discharge, were compounded by the five other offenses, two of which subject the grievant to immediate termination. All these offenses were not isolated instances of misconduct attributable to immediate personal emotional problems, but were, as the employer correctly noted, characteristic of the grievant's behavior throughout his brief employment with the company.

The employer has met its burden of proof: the evidence is overwhelming that the grievant committed offenses that subjected him to immediate termination. All union arguments discussed fail because they improperly seek to justify what is unjustifiable, that is, clear violations of the agreement and the *Employee's Handbook*. The union's attempt in its brief to blame the employer for procedural error also fails because the central issue is not company action but the grievant's misconduct.

Union Argument No. 1: The grievant's misconduct is attributable to his divorce. The grievant's divorce is not a valid excuse for his misconduct. His divorce does not explain his misconduct from December to May: his insubordination, his unauthorized use of company vehicles on January 27 and on April 13, his leaving work early, his unauthorized break, his falsified route sheet, his personal errand on company sick leave time and his habitual lateness. Furthermore, his consistently poor performance from February to May had nothing to do with his divorce. The grievant is an adult; equity to the employer demands that he be held to his contractual bargain.

Union Argument No. 2: The employer failed to apply progressive discipline. The union believed that before the employer can discharge, the employer must first warn and then suspend the grievant because the purpose of discipline is to help the grievant correct his misconduct. The employer can discharge only after the employee fails to satisfactorily respond to progressively more severe discipline. The union said that the grievant is "manifestly" amenable to correction because of his "sincere demeanor" at the hearing. He is honest: he admitted that he took a long break on May 5, and that he stopped at his lawyer's office on April 21. The grievant also corrected his insubordination after he got the letter of reprimand. The employer never gave the grievant a chance to improve because he was never warned that his allegedly substandard work performance or his "incorrect" route sheet could lead to discharge. Furthermore, the *Employee's Handbook* specifies that "reporting time inaccurately" and "failing to do your job in accordance with recognized standards" are "lesser" offenses which dictate "lesser penalties than discharge."

The employer countered that it had applied progressive discipline. First, it had considered the actual work environment. To discipline or to suspend, rather than to discharge in this instance, would not have helped or corrected the grievant, but it would have adversely affected customer service. In the operation, the three full-time installers must work together efficiently and cooperatively to maintain the system successfully. Second, the employer applied progressive discipline because it discussed the grievant's offenses with him, it gave the grievant repeated warnings, and it issued a final written warning. The employer gave the grievant many warnings, without rancor or animus; it sought to encourage the grievant to change his conduct, all to no avail.

The employer set out the record. First, the grievant was warned about the personal use of the company vehicle on January 27; on April 3 he repeated his misconduct, and again the employer warned him; on April 28 he ran a personal errand on company sick leave time in his vehicle.

Second, the grievant was told to keep accurate route sheets in Feburary; and he was questioned about discrepancies on his route sheets in mid-March, yet, on April 27, he disappeared 2 1/2 hours before quitting time and did not inform the employer of his whereabouts on the route sheet for that day. On May 5, the grievant falsified his route sheet to conceal an unauthorized break. Third, in February, the grievant was told that his co-workers believed that he was not carrying a fair share of the workload. In March he was questioned about how he was spending his day. In May, his conduct had not improved. Fourth, the grievant was warned on January 21 about his habitual lateness and warned again on Feburary 5 and on March 13, yet, he continued to be late in January, February, March, and through April. Only on the four days he worked in May did he report on time, because, as he said, he knew he was on thin ice. Fifth, the grievant was warned on December 11, on December 29, on January 21, and on February 25 to remove his tools from the shop. On February 25, only 2 1/2 months prior to his termination, he was issued a final written warning for failing to follow these direct orders. Sixth, he was warned in writing for failing to return a radio part as directed by his supervisor. He admitted that even after receiving this written warning, he did not immediately return the radio part but took care of it "sometime later," an attitude that prevailed toward later subsequent oral warnings about other conduct. During the same period, he was warned repeatdly for the commission of "lesser offenses" which included the listing of time inaccurately in March, April, and May, repeated tardiness in January, February, March and April; and repeated instances of quitting early in April.

The employer knew it could have terminted the grievant in Feburary; it tried warnings to secure an improvement in performance. The many incidents in April and May, however, made it clear that the grievant would not improve and should be terminated. The manager concluded that he "could have given him [the grievant] a written warning every time he talked to him" and to give the grievant more warnings "would not do any good."

Suspension in May was also inappropriate because the grievant had already committed three immediately terminable offenses within less than 2 1/2 months preceding his May 7 discharge, with no sign whatever of improvement: he had disobeyed valid orders in February; he had used company vehicles for personal business without authorization in January and again in April, and he had falsified company records to cover up an unauthorized break on May 5. On May 7, there was more than sufficient reason to terminate rather than suspend the grievant. The employer cannot be expected to tolerate an employee who repeatedly engages in misconduct and performs at unsatisfactory levels.

The employer was under no obligation to warn again, or to suspend, in other words, to follow the union's notion of what constitutes progressive discipline. The employer discharges for "proper" reason when it disciplines according to the prescription in the agreement and in the *Handbook*, the two authoritative and controlling documents that clearly and specifically enumerate those offenses that subject an employee to immediate termination.

Union Argument No. 3: The discharge is wholly disproportionate to the offense. The employer took an "inconsistent and unequal approach" in the grievant's case. The employer issued a letter of reprimand to one co-worker for a violation of the break policy and a letter of reprimand to another co-worker for inadequate job performance.

The question of unequal treatment does not and cannot arise because the overwhelming and objective evidence shows that the grievant committed immediately dischargeable offenses. This argument ignores the grievant's many offenses and assumes that the other employees misbehaved and that they had the same bad work record.

Union Argument No. 4: The discharge was arbitrary and unreasonable. The employer's laxity in the enforcement of the work rules "lulled the employees into a false sense of security." The employer did not act "arbitrarily" or "unreasonably" because it "properly" exercised its legal right to discharge: the grievant committed immediately dischargeable offenses.

Union Argument No. 5: The employer violated due process becauses the employer did not fully and fairly investigate the facts and circumstances surrounding the alleged misconduct. The employer did not give the grievant an opportunity to be heard and to present evidence to dissuade the employer from taking disciplinary action before it took a final action. The employer did not give the grievant an opportunity to respond to the three allegations when it terminated him during a meeting that lasted only ten minutes.

The employer did not violate substantive due process because the employer discharged for "proper" cause, that is, the grievant committed dischargeable offenses. The employer observed due process procedures: it investigated fairly, it discussed the grievant's misconduct with the grievant, it warned continually, it did not discharge hastily or with malice, and it gave the grievant plenty of time to respond to the allegations.

Union Argument No. 6: The employer's proof is not clear and convincing. The union argued that the allegations of misconduct without proof are insufficient. The employer must offer definitive proof that the grievant acted willfully, with intent to deceive.

The vague, gratuitous, subjective argument contradicts the overwhelming objective evidence that led to the conclusion that the grievant committed dischargeable offenses.

Conclusion

Question No. 1: Was the grievant, M., discharged for just cause?

Answer: Yes.

Question No. 2: If not, what is the proper remedy?

Answer: No remedy is needed.

Award

The employer's discharge action is hereby sustained. The grievant's misconduct is reprehensible and his work performance poor. He has failed to fulfill his part of the labor contract because he violated the agreement and the *Employee's Handbook*. I can find no substantial reason to reinstate the grievant. Reinstatement would adversely and seriously affect customer service, efficient operation, and the morale of his fellow employees. Additional warnings or even a suspension will not help. He has had many warnings and opportunities to correct his misconduct. He expressed no word of repentance or remorse; he gave no sign of willingness to reform. The employer has been very tolerant and patient with the grievant. In nine and one-half months he has not been able to make himself a competent and desirable employee. To the contrary, he has made himself an undesirable employee, now properly discharged.

EXAMPLE NO. 3

The school district discharged the school bus driver for off-duty alcoholism.

Facts

On May 12, E., the grievant, a school bus driver for the district for five years, was cited for driving while intoxicated (DWI). On May 21, the superintendent discussed the matter with her and suspended her with pay, pending the outcome of court proceedings. On June 10, she asked for and the court granted a deferred prosecution on condition that she undergo a two year course of treatment at the Community Alcoholism Services Association. On September 3, the superintendent's successor reviewed the incident with the grievant and discharged her on September 4. On September 11, the association filed a grievance on the discharge. Because the parties were unable to resolve the grievance in the grievance procedure, the association demanded arbitration.

Question

At the hearing, the parties agreed to the following formulation of the question:

Did the school district have just cause for discharging the grievant from her position of school bus driver? If not, what is the appropriate relief?

The association formulated the submission inaccurately in its *Brief*. Thus:

1. Was the district justified in discharging the grievant for an off-duty alcohol problem? If not, what is the appropriate remedy?
2. Did the grievant's conduct rise to level of just cause for discharge pursuant to Section 10.1 of the agreement? If not, what is the appropriate remedy?

I cannot accept the association's formulation of the issues because it is a legal error to unilaterally change, in any way, the jurisdiction of the arbitrator or the focus of the issue.

Argument

What is the issue? The following issues color, impinge on, and form the context of the dispute, but are not before me: the grievant's off-duty conduct; the validity of the grievant's driver's license under the state's Administrative Code; the legal effect of the court proceedings on her guilt or innocence; the district's liability for damages; the district's insurance coverage; community concern over the grievant's drinking problem; the effectiveness of antabuse (a liquid to control alcoholism); the rate of successful recovery from alcoholism; the district's misunderstanding, misinterpretation, or misapplication of a particular statute; the grievant's rights under Section 3.1 of the agreement and the law; the interpretation and application of the seven criteria for discharge in *Robert's Dictionary of Industrial Relations*; and the grievant's job performance history.

Stated directly, there are only three questions before me. I have asked and answered each in turn.

Question No. 1: Did the district deny the grievant procedural due process before it discharged the grievant, as the association alleged?

The district accorded the grievant procedural due process in all respects. The evidence shows that the district investigated fairly and objectively, it did not invidiously discriminate against her, and it did not mislead her when it first suspended her and waited for court proceedings before it discharged her. The following is my response to other union allegations. The district had no obligation to promulgate or disseminate a written policy statement that employees with alcohol problems would be subject to possible discharge; the grievant knew or should have known that the district would not and could not tolerate a bus driver who has an alcohol problem; and the district has no obligation to monitor an employee's treatment for an alcohol problem.

Question No. 2: Did the district have a just and sufficient cause to discharge the grievant?

The testimony and especially the written evaluataion of the grievant's drinking problem directly point to the unavoidable, stark, and unpleasant fact that the grievant is in the "middle" stages of alcoholism. Therefore, it is plainly evident that the district cannot allow the grievant to drive a school bus because, as a problem drinker, she poses a direct, immediate, and possible danger to the safety of students who ride the bus. The district not only has an abiding and compelling obligation to ensure their safety but it would also be derelict in its duty if it did not do so. Therefore, the district properly suspended her but, and this is the main question, is it fair to discharge her?

The district did not act fairly because the grievant, an excellent employee, did not offend or injure the district. Is the association's proposal that the district reinstate her and monitor her antabuse program fair? The association's proposal is also unfair because there is no guarantee that the grievant will not relapse into drinking alcohol while she is undergoing treatment. There is no proof that supervision makes it "much less likely that she would drink on the job now than before her arrest and treatment." The harsh fact is that no one knows, perhaps not even the grievant, whether or not she will relapse into drinking alcohol. I must reject the association's proposal because it assumes an unproved and an unprovable causal link between the abstract statistical success or failure rate of recovery and the grievant's future behavior. The proposal also unfairly and unwisely shifts the burden of recovery from the grievant to the district. Expert witnesses pointedly noted, and the association admitted, that the grievant must correct herself. I also have serious doubt that she is willing to change her habits. She testified that she no longer drinks alcohol but she frequents bars and taverns in spite of her counselor's advice that she not frequent these places. The stark fact is that the grievant can, and might, relapse into drinking. The fact that the grievant acknowledges her alcohol problem and now abstains from alcohol is not proof that she will not relapse into drinking. The danger of relapse is too great; a real danger, an every-present possibility. Experts testified that a person with an alcohol problem easily finds many reasons and opportunities to drink alcohol; problem drinkers are devious: they conjure a multitude of ways to avoid taking antabuse, a doubtful remedy, an ineffective crutch. The association's proposal also ignores the reality of driving a bus: a school bus driver cannot be supervised closely and continually; a bus driver exercises independent, unsupervised control over a bus.

Question. No. 3: What is the appropriate remedy?

This question properly phrased is: What remedy is fair to both the grievant and the district? Discharge is unfair to the grievant because she has not offended the district; the district cannot permit her to drive a school bus because she has an alcohol problem. I have sought to fashion a remedy that gives the grievant a chance and an incentive to overcome her alcohol problem and assures the district that if she once again drives a school bus, she will not jeopardize the safety of student riders.

Award

1. The grievant is hereby suspended for five calendar years, to run from the date of the DWI citation to the date of her possible reinstatement.

2. For the wrongful discharge, the district is hereby ordered to pay the grievant full back pay without benefits from the date of her discharge to the date of this *Award*. The district is also ordered to pay the grievant half pay without benefits from the date of this *Award* to the first anniversary of her discharge. During the remainder of the five year suspension period, she is to receive no back pay or benefits.

3. Thirty calendar days before the end of the five year period, the grievant may petition the district to reinstate her. The district must reinstate her if, at the end of the five year period, the grievant can convince the district's governing board by substantial, hard, concrete evidence and testimony of persons, that she has been completely and entirely sober for five years. If the district's board can show an arbitrator that she had lapsed into drinking alcohol once during the five year period, she automatically loses her right to reinstatement.

4. Thirty calendar days before the end of the first calendar year of her DWI citation and any time thereafter, the grievant may apply for a non-driving job with the district. To apply for and ultimately receive a non-driving job, the grievant must convince the district with the same level of proof set forth in No. 3 that she has remained entirely sober.

5. The district is hereby directed to formally invite the association, no later than April 30, to a meeting to arrange a mutually convenient date to discuss a possible severance settlement. Discussions on a severance settlement may take place at any time, but no later than May 19. If the district fails to invite the association, the grievant is automatically and immediately reinstated. If the association refuses to meet with the dis-

trict, the discharge stands. If the parties opt for the principle of a severance settlement but cannot agree on the details of the settlement, the district is hereby directed to so inform me no later than May 26. If so, I will determine the specifics of the severance settlement. If the parties do not accept the severance settlement principle, Orders No. 1 through No. 4 stand.

I hereby retain jurisdiction over the interpretation and application of this *Opinion and Award* until (date).

EXAMPLE NO. 4

The employer suspended the employee for failure to give notice before he left his work station. This opinion is an example of a summary opinion, a brief opinion that sets forth only the reasons why the suspension was unfair.

Questions and Answers

Question No. 1: Was the suspension of N. in violation of the contract?

Answer: Yes.

When the city suspended the grievant for five days because he failed to give the customary oral notice to his superior that he would not be at his duty station on a Friday, the city violated the just cause provision of the contract for two reasons. First, there is no contract provision or promulgated work rule that requires oral notice. Second, the five day suspension is not commensurate with the offense. The discipline is too severe because N., an exemplary employee for eighteen years, gave actual notice: he gave oral notice on Tuesday morning and written notice on Thursday afternoon that he would need to be off on Friday or on Saturday to get his wife from the hospital. Further, N. had always given oral notice, he is not a recalcitrant employee; he did not intend to, nor did he, adversely affect the employer's interests.

However, N. was negligent and exercised poor judgment: he neglected to effectively and efficiently contact either W. or C. N. knew that it was customary to give oral notice; he knew that it was most important for the continued operation of the plant that he give W. or C. effective and efficient notice. His failure to give oral notice disrupted W's schedule.

Question No. 2: What is the appropriate remedy?

Answer: The appropriate remedy is a letter of reprimand.

Award

(1) This *Award*, to be kept in the grievant's file for one year, nullifies the five day suspension, modifies the five day suspension to a reprimand, and orders the city to make the grievant whole, i.e., to pay the grievant for the five days he was suspended. The grievant is also entitled to one day "comp" time.

(2) I retain jurisdiction over the interpretation and application of this *Award* until (date).

EXAMPLE NO. 5

The employer discharged the employee for violation of a district safety rule. Discharge was too severe because the district incorrectly assumed that the grievant caused the automobile accident.

Facts

S., the grievant—a bus driver for the district for four years,—acceded to a request of a high school student, J., to leave the school bus for a few minutes at a convenience store. When J. left, another student, K. left with her. The grievant had arranged to pick them up when she returned on her route. To get to the return bus stop, the students had to cross two lanes of traffic on a busy highway which had a designated speed limit of 55 miles per hour. The students walked down the highway, and as they crossed the road, K. was struck by a car and injured. Approximately ten minutes later, when the grievant returned to pick up the students and take them to school, the grievant learned that K. had been struck by a car and seriously injured. She immediately reported the accident to school officials. After the district's investigation of the accident, the district discharged the grievant. The union grieved the discharge.

Questions

In their *SUBMISSION AGREEMENT*, parties agreed to the two following questions:

Question No. 1: Did the district violate Section 12.4 of the contract?

Question No. 2: If so, what is the appropriate remedy?

Relevant Contract Provision

Article XII, Severance of Employment

12.4   *Suspension or Discharge*—the employer shall not discharge nor suspend an employee without just cause. Just cause for immediate suspension of or discharge shall include, but not be limited to: gross insubordination, drunkenness on the job, proven dishonesty, excessive chargeable accidents, or a single chargeable severe accident.

12.4.1   Employer shall give at least one (1) written notice of complaint before suspending or discharging employees, except for the just causes stated above. A copy of the written notice of complaint shall not remain in effect for a period of more than six (6) months from the date of said warning notice. Warning letters, to be considered valid, must be issued within ten (10) days after the occurrence of the violation claimed by the employer in such warning letter.

Argument

The following facts are undisputed. The grievant knew that to allow students to get off at the convenience store violated both the district's work rule and the state regulation. Furthermore, the grievant had two chargeable (preventable) accidents on record. What is disputed is the answer to each of the following questions.

Question No. 1: What is the nature of the grievant's offense?

Is the grievant guilty of "gross insubordination," the "intentional, flagrant, inexcusable disobedience of the state regulation and district policy"? Did the grievant manifest a "willful disregard of express or implied direction of the employer"? Did she refuse to obey "reasonable order," as the district alleges, or is she guilty of a rule violation, as the union contends?

The grievant's non-observance of a work rule is not necessarily insubordination. To be insubordinate, an employee must be told orally, explicity, directly, unequivocally, and repeatedly (at least twice) that the refusal to obey an order constitutes insubordination. Here, there is no evidence to show that the grievant "willfully," "intentionally," or "blatantly" intended or directly did disobey or challenge the rule: she did not openly declare or adamantly refuse to comply with a direct, unequivocal, and repeated order. To the contrary, the grievant admitted that she was bound by the rule, and she declared that she is willing to abide by the rule in the future. The grievant is not guilty of insubordination; she is guilty of poor judgment (Union *Brief,* p. 4). The grievant erroneously concluded that the two high school students would abide by the drop-off and pick-up arrangements at the convenience store, that they would cross the highway safely and that she could ignore the safety rule.

Question No. 2: Did the grievant commit excessive chargeable accidents?

The grievant did not commit a chargeable accident. An accident is a chargeable (preventable) accident when the employee causes the acci-

220 An Introduction to Labor Arbitration

dent. Here, the grievant was not the direct or proximate cause of the accident. Therefore, the grievant's rule violation cannot be added to the grievant's two chargeable accidents to constitute "excessive chargeable accidents" because a rule violation is not a chargeable accident.

Question No. 3: Did the grievant commit "a single chargeable severe accident"?

The grievant did not commit a "single chargeable severe accident" because the grievant did not have an accident; she violated a work rule.

Question No. 4: Did the district violate Article XII, Section 4?

Was the district legally obligated to issue a warning letter before it discharged the grievant? The union thought so becauses the grievant had violated a work rule; she was not insubordinate. The district believed that it did not have to issue a warning letter because the grievant was insubordinate, an offense clearly enumerated in Section 12.4. Although I have concluded that the grievant violated a work rule, that she was not insubordinate, that she could not be charged with "excessive chargeable accidents," and that she did not commit a "single chargeable severe accident," the district did not have to issue a warning. Section 12.4 allows the district to discharge for offenses other than the enumerated offenses. Section 12.4 says: "Just cause of immediate suspension or discharge shall include but need not be limited to" the enumerated offenses. Section 12.4 allows the district to determine what other offenses are serious enough to warrant immediate suspension or discharge. Here, the district adjudged, correctly or incorrectly, that the grievant's violation of the safety rule was a serious matter. Because the matter was serious, discharge, not a letter of reprimand, nor a long term suspension, was the appropriate discipline.

Question No. 5: Was the discharge for just cause?

The district correctly asserted that insubordination constitutes a sufficient and just cause to discharge the grievant because insubordination immediately, substantially, and almost always irretrievably destroys the employment relationship. However, the grievant was not insubordinate: she did not "defy district policy, state regulations, and her trainer directives" (*Brief,* p. 6), nor did she refuse to obey district instructions "in flagrant disregard of the student's safety and security and her responsibility to the district, the students, and parents" (*Brief,* pp. 10–19).

Hence, the crucial question: was it just to discharge the grievant for violation of a work rule? It was unjust to discharge the grievant for her violations of a work rule because these violations do not and did not destroy or irretrievably impair the employment relationship.

Question No. 6: What is the appropriate remedy?

The district argued that the arbitrator should not substitute his judgment for that of the district unless he found the district's action arbitrary or capricious. It is true that the district's power to determine and to impose discipline is sacrosanct, that the district did not exercise its power arbitrarily or capriciously, and that the discharge would have been appropriate had the grievant been guilty of insubordination. However, I have power to review the district's judgment because the district assumed, incorrectly, that the grievant had been insubordinate. Discharge is not proportionate to the grievant's offense because her offense has not irretrievably broken or substantially impaired the employment relationship. Her poor judgment can be rectified. Neither is a letter or reprimand a sufficient remedy because the grievant violated not a "mere" rule, but a very important rule, a safety rule. The violation of a safety rule is a most serious matter: it frustrates the district's continuing, earnest, and diligent efforts to provide safety; it might impose a financial liability upon the district; and it might, and in this case did, have serious consequences: it might adversely affect the lives of students, teachers, and parents.

The appropriate remedy is a four week suspension. This judgment accords with the district's judgment: a district official testified that the district would not have discharged the grievant if the accident had not occurred.

Award

The district is hereby ordered (1) to reinstate the grievant at its earliest administrative convenience but no later than June 4, and (2) to make the grievant whole for all back pay, minus pay for the four weeks suspension, and to restore to the grievant any lost benefits which might have resulted from her discharge.

I retain jurisdiction over this *Option and Award* until (date).

EXAMPLE NO. 6

The employer discharged the grievant for failure to call in or report for work.

Facts

On May 28, B. (the grievant), an iron worker, asked his foreman, F., for leave for the week of June 1 to have his wisdom teeth removed. His supervisor, unauthorized to grant such a request, went to his own supervisor who, in turn, sent him to C. in the medical department because only the medical department could authorized sick leaves. C. advised F.

to tell the grievant to go on sick leave. On sick leave, the grievant would have to call in within three days, and he would need a doctor's release to return to work. On June 3, because the grievant had failed to call in or to report for work, the employer terminated him.

The union filed a grievance that alleged that the employer had violated Article 1, Article 2, Article 3, and Article 10 of the collective bargaining agreement. The employer denied the grievance and the union demanded arbitration.

Question

The parties agreed to submit the following question: Did the company violate the agreement between the union and the company as alleged by B. in his grievance dated June 11? If so, what is the proper remedy?

Pertinent Contract Clauses

Article 5, *Seniority*, Section 4, reads:

Seniority shall be terminated under this agreement if: ... (b) an employee's absence is unauthorized in excess of two (2) days.

Article 8, *Leaves of Absence*, Section 1, reads:

Leaves of absence for sickness or injury will be granted by management when the sickness or injury is substantiated by the doctor in charge of the case.

Article 9, *Employee Responsibility*, Section 2, reads:

All daily paid employees who anticipate missing a shift must report this to the Security Office at least one (1) hour before their shift starts. This does not necessarily constitute an excused absence. This report may be made in person or by telephone, or by telegraph, or through some other designated person. Excused absences will be granted for valid reasons.

Article 10, *Discharge-Layoff*, Section 1 and Section 2, reads:

1. In all disciplinary cases concerning a formal warning in the supervisor's office, the employee involved shall have the right to union representation.

2. Should any employee or former employee within ten (10) days excluding Saturdays, Sundays and holidays, of his discharge or layoff believe that he has been unjustly treated, he or his representative may present his grievance according to the grievance procedure starting at the Employee Relations Manager's level. If it is found that the employee has been unjustly discharged or laid off through recourse to the grievance procedure, he shall be reinstated to his former

position with like seniority and pay for all time lost if his case warrants such action, or such other disposition as may be agreed to by the company and the union or determined by an arbitration case. Warning slips which are two (2) years old will be removed from the employee's file providing no other warning slips have been issued during this two (2) year period. A copy of each warning slip issued and a list of those removed will be mailed to the union.

Argument

The union believed that the termination was unjust because the grievant did not deceive the employer and was honest about his surgery; he did not commit fraud; and he brought the required doctor's slip to his supervisor. This argument is irrelevant because the issue is not the grievant's integrity but his unauthorized absence.

The union implied that it was unfair to terminate the grievant because another employee, L. made only one call-in but was placed on sick leave. This argument also fails because, as the employer pointed out, L. was properly put on sick leave because the employer does make exceptions; the employer does put employees on sick leave after one call-in if they are absent because of an industrial accident or if they are hospitalized. The grievant was neither hospitalized nor absent because of an industrial accident.

The simple controlling fact is that the grievant violated the contractual bargain: he violated Article 5, Section 4, and Article 9, Section 2, of the collective bargaining agreement. The grievant's failure to call or report for work is a serious omission of a contractual duty. The grievant must be held to his contractual bargain. He is an adult, and there is no reason to excuse him. He cannot properly assume, as he argued, that he would be put on sick leave because his supervisor told him not once but twice that he would have to call in for three days. He knew the procedure, he had signed and received a copy of the call-in procedure, and he had used the proper procedure twice.

Conclusion

I can arrive at only one conclusion: the employer properly discharged the grievant because the grievant failed to abide by his contractual bargain.

Question No. 1: Did the employer violate the agreement as alleged by the grievant?

Answer: No.

Question No. 2: If so, what is the proper remedy?

Answer: No remedy is appropriate because the employer did not violate the agreement.

Award

The grievance is hereby denied because the employer did not violate the agreement.

EXAMPLE NO. 7

The employer improperly discharged the employee for off-duty dishonesty.

Facts

The grievant, D., a solo truck driver, pled guilty to a second degree felony charge of theft in Superior Court; he applied for and received unemployment benefits while he was unemployed. When the employer learned of the verdict, the employer promptly terminated the grievant. The union grieved the termination in the belief that the felony charge did not constitute dishonesty under Section 29.02 of the collective bargaining agreement. The matter went unresolved and the parties proceeded to arbitration.

Relevant Contract Provisions

Article 29.02 of Section 29, *SUSPENSION AND DISCHARGE,* provides that:

No employee(s) shall be warned or suffer suspension or discharge except for just cause.

Paragraph 29.06, *EXCEPTIONS,* reads:

Warning notices are not necessary if the grounds are dishonesty, recklessness, carrying unauthorized passengers while operating employer's vehicles, possession, sale or use of dangerous drugs or narcotics or drinking related to employment or engaging in business (directly or indirectly) in competition with the employer. Discharges or suspensions under these exceptions must be executed within five (5) days of the occurrence of the incident forming the ground. However, if the employer's knowledge of the incident is not immediate, a discharge or suspension founded thereon must be executed within five (5) days of the time the employer acquires knowledge of same, but in no event more than sixty (60) days following the incident, except for dishonesty. Circumscription of dishonesty is: Stealing time, materials, money or equipment.

Questions

(1)   Did the employer violate Section 29 of the collective bargaining agreement when it terminated the grievant?

(2)   If so, what is the proper remedy?

Argument

To sustain the discharge, the employer must show either (1) that Paragraph 29.06 legally permits the employer to discharge an employee for off-duty dishonesty, or (2) that considerations of equity justify discharge.

Question No. 1: Does Paragraph 29.06 empower the employer to discharge an employee for off duty conduct?

First, a procedural question: Does Paragraph 29.06 require the employer to issue a warning to be procedurally correct? The answer to this question is "No" because the contract clearly says: "Warning notices are not necessary if the grounds are dishonesty." Therefore, the employer committed no procedural error when it discharged the grievant for dishonesty.

The employer believed that off-duty dishonesty was "within the contract's definition of dishonesty." The union believed that the theft must be "from the employer and not from some unconnected outside person."

The employer's argument is that when the parties intended to limit certain offenses to on-duty behavior, they clearly did so: they used the modifying language "related to employment." Therefore, the parties must have intended to allow the employer to discharge an employee for off-duty dishonesty.

The employer's subjective and negative interpretation of Paragraph 29.06 is legally insufficient because the contract language is clear and unambiguous. It is a well-known, long-established, and fundamental postulate of contract interpretation that clear contract language prevails over any subjective reading of the contract, putative intent, and all understandings, because clear language objectively fixes the parties' intent. The contract language becomes even clearer if the definition of dishonesty is placed in its appositive position, next to the word "dishonesty," thus:

Warning notices are not necessary if the grounds are dishonesty (circumscription of dishonesty is: stealing time, materials, money, or equipment), recklessness, carrying unauthorized passengers while operating the employer's vehicles, possession, sale, or use of dangerous drugs or narcotics or drinking related to employment.

This simple transposition conclusively shows that the expression "related to employment" applies not only to the other enumerated acts but also to dishonesty. Therefore, the ineluctable conclusion is that the unambiguous language of Paragraph 29.06 empowers the employer to discharge only for on-duty, not for off-duty dishonesty.

The employer's interpretation of Paragraph 29.06 also contravenes the very notion of collective bargaining agreements. Collective bargaining agreements, essentially employment contracts, necessarily by their very terms, limit the employer's right to discipline employees to on-duty hours: an employee cedes his freedom and subjects himself to discipline only during the stipulated "hours of employment." It is inconceivable that a union would, or in fact could, bind its members to any employment contract whose reach would extend beyond the stipulated duty hours. If an employer could discipline or discharge an employee for off-duty misconduct, the employer would become a continuing employer and a moralizing agent, an ever-present moral judge of an employee's total conduct not only during working hours but also during off-duty hours. What the employer found reprehensible during work hours, the employer could find reprehensible during off-duty hours. Each and every employee off-duty act, even the most private act, would then be subject to Paragraph 29.06, a result not intended by the contracting parties.

Question No. 2: Do considerations of equity justify discharge?

Considerations of equity may justify an employer's discharge of an employee for off-duty dishonesty because an employer has the residual and inherent right to protect itself against harmful or undesirable employees. However, when the employer seeks to exercise its latent right to discharge an employee for off-duty dishonesty, the employer must establish a clear and easily identifiable causal link between the employee's off-duty dishonesty and the employer's interest. The employer bears a heavy burden of proof to show that the employee is either unable to perform his duties, or that the employer has actually been harmed or will be harmed in the near future.

Here, the employer advanced two arguments: first, the grievant was "no longer able to satisfactorily perform his job," and second, his actions "adversely affected the employer."

Argument No. 1: The grievant's criminal dishonesty makes the grievant no longer able to satisfactorily perform his job.

This argument fails for two reasons. First, the employer did not adduce any evidence to show that there was a direct causal link between the grievant's criminal dishonesty and his ability to perform his job. Second, the grievant's past record contradicts this speculative, and hence unwarranted conclusion. Undoubtedly, solo drivers must be trustworthy:

they make pick-ups and deliveries of customers' valuable goods, they have constant access to customers' loading docks and warehouses, they often make C.O.D. deliveries, and they keep time records that determine their own wages and customer charges. However, all employer witnesses readily admitted that the grievant had a clean record: he had never been suspected or guilty of any wrongdoing in his handling of short and damaged claims, or in cash collection or hours logged.

The grievant is able and willing to work; contractually, he is and has been honest.

Argument No. 2: The grievant's actions adversely affected the employer.

First, the employer argued that the grievant's dishonesty caused the employer to lose money because the employer spent much time in the investigations by the Employment Security Department and by the Department of Labor and Industries; and an employee had to stand by to appear at the grievant's trial. The union sought to minimize the hours spent by the employer in the investigation and trial and concluded that "overall, any harm to the employer in this respect must be held to be *de minimis.*"

The grievant's criminal dishonesty is directly and causally linked to the use of the employer's time. Since the grievant has injured the employer, I have sought to remedy this injury in my *Award.*

Second, the employer argued that the grievant's dishonesty triggered Paragraph 15 of the Employer's *Comprehensive Dishonesty, Disappearance and Destruction Policy,* which terminated the grievant's insurance coverage. If the grievant had been retained, he would have been the only driver not covered by the policy.

Third, the employer argued that the grievant's dishonesty might increase the employer's contribution to the unemployment and workmen's compensation systems because employer contributions to the Employment Security Department and to the Department of Labor and Industries depend on the employer's rate of experience and are directly related to the use of that system.

The union countered that a reading of RCW 50.29.020 shows that the effect upon the employer's contribution based on the grievant's claims would be remote, indeed, "so remote as to be unworthy of consideration."

The employer's argument fails because it is entirely speculative: the employer failed to adduce empirical or statistical evidence to show that the grievant's criminal dishonesty had affected or increased its contributions to the Employment Security Department or to the Department of Labor and Industries.

The employer's arguments fail. Considerations of equity do not justify discharge because the grievant's criminal dishonesty did not impair his ability to work, nor did his criminal misconduct seriously injure the employer. The union's conclusion that the employer did not show "any substantial, discernible adverse effect on its business interests as a result of alleged misconduct on the part of the grievant, even if taken as true," is only partially correct.

Conclusion

Question: Did the employer violate Section 29 of the collective bargaining agreement when it terminated the grievant, P.?

Answer: Yes.

Question: If so, what is the proper remedy?

Answer: The remedy is in the *Award.*

Award

1. The employer is hereby ordered to reinstate the grievant at its administrative convenience, but no later than April 1.

2. Reinstatement is with full back pay minus all interim earnings and without loss of any benefits from the date of his discharge to the date of his reinstatement. Back pay means all the money he would have earned had he worked or had he been offered work.

3. Reinstatement is conditional and probationary.

(a) The grievant must pay the employer no later than April 30 an equitable sum, either in a lump sum or in installments, for all the time the employer spent on the investigations, and on the trial. The employer and the union are hereby ordered to negotiate the amount of the sum payable to the employer. If the employer and the union cannot agree on the equitable sum by April 30, the parties are hereby directed to so inform the arbitrator and to set forth in writing to the arbitrator their specific proposals no later than April 30. Then, I will determine the amount payable to the employer.

(b) The grievant is hereby ordered to hand write a letter of apology to the employer which contains (1) a statement of apology, and (2) a statement of his appreciation for the opportunity to work for M.

(c) The grievant is hereby ordered to hand write a letter of thanks to his union to express his appreciation for its defense of his interests.

(d) The grievant is on probation for two years from April 30. During this probationary period, the grievant cannot avail himself of the protection afforded him by the just cause provision in all matters of honesty, whether on or off duty. If a court finds the grievant guilty of any off-duty dishonesty, the employer may discharge him at will. In a future arbitration on the grievant's on-duty dishonesty of the smallest sum, time, materials, or equipment, the arbitrator's jurisdiction shall be limited to a question of fact.

4. The union is hereby ordered to apprise the insurance carrier no later than April 15 that the grievant is willing and able to work, and that for purposes of employment, I have found him to be contractually honest. Therefore, the employer is hereby ordered to seek reinstatement of the grievant's insurance policy no later than April 30. If the insurance carrier refuses to insure the grievant, the employer is hereby ordered to notify the arbitrator no later than April 30. I will then order a remedy.

5. If the grievant refuses reinstatement on these terms, or if the grievant refuses to work for the employer for three months, the grievant must pay full union arbitration costs.

6. The union is hereby ordered to read this *Opinion and Award* aloud to the grievant, particularly the *Award*, to make sure he understands its terms.

7. The union shall certify to the employer no later than April 30 that both the grievant and the union have complied with all these *Orders*. If either the union or the grievant fails to comply with any one of these *Orders*, the employer may discharge the grievant at will.

8. The employer is hereby ordered to retain the complete record of this arbitration in the grievant's file for the two year probationary period.

I hereby retain jurisdiction on any and all disputes that might arise out of the implementation of this *Award* until (date).

EXAMPLE NO. 8

The employer discharged the employee for possession of cocaine. The opinion discusses the burden of proof that an employer assumes when it discharges an employee, circumstantial evidence, and credibility of the grievant.

Facts

In September, the employer discharged H., the grievant, a member of the union, and a crane operator. The crane operator performs an important and potentially dangerous task: he hauls log bundles and loose logs out of the water onto the log deck.

The grievant had worked the swing shift but he drew a mandatory second graveyard shift, a "double." At about 12:30 A.M., I., a friend of the grievant, called security to inquire whether the grievant was working a double shift. I. wanted to arrange a ride home. About 2:00 A.M., I. again called to tell security that he and R., another friend, were bringing the grievant a sack lunch. When security informed the wood room foreman that a sack lunch would be brought into the crane area, he became suspicious because on other occasions he had observed beer cans around the area. When he inspected the lunch, he found cocaine and a note that said: "H., there is some cocaine in your snack, so have a good one. Signed, R."

After they delivered the lunch to security, R. eluded security by going on the employer's property through a hole in the fence. He contacted the grievant in the crane and told him that the lunch contained cocaine. The grievant then asked his supervisor for permission to get his check (it was payday), but, as he testified, he really went to get his lunch. When he went to get his lunch, security told him that I. and R. had taken the lunch back. The grievant knew this was not true because R. had told him that they had just brought the lunch. The grievant returned to the crane. When security informed the personnel supervisor that the lunch contained cocaine, the personnel supervisor, after consultation with the wood preparation superintendent and the tour foreman, directed that the grievant be called to get his lunch. As the grievant passed the production department around 3:30 or 4:00 A.M., employer officials called him into the office and confronted him with the cocaine and the note. The grievant denied that he knew anything about the cocaine; the employer suspended him and asked him to report at 8:00 A.M. At 8:00 A.M., however, the grievant admitted that he knew the lunch contained cocaine. Consequently, the employer discharged him.

The union grieved the discharge, and the parties proceeded to arbitration.

Questions

The parties stipulated two questions in their *Submission Agreement*, namely,:

1. Was H. discharged for just cause?
2. If not, what is the appropriate remedy?

Scope of the Arbitrator's Authority

The *Submission Agreement* limits the arbitrator's authority and specifies his power and functions. The arbitrator's jurisdiction is limited to Section 17(a) because the employer in its *Letter* of April 4 sets forth the reason for discharge: "for aiding and abetting the bringing of intoxicants onto the mill site," or, in the words of the employer's counsel, for "aiding and abetting and really knowing the fact that there was cocaine coming to him and he went to accept it." Section 17(a), one of the causes for immediate discharge, reads:

Bringing intoxicants into or consuming intoxicants in the mill or reporting to duty under the influence of intoxicants onto the mill site.

Therefore, the *Submission Agreement* limits the arbitrator's jurisdiction to the "intoxicants" portion of Section 17(a). The arbitrator has no jurisdiction, as the employer seemed to imply, over "honesty" a portion of Section 17(a), or over Section 17(b), which requires the employer to notify the grievant of his discharge in writing.

Section 25 of the collective bargaining agreement specifies the arbitrator's function and limits his power on the remedy, thus:

The functions of the arbitrator shall be to interpret and apply the agreement and he shall have no power to add or to subtract from or to modify any of the terms of the agreement. The decision of the arbitrator shall be final and binding on the parties.

In suspension or discharge cases submitted to arbitration and as to which the arbitrator shall find the discharge or suspension to be unjustified, the amount of payment for lost time shall be determined by the arbitrator but shall not exceed payment for lost time at the employee's rate of pay of the job he was on at the time of suspension or discharge.

Argument

The strong verbs in the contractual language, written in the active voice and in the progressive present, impose a very strict and heavy burden of proof on the employer. The employer must present clear, compelling, concrete, and positive evidence that the grievant actually brought, possessed, or consumed intoxicants on the mill site, or that he was under the influence of intoxicants. An employee must commit a positive act, he must be caught red handed, in flagrante delicto; or witnesses must positively testify that they saw an employee possess, use, or appear under the influence of intoxicants. Circumstantial evidence, suggestions of possible or probable intent, suspicions, and surmises will not suffice.

The employer failed to meet its burden of proof, primarily and decisively because the employer's officials at the hearing, and the employer's counsel in his *Brief*, accepted the union's statement of facts: the grievant did not bring intoxicants into the mill, and he did not report for duty under the influence of intoxicants.

Second, the employer failed to adduce evidence to show that the grievant knew that cocaine was to be brought onto the mill site, or that he intended to consume the cocaine after he knew it was in the sack lunch. What the employer offered as evidence, (possible alternatives available to the grievant after he learned that the sack lunch contained cocaine), are polemical questions and speculations, not evidence. They fail to show that the grievant colluded with I. or R. to bring cocaine onto the mill site. On the contrary, the testimony of R. and I. supported the grievant's testimony that he (the grievant) knew nothing about the lunch or the cocaine before R. sneaked onto the mill site. It might be that both R. and I. perjured themselves; but they might be telling the truth. The best evidence is the objective evidence: the note itself. The note exonerates the grievant. If the grievant had known that the cocaine was in the sack lunch before R. sneaked onto the mill site, I. and R. need not have written the note.

It indeed might be, as the employer pointed out, that the grievant is not a credible witness. He lied to the employer on April 4 when he denied that he knew the cocaine was in the lunch; he lied to the employer on other occasions when he declared that he did not use drugs. The grievant's testimony that he did not cancel the security lunch conflicts with the testimony of company officials, who have no reason to lie, that he did cancel the security lunch after he was told that a lunch would be (or was) delivered to him from outside. The grievant's integrity is open to question but it is not the issue: the issue is the actual possession and use of cocaine.

Third, it may be, as the employer argued, that the grievant intended to take possession of and to consume the cocaine because the grievant, a known user, might be prone to do so. However, this is speculation without proof, an insufficient basis for discharge under Section 17(a).

Conclusion

Question No. 1: Was H. discharged for just cause?

Answer: No.

Although I find that the grievant was unjustly discharged under Article 17(a), I must draw the grievant's attention to two other considerations. First, he did not appear in arbitration with "clean hands": he lied to the employer's officials after the understandable emotional reaction to M.'s visit, whereas he could have apprised the employer that the sack lunch contained cocaine. I must and do suspect that he intended to consume the cocaine because he went to get the sack lunch on the pretext that he was going to get his check; I believe the employer's officials and not the grievant when they claim that he did cancel the security lunch; and the grievant shows little, if any, understanding of the importance of the ban on intoxicants because he went out of his way to ask O., at security, why she did not destroy the evidence when she discovered that the sack lunch contained cocaine.

Second, I remind him that the employer has a compelling, legitimate, and abiding interest and contractual right to immediately discharge any employee, particularly a crane operator, who possesses, uses, or is under the influence of cocaine on the mill site. The employer cannot tolerate the use of cocaine because a cocaine user can seriously damage company property and injure company personnel.

I must note that the employer is not blameless: Security lied to the grievant when she told him that I. and R. had taken back the sack lunch.

Question No. 2: If not, what is the appropriate remedy?
Answer: The proper remedy is in the *Award.*

Award

(1) The employer is ordered to reinstate the grievant at its administrative convenience but no later than September 21; to pay him all wages he would have earned minus all wages he actually earned from the date of his discharge to the date of his reinstatement; and to make him whole for all benefits.

(2) The grievant is hereby ordered to hand write a letter of apology to the personnel supervisor for the lie he told on April 4; the grievant is hereby ordered to hand write a letter of thanks to the president of his union and to his representative in arbitration for the time and money spent in his defense.

(3) The union is hereby ordered to read aloud and to discuss with the grievant the first two paragraphs of the answer to Question No. 1 of this *Opinion and Award.* The union must so certify in writing to the employer no later than September 21. If the grievant and/or the union fail to write, and to transmit a copy of these four letters to the employer on or before September 21, the employer may discharge the grievant at will.

(4) The employer is hereby ordered to keep this *Opinion and Award* and a copy of the four letters in the grievant's file for one calendar year after the date of this *Award.*

EXAMPLE NO. 9

The employer discharged the employee for theft of government property and for union activity. This classic example on just cause also illustrates a principle of contract interpretation and application: past practice can nullify clear contract language.

Facts

The Project Manager, D., saw the grievant, W. (a cashier and shop steward), undercharge another employee, K., for food that was on his tray. K. admitted to D. that the grievant had undercharged him. On the next morning, another employee, Y., asked D. why the grievant had charged him the full price for his breakfast. The grievant had never charged him the full price before. D. discharged the grievant for theft of government property. The union grieved the discharge and the parties proceeded to arbitration.

Questions

Question No. 1: Was the grievant discharged for just cause?

Question No. 2: Was the grievant discharged for her activities as a union steward?

Question No. 3: If not, what is the appropriate remedy?

Applicable Contract Language and Company Policy Provisions

Article XV, Discharge, p. 13, reads:

... In cases involving theft, malicious mischief, or violation of military regulations, the company may discharge without prior notice, but shall immediately notify the Union of all the facts. All discharges shall be subject to the Grievance Procedure as outlined in this Agreement.

Policy Letter #1, Employee Conduct, dated 8/17, reads:
Theft of Government property and/or property of this company is prohibited. Violation will result in termination of employment.

Policy Letter #8, Managerial Authority dated 8/17, reads:
The Project Manager works under the direct authority of the sole owner of the Management Group and is responsible for management of the Food Service Attendant Contract at the Air Force Base.

Policy Letter #9, Cashier's Duties, dated 9/30, reads:
Cashiers are expected to be courteous to patrons and to pay strict attention to identifying patrons, entering the correct food prices or meal card numbers, collecting money and returning correct change to the patrons. They shall offer cash receipts to patrons and account for all cash and meals furnished to meal card holders....

Cashiers are expected to be completely accurate throughout their performance of their duties. Cashiers found appropriating monies to their own use which belong to the company or to the government will be terminated.

Argument

Question No. 1: Was employee W. discharged for just cause?

Answer: No.

There is no argument over the employer's right to promulgate and to enforce rules or over the following facts: that both the collective bargaining agreement and the employer's policy letters explicitly make theft of government property a dischargeable offense; that the employer gave explicit notice that theft of government property could result in termination of employment; and that the grievant, a shop steward, was aware of the collective bargaining agreement and the policy letters. The argument is over the bindingness of the rule. The union's argument is simple and direct: past practice has destroyed the legal force of the rule against undercharging, construed as a theft.

For several years food service contract employees, under a variety of management companies at the air base, had either received their meals free or had paid less than the stated price at the dining halls where they worked. A previous Project Manager had directed cashiers to charge fellow employees for only a portion of what they ate. Persons, called "supervisors," knew and participated in the practice, both as purchasers and as cashiers. The various managements had never promulgated a rule to contravene the practice until D. terminated the grievant.

To counter the union's argument, the employer point out that management did not know of nor did it ever participate in the practice; only the employees did. Management never instructed cashiers to charge co-employees less for their meals. Further, the previous companies were not affiliated with the present company; these companies held different contracts with the government; and the present company was not a party to the contract between the other companies and the government.

The employer's arguments fail because the employer's arguments do not relate to nor do they justify the discharge.

The discharge was improper for many reasons. First, the employer incorrectly concluded that the grievant committed theft. The grievant was not guilty of theft, she did not appropriate monies which belong to the employer or to the government for her own use, a clear requirement in *Policy Letter #9*.

Second, past practice had destroyed the clear intent of the language. It is a primary, sacrosanct, and well-established principle of contract law that clear contract language is superior to past practice, but a well-established past practice can, and here did, nullify the legal force of a clear rule. The parties, by their daily, continuous, uninterrupted actions, have caused the rule to fall into desuetude. The past practice, not the clear rule, has concretely fixed the relations between the parties; it has given their relationship context, life, and vitality, and it has created and fixed a *modus vivendi et operandi,* an agreed upon, though tacit, method on "how things were to be done." The past practice, known by all, applied uniformly and consistently by all, and uncontested by the employer, has created a prescriptive right, the right to food at less than the stated cost. Therefore, employees are legally entitled to the right.

I find it hard to believe that the Project Manager, clearly an energetic and vigilant sort, was unaware of the practice. In any case, he should have been aware of the practice because it is his obligation to know what cashiers are doing. He should have known about the practice because his supervisors (shift leaders), who knew about and participated in the practice, should have told him about the practice.

Third, the employer discharged the grievant without an investigation.

Fourth, it is intrinsically unfair and arbitrary to seek to impose the strict observance of a rule after the employer or his agents had acquiesced in its non-observance and tacitly had tolerated violations of its rule. It is unfair to condone non-observance today and insist on strict observance by fiat tomorrow. To revive a rule, management must promulgate by publicly posting in customary and conspicuous places a written notice that, on a given date, the old rule will be strictly enforced.

Fifth, the employer invidiously discriminated against the grievant. The employer disciplined the grievant and only the grievant for the violation of the rule. If the employer had cause to discharge the grievant, it also had cause to discharge, and was obligated to discharge, all other cashiers, including his supervisors who had undercharged for meals.

> *Question No. 2*: Was the grievant discharged for her activities as union steward?
>
> *Answer*: Yes.

I have given great weight to the Project Manager's report to his supervisors and significant credit to the affidavit of A. because the employer did not dispute the facts in her affidavit.

These two documents show that the Project Manager not only disliked the grievant, but that he was "out to get" the grievant for her union activities. D. had conducted a survey of 25 management personnel at the air base. He had asked: "Are you satisfied with your days off?" He reported to his supervisors that during the survey he found the grievant's behavior "totally out of line" when he learned that the grievant had told employees "Tell him no, you want Saturday and Sunday off." He declared that her actions harmed good order and morale, and he believed that she had lost her "credibility." He told his superiors: "I feel that it would be in the best interest of the union and the working personnel to elect a new shop steward."

A., a former representative of the union and once in charge of food service at the air base, deposed that B., assistant management president, told her during a discussion of general problems at the air base that if the union were not careful and if it kept pressing on various problems, management would fire the shop steward, W., just as it had fired the union's shop steward at another base. She also deposed that D., in a discussion about the scheduling of employees on weekends, said that W. was a "trouble-maker" because she (the grievant) had encouraged other employees to register protests on working conditions. A. had defended the grievant and said that the grievant, as shop steward, had the obligation to speak to other employees about violations of the agreement and other job-related problems. A. also deposed that when she met with D. to discuss various matters, D. told her that he believed that it was the grievant who had told the base commander that he, D., was having an affair with one of management's employees. D. said that if the base commander confirmed the statement, he would fire the grievant. D. also said that the grievant had interfered in his management because she tried to get employees to sign a document that showed their dissatisfaction with their work schedules. A. replied that the grievant had every right to do so because she was the shop steward.

Question No. 3: What is the appropriate remedy?

Answer: The appropriate remedy is the *Award*.

Award

1. The employer is hereby ordered to make the grievant whole for all lost pay and benefits. Specifically, the employer is ordered to reinstate the grievant to her former position with full back pay, benefits, and seniority at its administrative convenience, but not later than (date).

2. The employer is hereby ordered not to make anti-union statements or to take any other action that might be construed to be anti-union action. If an arbitrator finds that the employer has willfully failed to comply with this order, the arbitrator may impose punitive damages payable to the union.

3. I retain complete jurisdiction over the interpretation and application of the *Opinion and Award* until (date).

EXAMPLE NO. 10

This opinion on the discharge of a service technician, though lengthy, is worth a complete reading because it discusses not only the reasons for the discharge, that is, the falsification of time records, unauthorized absences, harassing fellow employees, and causing morale problems, but also the many issues that might arise at a hearing: the admissibility of certain evidence, the credibility of witnesses, the sequestration of witnesses, the function of a union steward, the admissibility of post-arbitration evidence, and the arbitrator's power over the remedy.

Facts

From approximately (date) to (date), W., the grievant, a service technician, worked for the employer. After the grievant's property was devastated by a flood, he filed a claim with the Bureau of Reclamation to recover from the damage. During his employment, he had problems with his supervisors and other employees. The employer issued the grievant a warning letter which provided in part:

> Continued attitude problems and harassment which cause morale problems will result in your termination. This warning and all of the memos will stay in your file until the problem has been cleared up in two years. A six-months (minimum) follow-up will be written on these problems. Consider this as a warning letter and any more of this harassment will be considered as grounds for termination.

The warning letter specifically asked the grievant "to put the flood behind you . . . concentrate on your job and your attitude . . . quit looking for problems." The warning letter pinpointed the employer's complaints: "This constant harassment you are creating is causing morale problems throughout the company and very much more so in your division." The employer urged the grievant to "work toward harmony and getting along, doing your job and a feeling of togetherness. It is not us versus you. It is us working together."

The warning letter was explained to the grievant, he was told that the harassment of his supervisors consisted "primarily of his writing one-sided memoranda" to supervisors which he sent throughout the company. The memoranda contained "half-truths and innuendos about his supervisors," tended to malign their character and job performance, and caused a morale problem. The company also explained to the grievant that he was creating a morale problem throughout the division because he refused call-outs and because he had a recording device on his telephone to say conveniently that he had not received the calls or had not been at home at the time of the calls.

The grievant filed a grievance that objected to the contents in the Warning Letter (Union Exh. 9); he alleged that the employer violated Article I (Union Exh. 10), an article which obliged the employer to give its employees "considerate and courteous" treatment. The employer thought Article I inapplicable; its right to discipline employees could be found in Article V, Section I, to wit:

The Company has the function, right, and responsibility...to transfer, suspend, demote, discipline, or discharge for cause." (Union Exh. 10)

In the same exhibit, the employer said to the grievant "you still have a problem interpreting and understanding written procedures...even after we had a meeting...and a warning letter." The grievance was ultimately dropped at a meeting between management and a labor representative which also included the grievant. At that meeting, the employer told the grievant that the *Warning Letter* had had little effect on his conduct: he threatened lawsuits, he still kept sending memoranda, and he still objected to the dispatching and logging systems.

The employer reviewed the *Warning Letter* and concluded that the grievant had improved in some areas but that he had not improved in the area mentioned in the above-quoted portion of the *Warning Letter*. Since problems continued, the employer suspended the grievant for an indefinite period. The company supervisor wrote:

This letter is to substantiate in writing what we covered in a meeting this morning in the office notifying you of suspension from your work duties. Those in attendance at the meeting were myself, and as requested by you, J. You were notified by myself that you are suspended from your job until indefinite or further notice. We informed you at the time, that your suspension is based on your failure to notify your immediate supervisor or designate to request time off from your work.

After the company's vice-president and the director of personnel investigated the reasons for the suspension, they concluded not only that the suspension was justified but also that the employer had just, compelling, and legitimate reasons to discharge the grievant. Therefore, the employer verbally discharged the grievant in the presence of the business manager for the union and the union steward. The employer specified the reasons: the grievant had taken unauthorized absences, falsified certain time records, conducted personal business on the employer's time, engaged in the disruption of the work atmosphere, and precipitated or exacerbated morale problems. The employee had attempted:

constant derailment of management and their directives in the presence of other employees in the division. Additionally, our investigation indicated that you have made statements to employees that you were not going to comply with management directives which, indeed, causes morale problems and unrest in the office.

Unable to resolve the grievance in the grievance procedure, the parties proceeded to arbitration.

Questions

The parties agreed to submit the following questions:

Question No. 1: Was the discharge of W. from employment in violation of the employment contract between the company and the union?

Answer: If so, what is the proper remedy?

Argument

The answers to these two questions depend on (a) whether certain evidence is admissible, (b) on the probative value that I attach to the evidence, and (c) on the application of the criteria for discharge.

On the Admissibility of Certain Evidence

Sequestration of Witnesses. At the beginning of the hearing, I granted the employer's motion that no witness be allowed to hear the testimony of any other witness. Toward the end of the hearing, I denied the union's motion to reconsider the ruling because a change in procedure would place the prospective witness in a privileged position.

On the Admissibility of Post-Termination Evidence and on the Remedy. During the hearing, the employer sought to introduce evidence on the grievant's post-termination conduct. The employer believed that since the grievant's post-termination conduct was intimately tied to the question of reinstatement, the arbitrator had discretionary power on the reinstatement even if he found that the grievant was discharged without just cause. The union objected and argued that post-termination evidence was irrelevant to the just cause question because Article X reads:

> In the absence of just cause for such discharge, the employee shall be reinstated and shall be paid for the time lost at his regular rate of pay for the work being performed by him at the time of such discharge.

Since this clear language prescribed the remedy, the union argued that the arbitrator had no discretionary power over the remedy; the arbitrator must reinstate with back pay if he finds no just cause for discharge. If the parties had wanted to vest the arbitrator with discretionary power, they would have done so; he can neither modify nor add to that agreement.

Initially, after a quick reading, I ruled that Article X, Section 1, foreclosed all consideration of appropriate remedies: I could find no discretionary power in the clear and specific contract language.

The company moved for a reconsideration of the motion. To ensure that the company's argument was fairly and fully heard, I directed the employer to submit written answers to the following three questions before 8:00 P.M. The questions and the answers were as follows:

Question No. 1: Does the contractual language allow for arbitral discretion?

The employer admitted that the language might appear to mandate reinstatement with full back pay from the date of discharge if the arbitrator finds that "just cause" for discharge does not exist. However, the arbitrator does have discretionary power over the remedy because the parties seek to obtain the arbitrator's interpretation of the contract, the contractual language must be applied in light of the circumstances, the language contains ambiguities, and the parties have asked the arbitrator a second question: "What is the appropriate remedy?"

Such a submission confers on the arbitrator considerable discretion on the remedy despite the seemingly clear language of the contract. Further, when the contract does not cover the issue precisely and where there is no specific prohibition against the exercise of discretionary power, the arbitrator should fashion an award appropriate to the circumstances. The discretionary power to fashion remedies is inherent in arbitration. Hence, this discretionary power allows the arbitrator to take into account the grievant's post-termination conduct.

Question No. 2: Would not the exercise of this so-called discretionary power be tantamount to a change in the contractual language?

The employer argued that so long as the discretionary power is drawn from the contract, its exercise is proper; it does not modify or change the contract. Indeed, the contract does speak to the issue of remedy upon post-termination conduct. Therefore, under the broad submission of the remedy issue and under the accepted rulings of the discretionary power of the arbitrator, such exercise would be well within the confines of the contract itself.

Question No. 3: If the grievant is no longer an employee of the Company, how do the terms of the collective bargaining agreement reach him?

The employer's response was: the employer does not dispute the union's right to grieve the discharge of the grievant. Since remedies are within the arbitrator's discretion to fashion, he can only do so upon full hearing of all the proper evidence, including the post-termination evidence.

After I read the employer's lengthy *Memorandum*, prepared under the pressure of time, I ruled as follows:

Since the admissibility of post-termination evidence reaches the two most serious matters in this dispute, viz., (1) "discharge for just cause" issue, and (2) the very real question of justice to both the grievant and to the employer, I hereby rule that (1) I will hear all the post-termination evidence on the grounds that arbitration proceedings overwhelmingly favor more rather than less evidence, even hearsay, irrelevant, or inadmissible evidence; (2) I will determine the admissibility of the post-termination evidence after I have given the arguments of the parties extended consideration; (3) the reasons for my decision in the admissibility of post-termination evidence will be argued in full in my *Opinion and Award.*

It is true that the basis for the discharge was the grievant's conduct before the actual date of the discharge. But since reinstatement, if ordered, renews the old work relationship, the arbitrator should and must consider the grievant's post-termination conduct, i.e., his attitude and behavior toward that relationship, before he either restores or finally dissolves the relationship, i.e., he may reinstate either conditionally or absolutely.

Ruling No. 1.: The arbitrator has the right and the duty to consider post-termination evidence.

Ruling No. 2.: The arbitrator has the discretionary power to fashion a remedy if he finds that the grievant was discharged without just cause.

On the Evidence

At the lengthy hearing and in their *Briefs*, the parties entered extensive evidence on the three charges against the grievant, namely, 1) that the grievant falsified his time records, 2) that the grievant harassed fellow employees and his supervisors, and, 3) that the grievant caused morale problems.

Alleged Time Record Discrepancies. The employer charged that the grievant falsified his time reports in September, in November, and in August.

On September (date). Soon after the flood, the grievant filed for bankruptcy and turned control of his assets over to a bankruptcy trustee. Prior to September, the government determined the amount it would pay the grievant on his claim. The trustee was inclined to accept the offer to pay off debts, but the grievant wanted to appeal. The uncontested testimony is that on September (date), the grievant spoke by telephone to the government's claim verifier during his lunch hour. He talked to the verifier beyond 1:00 P.M. and returned to work at 1:45 P.M. On his time sheet on September (date) (Company Exh. 14), the grievant recorded "personal emergency," identified as code 9905 (Company Exh. 10) which is "unexcused absence without pay." At the bottom left-hand portion of the time report, the grievant wrote that he was eligible for payment of eight hours straight time. Upon discovery, his supervisor denied the request because the grievant had not requested a leave of absence from his supervisor. The grievant was not paid for the 45 minutes of unauthorized absence.

The employer did not consider this incident "cause for alarm," but it did view the incident as a "lack of concern for Company procedure" (Company *Brief*, p. 7). The union argued that the grievant reported his absence "accurately and honestly"; he "contemplated such a situation" where no excuse was possible; no one had ever told him differently; and previously, his supervisor had talked to the grievant whenever he discovered a mistake or an inaccuracy on the time sheets. In this case, however, his supervisor never said a word to the grievant about the incident until over two months later at his suspension.

On November (date). The grievant reported on his time sheet for November (date) (Company Exh. 15) that he was engaged in company business all afternoon. He recorded that he had worked on his truck for 15 minutes, from 1:00 P.M. until 1:15 P.M.; that from 1:15 until 4:30 he was at the office at a meeting (job code 9915—"training and meetings"); and that from 4:30 to 5:00 p.m. he was engaged in a pre-inspection of customer equipment (job code 1045—"pre-inspection, customer equipment").

The employer charged that the grievant falsified his time report. While at home for lunch on that day, he called S., the dispatcher, to tell her he was going to take the rest of the afternoon off to take care of his claim. However, upon call, he attended a service personnel meeting on the standby system in the afternoon.

The grievant's explanation was that he was preoccupied with his claim. He said that the bankruptcy trustee and court were pressing him to accept the claim by the end of December. If he did not do so he would lose approximately $100,000. The grievant's account was that during his lunch hour he returned S.'s morning telephone call. S. wanted more information on the claim by that afternoon. The grievant planned to take the afternoon off to take care of his claim.

The grievant explained his time sheet recording for the afternoon: the truck would not start, he fixed the truck, got gas, and attended the meeting. "Thinking he would use vacation time, he had not been paying attention to the time" (Union *Brief*, p. 5). Therefore, he allotted 15 minutes to service the vehicle (code 1098), and estimated his arrival at the office at 1:15 P.M., although he conceded that he actually arrived later.

How much later did he arrive? The employer's two supervisors remembered the time at 2:28 P.M. because they looked at the clock when he reported; two service technicians remembered 2:30 P.M. (Company Exh. 40 and 41). The union suspected the testimony of the two supervisors identical recollection. The union also challenged one supervisor's recollection that N., another service technician, arrived before the grievant and that everyone was waiting for the grievant to arrive because both N. and the grievant distinctly remembered that the grievant came before N., who estimated his arrival at 2:00 P.M. To reinforce his testimony, the union relied on the grievant's personal log (Union Exh. 24), which showed 1:15 P.M. as "estimated" time, the "truck tampered with," and that he had written "no way to charge vacation." Whatever the evidence, the union concluded that there was no discrepancy in his time sheet, and, in any event, "the misreporting was insignificant and unintentional" (Union *Brief*, p. 8).

The employer did not consider the matter insignificant. To take vacation in the afternoon without authorization is a serious violation of employer policy (Company *Brief*, p. 9). It did not seem reasonable to the employer that the grievant merely estimated the time at the meeting because the grievant generally reported accurately.

On November (date). The grievant reported on his time sheet for the afternoon of November (date), (Company Exh. 16), that he was on vacation from 1:00 P.M. until 5:00 P.M. The employer charged that the grievant took vacation time without authorization in spite of the fact that he knew, understood, and previously had conformed to the employer's vacation policy (Company Exh. 19).

The grievant's explanation was that his memo to his supervisor (Union Exh. 12) was notice that he would use vacation time whenever he "unexpectedly" needed time off to settle his claim. Admittedly, it was a general request for vacation time, but he could not know in advance exactly when he would need time off to work on his claim. Since his supervisor did not respond to the memo, he assumed, as in the past, that silence meant approval. On this assumption, the grievant called S. at the claims office; he also telephoned his supervisor, who was not there; and he also called the dispatcher to tell her that he would work on his claim in the afternoon, and told her to call him if necessary. He worked all afternoon at home, and he went to the claims office after 5:00 P.M. The union concluded that the grievant recorded his time sheet for November (date) honestly as "Vacation, personal emergency."

The employer countered that the union *Exhibit 12* requests no specific time off; it simply apprised the grievant's supervisor that some time in the future the grievant might need time off to work on his claim and certain legal matters. His supervisor's lack of response cannot be considered a blanket approval for vacation time off. The grievant simply took the matter into his own hands, took vacation time when he wanted, and interpreted his general request "so as to get himself out of trouble." The employer viewed its vacation policy as especially important for a service technician: a supervisor must know who is available, especially in emergencies.

On August (date). The employer discovered this alleged time discrepancy during its investigation of the suspension. The grievant reported in his time sheet for August (date) that he performed a pre-inspection of customer equipment from 3:50 P.M. until 4:30 P.M. The two employer investigators concluded that the grievant had not conducted this pre-inspection.

The employer relied on the testimony of S., the dispatcher, and W., a local dealer. S. testified that on the afternoon of August (date), W. called to request a service technician to perform a pressure test on a gas dryer he was hooking up for a customer. The dispatcher told him that a service man would not be available until 4:00 P.M. At approximately 4:10 she gave the grievant the customer order. Shortly after she gave the grievant the customer order, he picked up the telephone and talked to the claims office until approximately 6:00 P.M. She also testified that while the grievant was on the telephone, the local dealer called twice for a serviceman. Twice she interrupted the grievant to tell him that the dealer was waiting for him.

W. corroborated the testimony. He and his assistant waited until shortly after 5:00 P.M. At that time no service technician had yet performed the pressure test. However, when W. went back to the house the next day, the pressure test had been performed, the piece of equipment had been fired off, and a green tag had been left on the meter.

The union contended that the grievant's time sheet "accurately reflected the work he did that day." (Union *Brief*, pp. 7–8). The grievant directly contradicted S.'s and W.'s testimony: he categorically denied that he made a telephone call to the claims office. He testified that he performed the pressure test from 3:50 P.M. to 4:30 P.M.

Whom should the arbitrator believe: The grievant or S.? The union urged the arbitrator to believe the grievant, not S. The grievant always accurately recorded his contacts with the claims office. S. was not a reliable witness; her animosity toward the grievant was well-known. According to N., she makes false accusations against servicemen; according to M., she "lives in a fantasy world"; and according to M. and B., she lied about her tardiness, about the length of her breaks, and about doing personal business on company time. The work order (Union Exh. 27) shows that S. did the pressure test, and W. admitted that the test was done. W.'s three to four phone calls to the office were made from inside the house while the test was made outside the house on the meter; W. was a continual violator of the gas code who expressed displeasure at being "red-tagged" by going above the servicemen/inspectors' heads to their supervisors.

Neither S. nor the grievant are credible. Their interest colored their selective memory; personal differences obscured their judgments; their testimony, ostensibly candid and forthright, was coolly and designedly calculated. Several witnesses tellingly impugned S.'s credibility and character. The grievant's testimony is also suspect: too many witnesses contradict him; there is too much objective evidence against his statements.

However, the absence of overwhelming, positive, and probative evidence does not lead to the union's overall conclusion that the alleged time sheet irregularities were either "not irregular at all" or that they were "so insignificant and innocent that anyone could have made the same errors" (Union *Brief*, p. 9). The irregularities are there; he was not entitled to eight hours of straight time pay for November, as he claimed, and he did show a cavalier attitude toward the company's vacation policy even if he had had blank permission (a doubtful premise based on a doubtful assumption). Discrepancies in time sheets and non-compliance with company policy are neither "innocent" nor trivial matters. As the company pointed out, these matters are serious matters; they not only reach into the grievant's probity and moral character, but they also touch on the company's legal claim against an employee.

Nonetheless, the grievant's explanations are plausible, if somewhat shaky: he did report accurately, for example; "unexcused without pay"; he did apologize to his supervisor for his unauthorized absence; and he did request a memo of clarification so it would not happen again (Company Exh. 9). It is more than likely that the grievant's preoccupation with the resolution of his financial status with his claim could account for, but not justify, his time record inaccuracies and his apparent unwillingness to and carelessness about seeking formal permission for vacation time. The union's conclusion that "These time sheet problems do not constitute 'just cause' for discharge" and that "Discharge is far too severe a penalty for these mistakes" (Union *Brief*, p. 11) is correct but only if the discharge were based solely on the time record discrepancies.

Nor does the evidence support the employer's vague, broad, and all-encompassing conclusion that the grievant was "not willing to work with his employer," . . . "to allow his employer to provide a back-up for him when he was not at work," . . . that the grievant "took the matter into his own hands," . . . and that he attempted "to cover his tracks by calling non-supervisory personnel and telling them he was going to take time off or by writing a blanket memorandum telling his supervisor he was going to take some time off in the future." Certainly such activities, from the employer's perspective, are not "in the best interest of the Employer": they flout the "reasonable rules developed by the employer," and they "disregard the authority of supervisors."

To restate, the time record discrepancies alone do not justify discharge.

Alleged Harassment. The employer charged that the grievant harassed both his fellow employees and his supervisors even after the *Warning Letter* which specifically pointed to "continued attitude problems and harassment which causes morale problems" (Company Exh. 6). The employer contended that the grievant's conduct on numerous instances constituted harassment of his supervisors.

What the employer considered harassment, the union construed as the grievant's attempt to explain his situation as he did in his *Letter* of February. What H. considered "harassment" was what the grievant considered as "doing his job as steward" (Union, *Brief*, p. 10).

In general, the employer alleged (1) that the grievant constantly complained and griped about the employer's policies and about his supervisors; (2) that the grievant attempted to undermine his supervisor's authority because he questioned their decisions and he refused to cooperate in the collective endeavor; (3) that the grievant wanted to run the office his way; (4) that he misquoted, maligned, and made false accusations about his supervisors; and (5) that the grievant promoted dissension among his fellow employees. To substantiate these general allegations, the employer cited the specific incidents discussed below.

The Doctor's Certificate. The union steward suggested to management that it require the grievant to get a doctor's certificate. When management asked the grievant over the telephone to provide a doctor's certificate, the grievant, according to one supervisor, became angry, accused management of harassment, and presented management with a doctor's certificate which contained the following notation: "As W.'s supervisor, I have requested he go to a doctor for a note, to prove he has been ill the last two (2) days. W. has been off a total of eleven (11) days last year. At W.'s request, we will pay costs. We are trying to discourage any use of sick leave, if possible, by all employees." The bottom of the note also states "as per telephone conversation with R." (Company Exh. 11).

The employer thought that the grievant's writing of Company *Exhibit 11* was "direct and obvious harassment of the supervisor" because no member of management either wrote or authorized *Exhibit 11*. Furthermore, a supervisor flatly denied that the employer policy was to discourage the use of sick leave or that the employer would pay for the cost of the visit to the doctor's office. The employer believed that the grievant did this not only "to make the employer look bad with regard to sick leave policy" but as "ammunition for a grievance he intended to file against the employer on a matter which angered him" (Company *Brief*, p. 30).

The grievant claimed that he prepared the draft, that he read it to his supervisor over the phone, and that he had obtained his supervisor's approval. Both J. and M. corroborated the grievant's testimony; J. heard the grievant read and make changes in the draft; M. heard the conversation, and he typed what the grievant had written. However, the supervisor flatly denied that the telephone conversation ever took place. The employer disbelieved J. and M.: "It seems strange that both would recall the conversation when the supervisor, who testified under oath, said that no such conversation took place"..."they heard only one side of the conversation, they were not in any position to know whether or not R. really was on the other end of the telephone" (Company *Brief*, p. 31). The employer concluded that the grievant was "obviously setting the employer up for a grievance over a matter that disturbed him... the grievant feigned having such a telephone conversation...to build a case against the employer on the grievance."

The union simply said that the memo was "an accurate reflection of what was said to the grievant and approved by the supervisor" (Union *Brief*, p. 16).

On the Writing of Letters and Requests for Clarification. At the grievant's progress review, a meeting in April, the employer told the grievant to "stop unnecessary letter-writing." Again, after the grievant had filed a grievance on his *Warning Letter*, his supervisor's denial of his grievance included the admonition: "Again, I suggest that you put a stop to any unnecessary letter writing" (Union Exh. 11). At a meeting shortly after that, the grievant's supervisor told him that he would get in trouble if he continued to write letters.

The union admitted that the letter writing did get the grievant into trouble. The justification for all this letter writing was: "a union steward cannot be denied the right to effectively communicate in writing...the letter writing was not harassment but simply good practice for a union steward" (Union *Brief*, pp. 13, 14). The employer objected not to the letter writing but to the one-sided memoranda which contained "half-truths and innuendos" (Company *Brief*, pp. 36–39). One supervisor testified that even the union steward in another local thought that the grievant's letters contained false accusations and innuendos that constituted harassment.

The employer also objected to the grievant's "barrage of requests for clarification," but the union thought that these requests were "thoughtful, courteous questions about working conditions and policies that were not answered in the personnel manual"; they were "an attempt by a conscientious union steward to obtain written and explicit clarifications that affected the employee's working conditions" (Union *Brief*, p. 13). Furthermore, "the filing of grievances cannot be harassment because it is a protected activity. It cannot be grounds for discharge; H.'s ignorance of union matters demonstates his refusal to recognize the union, its steward, or its function as agent for employees" (Union *Brief*, p. 15).

The Letter of February 15—From the Grievant to H. This letter, a major source of harassment and the "straw that broke the camel's back," prompted the *Letter of Warning*. Although addressed to H., the uncontested fact is that H. never received a copy of the *Letter* until it was sent to him by L. In the *Letter*, the grievant stated that on the Wednesday after the day of the flood, a supervisor, B., went to his house and told him to be at work the next day or he would not have a job. B. flatly denied this testimony; he did not go to the grievant's house on that day but he did go to the grievant's house about ten days later. To support B.'s testimony, the employer cited the grievant's own *Letter* of September to Q. (Company Exh. 2), which states that the supervisor went to the grievant's house ten days later. B. testified that he merely asked the grievant how soon he would be finished with the work on his house, and said that the grievant should come back to work as soon as he finished. The employer concluded that the grievant's statement against this particular supervisor simply intended to "benefit the grievant and cast a bad light" on the supervisor, and purposely harass management.

The *Letter* also states that the grievant worked Saturday night and Sunday after the flood, took Monday, Tuesday, and Wednesday off, and returned to work the next day; that he worked seven days a week for two weeks; that he was denied all personal time, all vacation time, or a 40 hour work week; that he had very little time off; that a clash developed between him and the supervisor; and that the supervisor denigrated the grievant to anyone who would listen. The *Letter* also accused management of abusive treatment and lack of consideration.

Employer witnesses contested the accuracy of all these damaging statements. Q. testified that during the first two months after the flood, the grievant was absent from work for over 25 days for personal business, vacation or sick leave; that the employer gave the grievant approximately a week to ten days off right after the flood so he could get his personal affairs in order; that the employer provided two company men to help him dig out his basement; that the employer gave the grievant $1,000 to replace personal items; and that the employer obtained two pumps so the grievant could pump out water from his house.

The employer's conclusion is simple: the grievant was not treated unfairly during the aftermath of the flood; the employer did its best to ease the grievant's personal loss. In sum, the *Letter* of February (Company Exh. 7) constitutes "harassment of management by statements of half-truths, or, indeed, total falsehoods . . . the grievant maligned his operations manager because he sent the *Letter* to other supervisors but not to H." (Company *Brief*, p. 36).

The union says that "it is unfortunate that the letter was not at first received by H. but surely was not intentional" (Union *Brief*, p. 14) because the grievant had never been "shy about sending correspondence" and "it was intended to improve relations with H." Furthermore, the employer's charge that the *Letter* was one-sided is "specious" because communications between labor and management are by nature one-sided.

The *Letter* did not purport to be "an objective historical treatise by a neutral observer"; . . . the grievant admitted that it was the truth "as I see it."

The Company Manual. Shortly after the unsatisfactory employee progress review in April (Company Exh. 18), the grievant sent copies of certain pages and paragraphs of the company's personnel manual (Company Exh. 44) to E., the business manager of the union. The company regarded this action as a violation of manual procedure. At a meeting with the business manager and the grievant in May, the grievant admitted the transmittal but said he was not aware of this company policy and the company's interpretation of that policy. The grievant thought that a union official was "a part of the company and helped to run the company"; . . . he "could see no reason why he would be in violation of this procedure" (Union Exh. 6). The grievant wrote to W., a supervisor:

Please return, in writing, your permission to release all of Chapter I to E. Your interpretation that reproduced paragraphs constitutes release of the manual itself is highly questionable and will require a grievance to clarify. All information previously sent to R pertained to a pending grievance. (Union Exh. 23)

Later in May, the company filed an additional written warning against the grievant which charged that the grievant violated Section M of the Chapter entitled "That Little Bit Extra," paragraph 3, which reads:

While the Personnel Manual is available to you, it cannot be loaned to anyone and is not available to those outside the company except by approval of the director of personnel.

The company did not accept the grievant's interpretation of the rule that an employee could make public certain paragraphs and pages, but not the whole book. The company believed that the grievant used this type of policy "interpretation" and "clarification" to suit "his personal desires at a particular time" and as "an obvious trumped up request for policy or procedure clarification" (Company *Brief*, p. 38).

On the Dispatching System. On November 2, the grievant's supervisor conducted a six-month follow-up review of the April *Warning Letter* (Union Exh. 4). The review pointed to some improvement. Other areas needed to be improved, specifically point No. 8 of the *Warning Letter* stated:

Change your attitude about dispatching, the use of code 10 signal, and the keeping of the log. Several meetings have now been held on this subject. Your understanding of it should be completed, and we expect your cooperation to make it work the way it should and does elsewhere in the company system.

During the tenure of one supervisor, the division manager and the service technicians determined the priority of customer orders. After H. became manager, he required the dispatcher to do so. H. also required servicemen to call in on the radio whenever they changed locations, and to ask the dispatcher to record the calls on a radio log. All service technicians complained about the new procedure. The technicians believed that they were better qualified than the inexperienced S. to determine the priority of orders. They complained that they did not always receive a "clearing signal" when they called in on the radio, and that their calls did not always show up on the log.

The company recognized the inherent difficulties in the implementation of the new dispatching system, particularly since the dispatcher was inexperienced. After management explained its necessity and value, all technicians except the grievant ceased their complaints. However, the grievant "continued to make an issue of the dispatching and logging systems on a regular basis until the time he was discharged." He even questioned its necessity. He "continually complained about them and attempted to undermine them" (Company *Brief*, p. 19).

The union's defense was that the grievant did not object to the dispatching system but "to the way the dispatcher handled them"; . . . "his interest was in seeing that it was operated efficiently." . . . "He may have been more vocal than others, but his duties as a steward involved being a spokesman for the group" (Union *Brief*, p. 17).

On the Standby Procedure. H. also instituted a standby system whereby the servicemen were required to be available for calls on Saturday. Previously, call-out was voluntary. Supervisors explained the new standby procedure for Saturdays. At first, the Saturday standby procedure was explained only to J. and N. because the grievant was reading meters. Shortly thereafter, the grievant asked the company to hold another meeting on the standby system. The two supervisors met with the three service personnel, described the standby procedure, and pointed out that the answering service had not been able to locate servicemen in the area to take care of emergency situations and inclement weather had made it difficult and dangerous for servicemen outside the area to take care of the problems.

All three service technicians complained about the standby procedure; however, the grievant complained vehemently and vociferously. According to the company, the grievant engaged in protracted argument with his supervisors; the grievant told N. and J. that he intended to refuse standby orders because he had to devote all of his working with his verifier on his claim. He also removed the standby schedule from the bulletin board.

The union admitted that the grievant may have been more vocal than the others: this was his duty as steward. As steward, the grievant simply pointed to the contract which states, in Article XVII, Section 1: "On weekends every effort will be made to avoid change in the standby duty man which would result in breaking a man's weekend." The grievant simply insisted that every alternative be considered; he was doing nothing more than his steward's job to uphold the contract.

The union admits that the grievant removed the posted standby schedule. The union's explanation: the grievant sent the schedule to H. so that he could find a replacement and correct the schedule because the grievant's name was erased and R.'s name put on the schedule (Company Exh. 48a and 48c). The union concluded that the removal was based on a "reasonable expectation" and was not intended to harass (Union *Brief*, p. 19); nor did the grievant, in actual fact, ever refuse standby. All the grievant said was that "Personal emergency [was] making Saturday call impossible"..."I cannot work this Saturday" (Company Exh. 12). H. testified that along with Company Exh. 12, he received the standby schedule that had been posted in the office. The grievant wrote on the back of the standby schedule:

I have no options—during the flood I made a choice—THIS IS AN EMERGENCY AND I HAVE TO TAKE CARE OF MY CLAIM. I AM OUT OF TIME.

The company concluded that "It is obvious that Company *Exhibit 12* was a refusal to work the standby ordered by his supervisors." The company believed that the grievant made a choice: he put personal matters before the company business; "he took the matter in his own hands...he simply was refusing the order of his supervisors" (Company *Brief*, 41–42).

The company cited portions of this *Letter* as another example of "half truth and complete falsehoods." Subsequent to his suspension for time record discrepancies, the grievant wrote the *Letter* that justified his absences and his views and actions on standby. He said: "All my spare time was essential especially this Saturday because of claims pressure." Rephrased: he had to comply with the demands of the claims office made on his time without prior notice. He wrote:

Then asked J., no supervisors in office. Asked her not to plan any work after lunch I had another meeting. I called the other area but D. was out to lunch also. I was unable to call back and when I spent til 6:30 in the claims office I again had to charge vacation.

The company pointed out that the *Letter's* explanation of the occurrences in November is "in direct conflict with what he stated at the hearing...and that numerous other witnesses testified tht he was indeed at a meeting at the office from 2:30 P.M. until 4:30 P.M." H. denied at the hearing that he said that the grievant was indefinitely suspended to teach him a lesson and that "he would find other ways to teach the grievant a lesson if he had to." H. testified that the reason that the grievant was suspended was for unauthorized absences. The conclusion of the company was that "facts as you presented them are totally incorrect" (Company Exh. 19—*Letter* of December 7).

The company also concluded that the grievant's attempt to justify the discrepancies on his time sheet for the two times in November (Company Exh. 15 and Company Exh. 16) must also fail. The company disputed the grievant's statement of facts. The grievant said that he had called a company supervisor to tell her that he had to be out of service and would be back as soon as possible, because he was preoccupied with his claim. The company also disputed the grievant's contention that "a person has no choice if you wish to get your claim processed ... but to exceed [sic] to their demands [the claims office and the court] on your time without notice" (Company Exh. 9). The company disputed this statement. The depositions (Company Exh. 23 and 22, respectively) of S. and L., verifier for the claims office, stated that the office "made no demands on the grievant's time other than ones which could easily be worked into his schedule. Any demands that were made on his time with regard to his claim were placed there by the grievant himself."

The union's defense was that "whatever" the grievant did, he did it as union steward. He did not do it to harass either his fellow employees or his supervisors:

He would not be deterred from engaging in his protected activities as steward, of requesting clarifications, of writing letters, of filing grievances, of upholding the contract, and of being spokesman for the other employees. Federal law protects his right to engage in doing them. (Union *Brief*, p. 19)

Admittedly, it is difficult for the company or anyone else to "prove" that the grievant harassed both his fellow employees and his supervisors. Incidents can always be construed as misunderstandings, as results of personality conflicts, or as unfortunate circumstances, yet the incidents reported here can and do manifest a spirit, an attitude that governs behavior, and an approach to one's fellow employees and to one's supervisors that can properly be called harassment. The evidence on the doctor's certificate is inconclusive, but it is very difficult to believe the grievant and very easy to believe his supervisor. Again, it is very difficult to believe the union's explanation that the date discrepancy in the *Letter* of February was "incorrectly typed by someone else than the grievant." It is also hard to believe that the company, and in particular H., had animus against the grievant. The undisputed evidence is that the company did help the grievant immediately after the devastation of the flood; and that the company did not, and had not treated him in a discourteous, unfair, or unjust way. The union's explanation that it is "unfortunate" and "unintentional" that the letter addressed to H. did not reach him is lame and insufficient. The letter clearly bypassed channels, affronted authority, and antagonized management. If the grievant is the experienced union steward that the union claimed him to be, he would certainly know the importance of consultation with his supervisor. The incident of the company manual is a serious matter: the grievant violated company procedure; his specious interpretation and defense were both inadequate and puerile, and the *Letter* of May simply exacerbated the tense relations. On the dispatching issue, the grievant is a constant and unwelcome complainer, not one who wants the system to run efficiently. On the standby issue, the grievant is clearly a troublesome and uncooperative employee. Obviously, after discussion and decision, an employee must perform his assigned task or quit. The workplace is not the place for long, bitter, and protracted argument; work must be done according to rules. Although the evidence is not conclusive that the grievant actually refused standby, his open intention to refuse it is very close. The spirit of disobedience precedes the disobedience itself. If, as the union argued, the grievant thought that the new standby procedure violated Article XVII, Section 1, he had the right to file a grievance. It is exactly at this point that he could properly have acted as union steward. Finally, it cannot be doubted that the claim, in process for two years, consumed a great deal of the grievant's time, but the uncontested testimony of two neutral verifiers was that the grievant's work time was never controlled by the claims office.

Even if "harassment" is not the right word to characterize the grievant's actions, other words are appropriate: the grievant is uncooperative, belligerent, hostile, and insensitive to his obligation to obey lawful orders. In short, though an excellent technician, he is an undesirable employee in the workplace. He cannot be called in any sense of the word a cooperative employee; he would work as he willed, but not at the will of another.

The Morale Problems. The company charged that the grievant's "attitude and actions combined either to cause or intensify a morale problem among his fellow employees within the division and particularly in the local office" (Company *Brief*, p. 15). The union disputes even the existence of a morale problem, and, even if one did exist, it arose out of the company's difficulty "in accepting the union and the agreement as a limitation of its unfettered discretion in operating its business" (*Prehearing Brief*, p. 2).

The company admitted that the grievant was not the sole cause of the existing morale problem because personality clashes are inevitable and personal problems affect job performance. However, the company did charge that the grievant "refused to cooperate with his fellow employees and his supervisors" and that the grievant created "an atmosphere of mistrust, confusion, and unrest among employees... not only among themselves but also toward supervision" (Company *Brief*, p. 16). The testimony of both management witnesses and the grievant's co-workers was that the grievant continually and vociferously griped about his supervisors and management policy. He questioned the authority of supervisors in front of other employees, and he incited other employees against their supervisors.

Testimony of H. H., a supervisor, testified that several of the servicemen complained to him: they continually had to cover for the grievant on call-outs in the local area. Further, the answering service could not get a hold of the grievant in the evenings for emergency situations because he had a tape recording device on his telephone, and the union steward in another local complained that the recording device on the telephone angered his servicemen.

The Testimony of S. S., the inexperienced dispatcher for the local office, testified that the grievant caused her innumerable difficulties: he constantly criticized her general job performance, particularly her log keeping of the servicemen's time which they reported over the radio. S. testified that her log was missing during the summer. After a couple of weeks she found it in the back room on a shelf. S. would move papers and boxes in front of the log but on the next day, she would find the papers and boxes shoved aside to expose the log again. S. confronted the grievant with her suspicion that he had taken the log, and the grievant responded that he had taken the log to show her incompetency. The company concluded that this evidence shows that the grievant refused to cooperate; he would not implement the system, he worked to undermine it, and he caused S. difficulties.

Testimony of B. B. testified that in November, the grievant griped and complained loudly and agitatedly in front of several employees and customers of the company: the grievant said that the standby system was unfair, it ruined his weekends, the pay was insufficient, and supervisors were incompetent and not well-disposed toward the local servicemen. These tirades were common, frequent, continuous, and different from the usual employee complaints against management.

Testimony of M. M., a friend and an apprentice, testified that the grievant not only taught him the job but that he attempted to direct his attitude and actions toward his supervisors. M. testified that the grievant griped about management nearly every day, that the grievant said to him and to other employees that the supervisors were "out to get" the employees in the local office, and that he suggested that the service personnel in another office get into their trucks and act as if they were working when supervisors were coming. M. also testified that the grievant advised him to keep his service manual available in his truck. In this way he could sleep or rest in his truck. If a supervisor came upon him unexpectedly, he could grab his manual and pretend that he was studying it. M. further testified that the grievant advised him never to talk informally with supervision; he should force supervisors to put everything in writing. He should make every effort to "pin-down" management. M. also testified that the grievant told him that the purpose of the recording device in his telephone was to monitor the calls that were coming in. This way he could accept those he wanted and reject others. M. admitted that after a while he himself got tired of the grievant's constant complaints about the company policies and supervisory personnel: that he hated to go to the office, that he himself had a bad attitude toward his job and toward his supervisors, and that all were attributable to the grievant's continual criticism of the company and its supervisors.

Five employees testified that: the grievant was a constant complainer, that he promoted unrest, and that he incited employees against management. All are intolerable actions, particularly in a senior serviceman. The company believed that they demonstrate "a wholly uncooperative attitude combined with an insidious design to wield his brand of power over other employees and supervisors" (Company *Brief*, p. 27).

In defense, the union pointed to conflict in the testimony. S. and M. said that the grievant caused the morale problem but C. testified that no morale problem existed and that the grievant "was good for morale," and J. testified that it was S. who caused whatever "upset," confusion, and "tension" existed. The office ran better when she was not there.

The union attacked the credibility of the witness: S. could not be believed because of her "obvious animosity"; M. could not be believed either because he too complained until he got the long-sought transfer and became a "re-born company man." M. was the source of the "unbelievable" testimony that the grievant used profane language "frequently" and that the grievant engaged in "doughnut and yogurt discrimination" (unfair distribution of food), testimony that was unsubstantiated by others.

The union urged the arbitrator to believe N., J., and C., because they "had no axes to grind" (Union *Brief*, p. 21). The mixed and contradictory testimony simply reflects "valid differences of opinion" and shows that the company had not met its burden of proof to establish the existence of a morale problem.

The union explained the grievant's actions about the recorder, about his advice to M., and about his griping. The grievant had the answering device and recorder on his telephone to avoid harassing phone calls from his creditors. In any event, there is no obligation to be near a telephone, there is no obligation to take the call-out even if it is recieved, and the grievant did take call-outs. The act is lawful, the servicemen's perceptions and resentments are immaterial, and the recorder had no discernible effect on morale in the office. The grievant's advice to M. made common sense: it is good practice to ask management to respond in writing and it makes good sense to be out in the field doing work rather than sitting around the office. The grievant was simply repeating a story he had heard when he advised M. to keep the manual close by in the truck so that if a supervisor ever checked, the employee could say he was reading the manual. The incident was taken out of context. None of the advice was significant, continual or disruptive enough to cause a morale problem.

The union admits that S. and the grievant "griped about everything," that he disparaged all members of management, and that M. said "the grievant complained a lot"; but S. was not very specific and M. admitted that "some were legitimate complaints." N. said "everyone griped about management," but the grievant more loudly so than the others; B. said that the grievant criticized management loudly in front of customers but he admitted it was only once. J. thought that the "griping" was simply a discussion about matters the employees did not think were right. The union's explanation is that the grievant, as steward, was simply "the most vocal and visible proponent of the group." As a result, some people naturally thought he griped more than others (Union *Brief*, p. 24), particularly when he thought employees were not being treated fairly. Hence, "there was no convincing testimony that the grievant said or did anything out of the ordinary role for a steward" (Union *Brief*, p. 26). The grievant did not cause the morale problem. H. came into the division "like a bull in a china shop," he made the employees feel that they were not doing things right. Unpopular changes, the dispatching and standby, caused the morale problem. The grievant cannot be blamed for whatever morale problem existed: his part was insignificant, he should not be fired for "simply doing his steward's job" (Union *Brief*, p. 27).

Whether or not a morale problem existed in the local office is immaterial to my conclusion: the grievant's actions seriously and adversely affected people. The strong, convincing, and overwhelming testimony is that the grievant disrupted the peace; he fostered dissension, and he heightened discord. He stirred unfruitful and acrimonious controversy, not orderly and rational debate. He was not the effective union steward that he claimed to be: he did not resolve his or others' problems in a cool, positive and professional way. There was no evidence that he represented the bargaining unit's interests or that he had won the allegiances of his fellow employees. It is impossible to reject and to impugn the testimony of so many witnesses who came forward against him. Even his former friend testified against him. Only one witness half heartedly testified on his behalf. The union's defense was insufficient: its polemics and rhetoric lacked specifics. The expression "reborn company man" is one of obloquy, not one of evidence; evidence is fact, not a "valid difference of opinion." It is not defense to say that to put everything in writing is better than to "sit around the office all day," and the incident about the manual in the truck cannot be dismissed so cavalierly and without proof as a "story" the grievant heard in a different state.

The Grievant's Post-Termination Conduct. According to the company, the grievant accused the company, its supervisors, and certain employees of falsehoods, of illegal practices, and of gross unfairness (Company Exh. 21, 25, 29, 26). He spread these accusations throughout the company, and he threatened to send documents that purported to support these accusations to numerous public officials throughout the state and the United States. The grievant does not deny that he wrote and disseminated over three dozen packets of materials to employees throughout the company.

Letter of December 12. The first packet contained letters to S., J., N., and C. The grievant accused S. of lying about several employees, defaming his character, falsifying the log, leaving out call time, spying and reporting back to management about anything of a negative nature on everyone she worked with, and gross incompetency in her job. He wrote: "you have deliberately lied"..."I have documented all your misconduct";..."a damage suit against the company will name all parties contributing either directly or indirectly to my loss of employment" (Company Exh. 21).

In the letter to N. (nine copies were circulated), the grievant accused N. of certain indiscretions: he allowed his dog to destroy the seat covers of a company truck, and he took time off to baby-sit his child; the grievant charged N. with alleged abuses of company time, and he accused N. of lack of concern for company procedures. The grievant also informed N. that he had recorded N.'s movements, and he implied that he would hire a private investigator to look into N.'s job performance (Company Exh. 25).

The letter to J. (Company Exh. 37) and the letter to M. (Company Exh. 49), which were included in the same packets with the letters to N. and S., praise both J. and M. highly, but the company believed that the grievant emphasized the praise "quite blatantly" to demonstrate that the grievant "obviously wanted M. and J. to support him in his actions against the company" (Company *Brief*, p. 53).

Statement of December. In December, one day after his discharge, the grievant disseminated a statement entitled *Preliminary Statement of Issues* (Company Exh. 29). As the company noted, the document clearly reflects the grievant's emotional state:

If we lost to your superior talents I will have done everything humanly possible to restore my career and life.... I will have written and informed all the board of directors... another front page story about management's falsely depriving me of my employment... I will have written all congressmen and senators and the president I have received help from on my claim... I will apply for support and aid from employees fired, on disability or generally unhappy with management's treatment of themselves... I will have made full use of the PUC, federal pipeline safety standards, all errors I have seen and made and reported while employed will be made available to whoever it concerns for corrections, fines, penalties and/or criminal prosecution.

The grievant also disseminated throughout the company several letters that he had sent to the president of the company (Company Exh. 26). One paragraph reads:

Your supervisors with a few exceptions say one thing and do another out of your sight. I wish we could make a compromise and avoid what I have to do to restore my standing in my career. I have never had to do to a fellow worker what I have had to do now to get at the truth.

In another letter (Company Exh. 27), the grievant wrote:

I have no choice—you have, you can prevent all of the expense of court, the bad press, and all the things I will have to do but don't want to. I have no choice but to fight—I would rather work.

The grievant sent two other letters to the president of the company (Company Exh. 28 and 30). In those letters, the grievant blamed all his troubles on H.'s dictatorial attitude. He wrote in Company *Exhibit 30*:

I have never been terminated from a job in my life or drawn unemployment. If I am reinstated and H. cannot cope with my personality or does not feel I can satisfy his emotional needs I will transfer or seek employment out of state.

On January 3, the grievant wrote another letter to the president of the company (Company Exh. 31) which caused the company "considerable expense and anguish." In the letter the grievant hoped to "prevent a few individuals from spending the company's money to carry on a personal vendetta" and said "you remember how Watergate grew and grew." The company tried to trace all accusations to determine whether such accusations would be made to public officials.

On January 24, the grievant sent an *Open Letter to All Employees* (Company Exh. 32). In that letter he stated:

Some of you may laugh at my bringing a $1,000,000 dollar suit against the company, but you underestimate me as company management and the union has, bear in mind larger suits have been won on one printed line of libel, one whispered rumor that slandered someone, and less pain and suffering and public ridicule than my termination has caused me.

Further on in that letter, the grievant said that both his attorney and the union asked him "to stop complaining and publicly airing the issues," but he said: "I am only airing letters that were public as a steward's work for the union must be."

The grievant disseminated another document throughout the company in December entitled *TABLE OF CONTENTS* (Company Exh. 33). The document begins:

Everything you always wanted to know about company supervision, and our union but were afraid to ask.

This is a true story of conspiracy, intrigue, suspense, action and human suffering. One employee's quest for truth, justice and the American way.

"Boy, really sounds corny right." We are all part of an experiment. I will attempt to make my points in a court of law. The company's management and the union are in for a new understanding of an individual's right to freedom of speech, and the right to considerate and courteous treatment while employed to provide a service.

The company cited the quotation above, but I must cite other passages that capture the flavor of the document.

I will try and teach everyone that there are legal definitions of libel, slander, character defamation, ect [sic]. Every employee that has stepped over the line of reason and helped cause my financial or emotional harm will be able to defend their actions in a court of law. . . . I will bring a $10,000 judgement [sic] against each of those people, I will make the point that gossip and unsupported opinions that cost someone their professions, community standing, emotional pain and suffering are not to be repeated against anyone else ever again!

From a lengthy attack on H., his immediate supervisor, I have culled these excerpts:

I will communicate with you again. These letters are not all the paperwork dealing with H. I have. I will continue working and fill in the other issuing chapters and correspondence later on. . . . H., how do I love thee let me count the ways. H. does feel he has control over all our time a point you should all worry about. . . . H. has tried to provoke me. . . . H. is really into the spirit of peace on earth and good will as you can all see.

On the letter of termination, he wrote:

There will be another whole book on this area...he [a supervisor] will be sued.

About E., business representative for the union, the grievant wrote:

E. has a saying, "if it hurts, it hurts, but I gotta tell it like I see it."...Well, E. is either lazy, incompetent or just plain agrees with management and doesn't want to fight the company. I am going to check with the national union mangement before I decide if our union is afraid to work.

About the president of the company, he wrote:

I have not received one call, letter or any other acknowledgement from the man who writes bring me your problems. Too soon to tell if he is interested in the company or the conspiracy to fire me.

As union steward, he claimed:

I have handled every employee's problem as a steward just as thoroughly and seriously as if it were happening to me and always will.

In January, the grievant wrote *To All Employees Beware* (Company Exh. 34). These quotations comment on the voluminous correspondence between the grievant and others.

I found out today that H. and F. sent numerous letters I had no knowledge of to a secret file kept by W.?

Letter dated October from H. and W.'s secret file. He handled problem by blaming me for S.'s problems as a dispatcher. Completely distorted the facts. Then demand I be terminated for trying to improve communications. Real nice guy and so straightforward and honest with an employee?

It appears H. used the full week before my termination to entrap me into using vacation time for personal emergency's [sic] my time off? Than [sic] at the end of the week closed his trap.

On a line break, he wrote:

No contractors fault because S. failed to issue order as I instructed. The memo ruined part of managements conspiracy to wrongfully terminate me. And the letter from R. "Letter of conspiracy" Shame they were unable to use it. Note words written by R. on bottom of page. I have been told several things about R. and if I prove them I will see R. in court. R. is one of three phony reasons why I was terminated.

Letter dated November H. for W.'s secret file. Be sure and read D.'s letter on same meeting? Something smells bad.

Letter written to test M. (the grievant's attorney in arbitration proceedings) and see what his instructions were. . . . Letter sent to president and assistant president of our union in Washington D.C. . . . Letter to M. I still am not sure of him. I will let him prove himself. He will be reinstated to assist if hearing necessary.

Company *Exhibit 35* is another of the documents sent out by the grievant to employees of the company. In addition to parts quoted by the company, I have included several other quotations that show the tenor and spirit of the document.

anyone being used by management to support this conspiracy better have first hand witnesses and supported statements or be held legally responsible.

If I win every one of you working and supplying your time and efforts for an hourly wage will also have made progress.

Bless the ones of you who have openly supported me, the ones who secretly support me, and the ones who are waiting to join the winning side.

God bless and be with you all.

Many people are afraid to stand up for fair play and justice. We need employees that demand the union process grievances and complain. I am probably the only employee who has ever filed a grievance or demanded the union be given proper recognition. . . . We must demand aggressive union representatives who file grievances and use all steps even arbitration regardless of the cost to secure due process. It's your union, get your monies worth, elect stewards that will work on your behalf. Write to the president of the union.

The grievant's post-termination conduct can only be characterized as malicious, unfair, and outrageous. The menacing threats, the inflammatory language, and the unverified accusations point to a tyrannical and obsessed mind, one insensitive to others' feelings, one without respect for the truth, and one blinded by some passion. The grievant's attacks on his co-workers, his supervisors, and the president of the company can neither be excused nor tolerated.

The arbitrator must reject the union's vague and inadequate explanation that the letters to the president of the company were "pleas for help from someone who thought he had been wrongfully accused of being dishonest, and harassing management by doing *bona fide* union steward activity" and that the packets sent to other employees were sent "in the spirit of outrage at injustice" but also with a determination "to see justice done."

Criteria for Discharge

What constitutes "just cause"? A "just cause" exists when the arbitrator finds sufficient, not necessarily overwhelming evidence that the original labor agreement, the *quid pro quo* specified in the labor contract, has been irretrievably and irreparably broken. When the employer so adjudges, the arbitrator must then determine whether the evidence is sufficient to restore the original labor relationship by reinstatement or whether he shall forever dissolve it. This practical judgment arises not only from the consideration of the normative notions of "fairness" and "justice" but also from a scrutiny of the probative value of the adduced evidence. The sufficient evidence rule must consider the wisdom, prudence, and fairness of reinstatement because reinstatement contravenes the judgment of the employer that the discharged employee has not, and probably will not, fulfill the requirements of the employment contract.

Is the evidence sufficient to show that the grievant violated company rules, that he refused to follow the orders and directives of his supervisors, that he downgraded and maligned them, that he challenged their authority, that he caused unrest, that he infected his fellow employees with uncooperative attitude, and that he caused serious morale problems? Although the evidence against the grievant is not firm, definitive, and conclusive on some minor points, particularly on the time record discrepancies, the company advanced convincing, strong, and specific evidence on the harassment, morale, and post-termination issues. The cumulative evidence is certainly sufficient, and in many parts overwhelming.

The union advanced the most formidable argument in labor relations: whatever the grievant did, he did as union steward. As the union said, whatever "mistakes" the grievant made were "unintentional and done in good faith" and could not be "just cause" for discharge. The suspension based on these "relatively insignificant" mistakes gave the company the "pretext" to launch an extensive investigation. The "real" reason the grievant was fired was not "harassment of supervision" and "creating a morale problem" but because he "performed the normal and proper activities of a union steward, i.e., requesting clarification of policies and practices, upholding the Collective Bargaining Agreement, documenting his activities, trying to help other employees, and acting as spokesman for the group" (Union *Brief*, pp. 1–2). The union explained that the grievant came out of Southern California where union activities were taken in stride and expected, but in the small and relatively isolated community, the company construed the union actions as threats and attempts to "derail management." The arbitrator cannot conclude that the company had just cause to discharge the grievant for union ativity; if he were to do so, he would, in effect, say that "a union steward may not do his job."

It was all H.'s fault that the grievant lost his job because H. "having never processed a grievance in 21 years as a manager for the company . . . was probably no more ready for the grievant as a union steward who had extensive training in Southern California, than the tiny community was ready for the flood which devastated the area" (Union *Brief*, pp. 1–3).

Substantively, and in legal terms, the union argued that the grievant never broke the original labor agreement; his actions as steward were legally within it. There is no evidence to support the union's argument. Nowhere did the union specify what the union steward's duties were, and that the grievant performed those duties. There was no evidence to show that the grievant represented the membership, that he processed claims other than his own, that he was their champion and leader, that, as he said, he "handled every employee's problems just as thoroughly as if it happened to me." Furthermore, the grievant did not represent the union in contract disputes, nor did the bargaining unit members rally to his defense. The evidence is to the contrary. Union members testified against him; and at the hearing, the union's official support of him was minimal and, at best, lukewarm. The record shows that the grievant attacked not only the members of the bargaining unit but the business manager of the union, whom the grievant characterized as lazy and incompetent. In the incident of the transmittal of the personnel manual, the grievant said that the business manager was "a part of the company and helped run the company." This phrase is either a misconception of the role of the union or a derogatory comment against the business manager. He also derogatorily implied that "the company management are in for a new understanding," that the union was not furthering the membership's interests, that the union underestimated him, and that the union did not want to fight the company. Furthermore, he disagreed with the counsel of the union to "cease airing disputes in public."

Even so, a shrewd, sophisticated, and experienced steward seeks accommodation, compromise, and adjustments in matters that do not affect the union's legal rights. He seeks to avoid confrontation, bitterness, and unfruitful behavior. In these matters, the grievant is wanting. Stewardship does not justify slicing the truth, a belligerent attitude, an insensitivity to others, or niggardly and reluctant obedience to work procedures and lawful orders.

The grievant cannot blame H. There is no evidence that H. was "dictatorial," that the management had animus toward him, or that there was a conspiracy to terminate him. Nor is there evidence that H. refused to recognized the union and its agents; in fact, H. has no power to recognize or not recognize the union. The fact and conclusion is that the grievant discharged himself. All the charges against the grievant— the possible falsifications of records, the harassment of fellow employees, the unauthorized absences, the destruction of or the exacerbation of morale, and particularly the grievant's post-termination conduct—are not related to union activity.

All the evidence, and in particular, the grievant's post-termination conduct, makes reinstatement, even conditional reinstatement, under any circumstances, a practical impossibility. It would not be fair to the company to give him another chance. His conduct after the *Warning Letter* did not improve, his conduct after the termination did not improve. His reinstatement would work a hardship on his supervisors, and on his fellow employees. His post-termination conduct alone seriously injured the company, a small service company that depends and thrives on its local reputation. Employees would find it difficult to work with the grievant no matter where he was assigned. His supervisors have had enough of him; the company has spent enough time and money to defend itself against his attacks. Indeed, the grievant "burned his bridges behind him." At the end of the hearing, the grievant made an impassioned plea for another chance. He said he was sorry for the things he had written in the documents he distributed after his termination, but as the company pointed out, this was not the first time the grievant had made such an impassioned plea. He has been given many chances: he had a chance on every occasion when the company confronted him with his problems.

The company has given the grievant chance after chance to recognize and correct the damages he has caused to the employees and supervisors with whom he works. It has been the grievant, not his supervisors or any of his fellow employees, who has caused the problems that led to his discharge. It is the grievant who has prevented himself from being a valued and needed employee at the company. It is the grievant who has created the just causes for his termination. (Company *Brief*, p. 60)

Perhaps the best summary is the grievant's own words: "I am sorry my lack of understanding or judgment has left me open to disciplinary action."

Conclusion

Question No. 1: Was the discharge of the grievant from employment at the company in violation of the employment contract between the employer and the union?

Answer: No.

Question No. 2: If so, what is the appropriate remedy?

Answer: No remedy is needed.

Award

The union grievance is hereby denied. The company's discharge of the grievant is hereby sustained.

Conclusions and Reflections

Now I address myself to four questions that confront practitioners and labor arbitrators. First, what is the status of labor grievance arbitration? Second, has labor arbitration lost its original virtues? Third, should an arbitrator interpret a statute to determine rights under a collective bargaining agreement? Finally, what is the future of labor arbitration?

Today, labor arbitration is not only alive and well, it is a robust and thriving institution. Grievance arbitration, as we know it today, found little acceptance before the Wagner Act. Today, it is an integral part of almost every collective bargaining agreement because parties have rightfully concluded that arbitration is a relatively inexpensive, informal, and speedy method for the resolution of labor grievance disputes. Today, parties routinely provide for labor arbitration and recently the federal government has made arbitration of grievances mandatory for federal employees. Therefore, I think it fitting and proper to recognize and credit those persons and institutions that have contributed to its development, a development congenial to the spirit of the United States and to democracy. Present day arbitrators and practitioners owe a debt of gratitude to the early labor-management practitioners who recognized, accepted, experimented with, and refined labor arbitration, a method preferable to litigation or economic contest. They are indebted to the labor-management leaders who agreed to arbitrate their disputes during World War II; to the War Labor Board which embedded labor arbitration into U.S. labor practice; to AAA for its constant and devoted advocacy of arbitration and for the critical and fundamental distinction it made between mediation (a political settlement) and arbitration (a judicial settlement); to the Supreme Court for its *Trilogy* and other decisions that praised the expertise of arbitrators, directed courts to shed their traditional hostility to arbitration, and gave labor arbitration a unique, favored, and protected place in the U.S. judicial system; to Congress for its declaration that the voluntary settlement of labor disputes was national policy; to FMCS for fostering its use; to past and present arbitrators for their probity, learning, and commitment to labor arbitration, and for their intelligent and literate opinions; to the National Academy of Arbitrators whose *Proceedings* record discussions on labor arbitration, to today's practitioners who continue, diligently and expertly, to prepare cases before arbitrators; and to workers and supervisors who accept an arbitrator's award as final and binding.

Has labor arbitration lost its original virtues? Although critics of labor arbitration do not dispute the value and vitality of grievance arbitration, they assert at conferences, seminars, and at the annual meetings of the NAA that labor arbitration has lost its three original virtues. They assert, often without specific evidence, that labor arbitration is too "expensive," "no longer speedy," and too "legalistic." Robert Coulson, President of the AAA, in his January 20, 1987 statement to the Members of the Labor Panel, cites some statistics, asks how arbitrators can resist tendencies to "lawyerize" the process, and points to the problem of increasing delays and expense. My experience has been and I must conclude that parties are primarily responsible for increased costs, delays, and "creeping legalism" because the ultimate reality in arbitration is that parties can control every facet of arbitration practice: they make arbitration what it is. However, the experience of a practitioner in the federal sector is quite different. He wrote:

In our experience, arbitrators share their responsibility with the parties and should properly be called to task as well to account for their individual and collective behavior. For example, it is no longer uncommon for arbitrators, especially the very busy ones, to take excessive time after the hearing ends and the record is closed to render awards. Also, too many arbitral opinions are much too long and include extraneous material. Many of these are frequently accompanied by unreasonable charges of study time and per diem payments.

I cannot exonerate or defend arbitrators who delay or increase cost. If parties object to a particular arbitrator's judgment, competence, wisdom, impartiality, objectivity, charges, and negligence, or if they are dissatisfied with an administrative agency, the remedy is available: bypass the arbitrator or the agency.

If parties want to reduce cost and delay, they can devise their own expedited procedures, adopt the expedited procedures of AAA, or adopt a variety of suggestions. Expedited procedures did not exist during the early days of arbitration: today's expedited procedures are yesterday's "regular" procedures. Many federal agencies have devised regular and expedited procedures. Certain expedited procedures call for the selection of the arbitrator from a permanent rotation panel and require that the arbitrator hold a hearing and render either a bench or a written decision within 48 hours. Other procedures prohibit the use of transcripts or briefs. One expedited procedure allotted only two hours to examine witnesses and to make opening and closing statements.

Parties can reduce costs and delays by adopting the *Expedited Labor Arbitration Rules of the AAA.* In 1971 the AAA, concerned about complaints on cost and delays, developed expedited procedures that modify the regular AAA rules in several ways: the AAA appoints an arbitrator who must issue a written summary decision no later than five days after the hearing. Parties can reduce costs and delays by eliminating expensive transcripts and post-hearing briefs. If post-hearing briefs are necessary, they should not cite a long list of cases; they need quote only the governing principle and the reasoning in the cited case. Parties also can eliminate the formal hearing in disputes over contract languages by a joint submission of facts, questions, arguments, and conclusions. Parties also can ask the arbitrator for a *Summary Opinion,* usually a one or two page opinion or an award-only decision, that is, a yes or no decision to a given question. In several discharge cases, parties have asked me to answer "yes" or "no" within five days concerning whether or not a grievant was discharged for just cause. This was quick, inexpensive, informal arbitration: arbitration at its best. Parties can eliminate frivolous or doubtful grievances by adopting a "loser-pay-all" clause, or parties can allow an arbitrator to apportion costs according to the relative merits of each party's case. To save time and money, parties can select an experienced local arbitrator who will hear several cases in a single day. With care and foresight, parties can avoid travel costs, administrative/docket fees for postponements and cancellations, and hearing room costs.

Parties can adopt a variety of special provisions to reduce costs and delays. It has been suggested that parties can provide that an arbitrator forfeit all or part of his fee and his position on the panel if he does not comply with time limits. Parties can stipulate that all grievances be submitted to expedited arbitration unless parties agree to use the regular procedure. Parties can require that all grievances be submitted to a Board of Adjustment, composed of one neutral and two or four representatives in arbitration. The Board would hear all grievances but only after the parties had stipulated all facts and the question(s) in writing. The neutral on the Board of Adjustment would first serve as friend, consultant, and mediator, and as arbitrator only if the parties became stalemated.

But if parties adopt expedited arbitration, does an expedited procedure "adversely affect the process and quality of arbitration" as some writers assert?

I find some merit to the critics' observation that labor arbitration is losing some of its informality, but contrary to the often-stated view, it is not the well prepared lawyer, a regular procedure, or the filing of papers that "legalizes" arbitration or deprives labor arbitration of its informality. The advocate or the arbitrator who uses formal court procedure and court jargon contributes to creeping legalism. Inevitably, the tone and coloration of court procedures and court language influence the practice of arbitration. This practice may some day convert arbitral proceedings (now private, informal, and expeditious) into "court" proceedings: public, extended, formalized proceedings. The evidence of "creeping legalism" is everywhere. The following language, which I found in the literature, in the *Proceedings* of the National Academy, in briefs, and in speeches at seminars and conferences, unmistakably points to the trend. Speakers or writers incorrectly call arbitration "a system of jurisprudence"; they equate the verb "to litigate" with "to arbitrate"; they call a grievant "the complainant," and the employer "the defendant"; the hearing a "trial"; they often refer to or equate a collective bargaining agreement (a private agreement) with "legislation" or "law," a rule imposed by public authority; they refer to an arbitrator as a "judge," a "trial judge," an "appellate judge," an "industrial judge," that he issues a "judgment" not an "award," and that he meets with parties "in chambers." They use words that are strange to workers and supervisors: laches, estoppel, pleadings, per curiam. They describe persons as testee, declarant, proferror, deponent. They incorrectly compare arbitral proceedings to judicial proceedings. For example: "Criminal law is an inexact analogy, but it does provide a good basis for comparison."... "The requirements would not be the same as a court proceeding."... "The legal practice is analogous to the ancient common law demurrer." ..."From the strictly legal point of view"..."Corpus Juris Secundum says"..."Federal Rules of Legal Procedure require"..."The treatment of arbitrators and courts on certain issues arising in arbitration corresponds to criminal procedure." They assume the existence of a "common law," a doubtful premise, and refer to the "common law in industrial relations," to a "body of case law," or to the ominpresent "weight of authority." And, almost inevitably, writers quote a Supreme Court decision or some other "authority."

Legal jargon disserves arbitration because it clothes arbitration in false garments: it makes arbitration look like a "labor court," an institution unknown and alien to U.S. workers. I have an impression, a tentative conclusion without empirical proof, that the present and ever growing use of court procedures and legal jargon is subtly changing the original spirit and tenor and, to some extent, the institution of arbitration, a trend that might ultimately destroy arbitration as we have known it—

an informal, expeditious, and inexpensive method to resolve grievance disputes.

Parties necessarily contribute to creeping legalism and to an increase in costs and delay when they ask a court or the FLRA to review an arbitrator's award. This tendency to review an arbitrator's award raises the third question. Does review signal the "death knell" of the "final and binding" clause? One writer thought that review marked the demise of the "Golden Age" of arbitration, a felicitous term used to describe that early period of labor arbitration when courts seldom reviewed arbitration awards. Review unequivocally means that an arbitral award is not final and binding. Although courts seldom reviewed an arbitrator's award in the past, an arbitrator's award was always subject to review because courts have always asserted the supremacy of law over a collective bargaining agreement. The only difference today is that the plethora of federal legislation on wages, hours, and working conditions makes review more likely, but it is clear that the spirit and intent of judicial decisions and CSRA is not to review but to defer to an arbitrator's award. *Gardner-Denver* unequivocally and specifically holds that an arbitrator's award on contractual rights under the collective bargaining agreement is final and binding. In *Gardner-Denver* the court reviewed the award only because the arbitrator's award affected an employee's statutory right. In *Vaca* the Court reviewed only to protect an employee's statutory right to fair representation. The spirit and intent of CSRA is not to review arbitration awards but to protect statutory rights. CSRA not only acknowledged the value of grievance arbitration as an effective means of dispute resolution, it also broadened the definition of a grievance, expanded the scope of the negotiated grievance procedure, and required binding arbitration as the final step in the negotiated procedure. Congress authorized FLRA to review an arbitrator's award only on narrow statutory, not contractual grounds: to determine if an award is contrary to law, rule, or regulation, or if an award was deficient on grounds similar to those applied by federal courts in private sector labor relations. FLRA's unequivocal and stated policy is not to review an arbitration award if the appealing party simply disagrees with an arbitrator's interpretation or application of the collective bargaining agreement, his findings of fact, his evaluation of the evidence and testimony, or his reasoning and conclusion. Furthermore, FLRA rejects those exceptions that seek review on the merits of a dispute.

Should an arbitrator interpret a statute to determine rights under a collective bargaining agreement? This question arises only in private sector arbitration, not in federal sector arbitration, because CSRA specifically directs an arbitrator to interpret and apply relevant laws, rules, and regulations. Two dominant views have emerged among arbitrators and practitioners. Some hold that an arbitrator must "always" interpret and apply the statute because the agreement implicitly incorporates law; others assert that an arbitrator must "never" interpret or apply the statute because he has no jurisdiction over it. In private sector arbitration an arbitrator must interpret and apply a statute if parties incorporate the statute in their collective bargaining agreement, if the agreement directs him to interpret and apply the agreement "consistent with applicable federal, state, and local law," or if they explicity enpower him to do so in a *Submission Agreement.* In these cases parties have absorbed and made the statute their private rule, a rule subject to the arbitrator's jurisdiction.

It is clear, as the Supreme Court has often said, that an arbitrator's task is "to effectuate the intent of the parties," that his award must draw "its essence" from the agreement, that he has "no general authority to invoke public laws," and that his competence is "in the law of the shop not in the law of the land." However, the Supreme Court also has said that an arbitrator may look to "many sources" when he interprets or applies an agreement. Therefore, I conclude that an arbitrator should interpret and apply the statute, that is, use the statute as an auxiliary aid, like any other source, to ascertain the parties' contractual intent. However, it is pertinent and critical to note that when an arbitrator interprets and applies a statute he does not determine a grievant's public law rights but a grievant's private contractual rights. His judgment on private contractual rights is necessarily final and binding even if a court or the FLRA reviews his award because these public authorities do not enter a judgment on private contractual rights but on a grievant's statutory rights.

What is the future of grievance arbitration? Of course, I do not know the future, but I forecast that, first, arbitrators will not mediate; their function will be a narrow one: to interpret and apply the collective bargaining agreement. Second, arbitration is here to stay, it has become a "way of life" because parties have found it an acceptable and valuable means to resolve contract grievances. Parties have concluded that contract grievances are better resolved through arbitration than by a strike or lockout, but the continuing trend toward "legalisms," increase in cost, and delays will weaken the acceptance of arbitration. Hence, they might use arbitration fewer times but will use it as a means in their continuing struggle for accommodation. Parties will turn more and more toward expedited arbitration, constitute permanent panels for arbitrator selection, and experiment with alternate dispute resolution systems, for example, grievance mediation. Third, courts, FLRA, and the Board will defer to arbitration awards but will continue to review them especially when statutory rights are at issue. Recourse to review will formalize the process, increase costs and delays, destroy the original intent and practice of industrial arbitration, invite and require more attorneys to process a grievance, and make arbitration an appendage to the judicial system.

Bibliography

Aaron Benjamin, et al. *The Future of Labor Arbitration*. New York: American Arbitration Association, 1976.

Abersold, John, R. and Wayne E. Howard. *Cases in Labor Relations: An Arbitration Process*. Englewood Cliffs: Prentice Hall, 1967.

American Arbitration Association. *Arbitration Journal*.

————. *Expedited Labor Arbitration Rules*. 1988.

————. *Grievance Arbitration in the Private Sector: Selected References*. 1981.

————. *Lawyer's Arbitration Letter*.

————. *Voluntary Labor Arbitration Rules*. 1988.

American Arbitration Association, National Academy of Arbitrators, and Federal Mediation and Conciliation Service. *The Code of Professional Responsibility for Arbitrators of Labor-Management Disputes*. Washington, D.C., 1972.

Baer, Walter E. *Discipline and Discharge under the Labor Agreement*. New York: American Management Association, 1972.

————. *The Labor Arbitration Guide*. Homewood, Illinois: Dow Jones-Irwin, 1974.

————. *Practice and Precedent in Labor Relations*. Lexington: Lexington Books, 1972.

————. *Winning in Labor Arbitration*. Chicago: Crain Books, 1982.

Baker, Sheridan. *The Practical Stylist*. New York: Harper and Row, 1985.

Bernstein, Merton C. *Private Dispute Settlement*. New York: Free Press, 1978.

Britton, Raymond L. *The Arbitration Guide*. Englewood Cliffs: Prentice Hall, 1982.

Bureau of National Affairs. *Grievance Guide*. Washington, D.C.: Bureau of National Affairs, Inc., 1978.

Coulson, Robert, *Labor Arbitration—What You Need to Know*. New York: American Arbitration Association, 1981.

Cox, Archibald. *Labor Law—Cases and Materials*. Mineola, N.Y.: Foundation Press, 1977.

Edwards, Henry T., Theodore R. Clark, Jr., and Charles B. Craver. *Labor Relations in the Public Sector*. Indianapolis: Bobbs-Merrill Company, 1979.

Elkin, Randyl D. and Thomas L. Hewitt. *Successful Arbitration: An Experimental Approach.* Reston, VA: Reston Publishing Co., Inc. 1980.

Elkouri, Frank and Edna Asper Elkouri. *How Arbitration Works.* Washington, D.C.: Bureau of National Affairs, 1986.

Fairweather, Owen. *Practice and Procedure in Labor Arbitration.* Washington, D.C.: Bureau of National Affairs, 1973.

Federal Mediation and Conciliation Service. *Arbitration Policies Functions, and Procedures.* Washington, D.C.: Government Printing Office, 1974.

Fleming, Robben. *The Labor Arbitration Process.* Urbana: University of Illinois, 1965.

Fowler, H. W. *A Dictionary of Modern English Usage,* 2d. ed. revised by Sir Ernest Gowers. Oxford: Claredon Press, 1965.

Fowler, Roger. *Essays on Style and Language.* New York: Humanities Press, 1966.

Garman, Philips L. *Grievance Arbitration Manual.* Champaign: University of Illinois, 1972.

Government Printing Office, Office of Comptroller General. *Manual of Available Remedies.* Washington, D.C., 1977.

Grossman, Mark M. *The Question of Arbitrability.* New York: Industrial Relations Press, Cornell University, 1984.

Hays, Paul. *Labor Arbitration: A Dissenting View.* New Haven: Yale University Press, 1966.

Hill, Marvin, Jr. and Anthony V. Sinicropi. *Evidence in Arbitration.* Washington D.C.: Bureau of National Affairs, 1980.

———. *Remedies in Arbitration.* Washington, D.C.: Bureau of National Affairs, 1981.

International Labour Office. *Grievance Arbitration.* Geneva: ILO Publications, 1977.

Kagel, Sam. *Anatomy of a Labor Arbitration.* Washington, D.C.: Bureau of National Affairs, 1961.

Kochan, Thomas A., et al. *Dispute Resolution under Fact-Finding and Arbitration: An Empirical Analysis.* New York: American Arbitration Association, 1979.

Koven, Adolph M. and Susan L. Smith. *Just Cause: The Seven Tests.* San Francisco: Coloracre Publications, Inc., 1985.

———. *Labor Law Journal.* Chicago: Commerce Clearing House.

Levin, Edward, and Donald Grody. *Witnesses in Arbitration.* Washington D.C.: Bureau of National Affairs, 1987.

Marmo, Michael. *Arbitration and the Off-Duty Conduct of Employees.* Washington, D.C.: International Personnel Association, 1985.

Munro, Robert J. *Grievance Arbitration Procedure,* Tarrytown: Associated Faculty Press, 1982.

National Academy of Arbitrators. *Code of Ethics and Procedural Standards for Labor-Management Arbitration.* Ann Arbor: University of Michigan, 1974.

———. *Proceedings of the Annual Conference on Labor Arbitration. 1948 through Present.* Washington, D.C.: Bureau of National Affairs.

Nolan, Dennis. *Labor Arbitration Law and Practice.* St. Paul: West Publishing Co., 1979.

Patterson, Lee T. and Reginald T. Murphy. *The Public Administrator's Grievance Arbitration Handbook.* New York: Longman, 1983.

Peterson, Craig A. and Claire McCarthy. *Arbitration Strategy and Technique*. Charlottesville: Michie Co., 1986.

Prasow, Paul and Edward Peters. *Arbitration and Collective Bargaining: Conflict Resolution in Labor Relations*. New York: McGraw Hill Book Company, 1970.

Reischl, Dennis K. and Ralph R. Smith. *Grievance Arbitration in the Federal Service*. Huntsville: Federal Personnel Management Institute, Inc., 1987.

Robinson, James W., Wayne L. Dernoncourt, and Ralph H. Effler. *The Grievance Procedure and Arbitration: Test and Cases*. Washington, D.C.: University Press of America, 1978.

Rothschild, Donald, Leroy Merrifield, and Harry Edwards. *Collective Bargaining and Labor Arbitration: Materials on Collective Bargaining*. Indianapolis: Bobbs-Merrill Company, 1979.

Scheinman, Martin F. *Evidence and Proof in Arbitration*. Ithaca, N.Y.: Cornell Univ., 1977.

Seide, Katherine. *A Dictionary of Arbitration*. Dobbs Ferry: Oceana Publications Inc., 1970.

Siegel, Boaz. *Proving Your Arbitration Case*. Washington, D.C.: Bureau of National Affairs, 1961.

Smith, Russell, A., Harry T. Edwards, and Theodore R. Clark, Jr. *Labor Relations in the Public Sector*. Indianapolis: Bobbs-Merril Company, 1974.

Stone, Morris. *Labor Grievances and Decisions*. New York: American Arbitration Association, 1970.

Stone, Morris and Earl Baderschneider, eds. *Arbitration of Discrimination Grievances*. New York: American Arbitration Association, 1974.

Strunk, William and E. B. White. *Elements of Style*. New York: MacMillan, 1979.

Teple, Edwin R. and Robert B. Moberly. *Arbitration and Conflict Resolution*. Washington, D.C.: Bureau of National Affairs, Inc., 1979.

———. *Arbitration as a Method of Resolving Disputes*, Washington, D.C.: Bureau of National Affairs, 1972.

Thomson, A. W. J. *The Grievance Procedure in the Private Sector*. New York: N.Y. State School of Industrial and Labor Relations, 1974.

———. *Grievance Procedures*. Lexington: D.C. Heath, 1976.

Tracy, Estelle, R. *Arbitration Cases in Public Employment*. New York: American Arbitration Association, 1969.

Trotta, Maurice M. *Arbitration of Labor-Management Disputes*. New York: American Management Association, 1974.

———. *Handling Grievances, A Guide for Management and Labor*. Washington, D.C.: Bureau of National Affairs, 1976.

United States Bureau of Labor Statistics. *Major Collective Bargaining Agreements: Arbitration Procedures*. Bulletin 1425–26. Washington, D.C.: Government Printing Office, 1966.

———. *Major Collective Bargaining Agreements: Grievance Procedures*. Bulletin 1425–1, Washington, D.C.: U. S. Government Printing Office, 1964.

Updegraff, Clarence. *Arbitration and Labor Relations*. Washington D.C.: Bureau of National Affairs, 1970.

U. S. Arbitration Act, 1926.

U. S. General Accounting Office. *Manual on Remedies Available to Third Parties in Adjudicating Federal Employee Grievances.* Washngton, D.C.

U. S. Bureau of Labor Statistics. *Monthly Labor Review.* Washington D.C.

Zack, Arnold (ed). *Understanding Grievance Arbitration in the Public Sector.* Washington, D.C.: U. S. Government Printing Office, 1974.

Zack, Arnold M. and Richard I. Block. *The Arbitration of Discipline Cases: Concepts and Questions.* New York: American Arbitration Association, 1979.

————. *Labor Agreement in Negotiations and Arbitration.* Washington, D.C.: Bureau of National Affairs, 1983.

Zack, Arnold M. et al. *Arbitration in Practice,* New York: Industrial Relations Press, Cornell University, 1984.

Zinsser, William. *On Writing Well.* New York: Harper and Row, 1980.

REPORTING SERVICES

American Arbitration Association. *Arbitration in Government.* New York.

American Arbitration Association. *Arbitration in the Schools.* New York.

American Arbitration Association. *Summary of Labor Arbitration Awards.* New York.

Bureau of National Affairs. *Labor Arbitration Reports.* Washington, D.C.

Commerce Clearing House. *Labor Arbitration Awards.* Chicago.

Labor Relations Press. *Labor Arbitration Index.* Fort Washington, PA.

Index

About the Author

CHARLES S. LaCUGNA received his B.A. from Manhattan College, his M.A. from Fordham University, and his Ph.D. from the University of Washington. He has taught political science at Seattle University for forty years. During that period, he served as mediator, fact finder, and arbitrator for private and public parties in many industries, and in regular and expedited systems throughout the Northwest and Alaska. He is listed on the national panel of the American Arbitration Association, the Federal Mediation and Conciliation Service, and state agencies in the Northwest.